FATHER LOSS

Also by Elyce Wakerman

AIR POWERED

ELYCE WAKERMAN

FATHER LOSS

*Daughters Discuss
the Man That Got Away*

DOUBLEDAY & COMPANY, INC.
GARDEN CITY, NEW YORK
1984

authors and publishers
eprint
hted material:

"The Man That Got Away." Lyric by Ira Gershwin; music by Harold Arlen, from *A Star Is Born*, © 1954 Harwin Music Co. © Renewed 1982 Harwin Music Co. Sole selling agent: Edwin H. Morris & Company, a Division of MPL Communications, Inc. International copyright secured. All rights reserved. Used by permission.

"Soliloquy," from *Carousel*, written by Richard Rodgers and Oscar Hammerstein II. Copyright © 1945 Williamson Music, Inc. Copyright renewed. Sole selling agent: T. B. Harms Company (c/o The Welk Music Group, Santa Monica, Calif. 90401). International copyright secured. All rights reserved. Used by permission.

"I'm the Greatest Star," from *Funny Girl*. Copyright © 1963, 1964, by Bob Merrill & Jule Styne. Chappell-Styne, Inc. and Wonderful Music Corp., owners of publication and allied rights. International copyright secured. All rights reserved. Used by permission.

"Daddy," from *The Collected Poems of Sylvia Plath*, edited by Ted Hughes. Copyright © 1963 by Ted Hughes. Reprinted by permission of Harper & Row, Publishers, Inc.

The Journals of Sylvia Plath, by Ted Hughes. Copyright © 1982 by Ted Hughes as Executor of the Estate of Sylvia Plath. A Dial Press book, reprinted by permission of Doubleday & Company, Inc.

Your Inner Child of the Past, by Dr. W. Hugh Missildine. Copyright © 1963 by W. Hugh Missildine. Reprinted by permission of Simon & Schuster, Inc.

The Way of All Women, by M. Esther Harding. Copyright © 1970 by the C. G. Jung Foundation for Analytic Psychology, Inc. All rights reserved.

Library of Congress Cataloging in Publication Data
Wakerman, Elyce.
Father Loss.
1. Daughters. 2. Fathers and daughters.
3. Paternal deprivation. 4. Women—Psychology.
I. Title.
HQ777.W35   1984   306.8'742

ISBN 0-385-18865-X
Library of Congress Catalog Card Number 84-4189
Copyright © 1984 by Elyce Wakerman
All rights reserved
Printed in the United States of America

First Edition

In memory of my father, Hyman Wakerman
And for my mother

ACKNOWLEDGMENTS

Though writing is certainly a solitary endeavor, the making of a book depends on the participation of others. And so it is with deep appreciation that I would like to thank: Elizabeth Smith, Susan Schwartz, and Jean Naggar for their early and steadfast support; Dr. Debra Decker, Dr. Janice Abarbanel, Marty Gwinn, Pat Walter, Tim Carnasale, Michael Monigan, the Los Angeles Public Library (the public library being one of our great institutions), the United States Bureau of the Census, and my father-in-law, Herbert L. Werner, for their generosity in providing me with leads and materials; and Wendy Sharp for her conscientious transcribing.

To the 608 women who participated in the study, and particularly to the scores of women who spent hours talking to me, a very special "Thank you."

The measurable facts and figures accumulated by Dr. Holly Barrett added immeasurably to the scope of the book, as did her less calculable but equally edifying interpretations of the data.

To my friend Jane Welkowitz Rosen, who was always "ready to read" the pages as soon as they were out of the typewriter, my abiding admiration and gratitude for lending her intelligence, insight, and scholarship to the project.

And, of course, lest it go without saying, very little would be possible were it not for Jeff.

Elyce Wakerman
January 1984

FOREWORD

Fatherless daughters have not received much attention from behavioral science. If the amount of research is an indicator, motherless children or fatherless sons are far more likely to evoke interest as victims of parental deprivation. It is my guess that this gap in the research literature has appeared less out of lack of interest than out of the romantic, mysterious aura surrounding the father-daughter relationship itself. Certainly, E. Mavis Hetherington's pioneering 1972 study of adolescent girls without fathers was instrumental in bringing the nature of the father-daughter relationship into sharper focus. Similarly, this book is as much about the father-daughter relationship as it is about father absence. From the very specific and poignant perspective of women who lost their fathers—owing to death, abandonment, or divorce—we gain a deeper understanding of the significant role that father plays in his daughter's development. Indeed, it is my greatest wish that many, many fathers will read this book, for what makes the man that got away so important is precisely what makes the man that stayed so important.

As a woman who grew up without a father, Elyce Wakerman knew that she had missed a vital relationship in her life, yet information on the psychological impact of her loss was cloaked in the same silence as were the texture and dynamics of the relationship itself. To fill both the personal and the research voids, she decided to write this book. The result, I believe, is a moving and informative narrative on the first male-female relationship in every woman's life, and what it means to have had that relationship end prematurely.

". . . [F]uture work on the effects of father absence on females," Hetherington's paper concluded, "may find its most important evidence in the lives of mature women." As a way of augmenting the information she was gleaning from interviews, and as if fulfilling Hetherington's prophesy, Elyce Wakerman asked me to create a study of adult women who had lost their fathers before the age of eighteen. We expected to collect a sample of perhaps a hundred women, but the response to our call for volunteers was overwhelming. Over seven hundred women wrote to ask for questionnaires, many of them remarking, "It's about time" or "I've been waiting for someone to ask me about this." The enthusiasm generated by our query produced:

- 144 women whose mothers divorced and did not remarry;
- 125 women whose mothers divorced and remarried;
- 200 women whose fathers died and whose mothers did not remarry;
- 88 women whose fathers died and whose mothers remarried.

While ours was a pilot study and therefore not as rigidly controlled as an experimental study would be, we did also include a group of fifty-one women who grew up with fathers so that we might discern trends in the difference between fathered and fatherless women. The mean age of our subjects was forty-two years.

Our sample is largely middle class, because we advertised for volunteers through national and local media, schools, clinics, women's groups, senior citizen centers, and other organizations that serve the middle class. However, the origins of the women in our study varied widely. Once the father loss occurred, the majority of our subjects experienced a decrease in social and economic status. This pattern is not likely to change without extensive cultural reorganization, and we can anticipate hearing many more of the kinds of tragic, moving, and thoughtful stories that fill this book.

Many women, upon hearing about the focus of our project, believed that they would be suitable subjects even though their fathers had been more or less physically present during their childhoods. These women felt that their fathers had been out there somewhere in the "real" world, possessing some magical qualities that made them effective, if remote. Yet, while it is true that the father-daughter relationship is tinged with a quality of fantasy, one of the many points of this book is that fathered daughters have the advantage of glimpsing what is ordinary and human in men. If they are lucky enough, as I was, to have active and interested fathers, paternal influence is profound.

With her customary insistence on getting to the truth of the matter, Elyce has asked me repeatedly, "What exactly *is* it that fathers give their daughters?" It is not necessarily strength, for the stories in this book are a testament to strength and to courage. Perhaps a father's best gift could be an underpinning of support that would allow his daughter to dare, a confidence in both her femininity and in her ability to achieve that enables her to acknowledge and develop the many aspects of herself.

Whether women idealize their absent or remote fathers, or condemn them as worthless, they maintain a picture of Daddy, and of men, that is somewhat drawn from fantasy. Some of the illusion around what Daddy is, was, or could have been to a little girl is healthy, as it dilutes hopelessness and a sense of complete isolation. Yet our exploration into women without fathers reveals much about the ways in which an unrealistic picture of father may negatively affect childhood, adolescence, and overall attitudes toward self, relationships, careers, and family. Today's girls without fathers—there are currently five and a half million in the United States alone—may not suffer the same intensity of social stigma that our subjects endured, but they will probably experience the emotional confusion and the difficulties with love relationships that seem to accompany father loss. Therefore, we hope that this study will provoke more questions and more research not only because of its relevance to all daughters and fathers, but because the incidence of single motherhood is rising, and fatherless daughters may someday constitute a large social group.

Illusion, for a time, may help us to absorb our losses, but as Elyce Wakerman emphasizes in the following pages, we women need to mourn the men that got away so that we can get on with the business of living.

Holly Barrett, Ph.D.
January 1984

CONTENTS

FATHER LOSS

PART ONE

INTRODUCTION

ONE

A SUBJECT I CAN SPEAK OF

"My Father Died When I Was Three"

I sit taut with anxiety at my wooden desk, eyes fixed on the empty inkwell. Although I am only eight years old, this tension is not new to me: it is the agony that goes with the first day of school.

Once again, just as in kindergarten and first grade, my classmates and I must stand up in alphabetical order and say what our fathers do. A small blessing, I am grateful for the *W* with which my last name begins. It gives me time to think. I can't possibly stand in front of everybody and say, "He's dead."

I am angry at the pretty, young teacher in front of the room. When I first saw her, just an hour ago, with my young girl's faith in pretty, young women I hoped that she would be different, that the bright red lips and perfumed smile would grant me a reprieve from the dreaded question. She would have original ways of getting to know her new students, I thought; she would forgo the cruel ritual. But the rhythmic recital of paternal professions drones like a litany around me. Debbie Rosenthal has just pronounced her father's affiliation with the garment industry, and I better think fast.

Damp with sweat, I feverishly run down a list of believable things a father might do for a living. I don't want to copy what anyone else has said or they'll be on to me. I could say, "Lawyer" (maybe I'll ask to go to the bathroom) or "Accountant"; my Uncle Norman, after all, is an accountant. Heart pounding with my impending falsehood, I settle on the closest thing to the truth that I can think of. He *used* to own two fruit and vegetable markets. It wouldn't be *such* a lie. "Elyce," the word like a reflex hammer jerks at my knees and I am standing. "He owns a fruit and vegetable market," I lie in a barely audible voice, eyes straight ahead, and I sit. Miss Hogan lets the mumbled presentation pass. True to the profound sensitivity with which I had previously imbued her, she doesn't require that I "speak up" as she did some of the other children.

She knows, she must know, I decide. It must be noted in the record book she has just glanced at. And she is sorry for having put me through this. . . . The sweat is evaporating, cold on my forehead, and the panic subsides. Obediently, I turn my attention to *Dick and Jane*.

*

My earliest recollection of not having a father is associated with shame. To have a parent who was DEAD was to live in the shadow of something ominous. I had no comprehension of death, but felt that my father being dead said something about me: my worthiness, my right to think of myself as just like anyone else. A mysterious event loomed in my background, an event that I neither understood nor remembered, but it branded me. I was convinced that there were dark implications connected to the fact that my father was dead, and I had no reason to believe that my classmates, or my teachers, would think otherwise.

In addition to my fears about being *less* than everyone else was the threat of being discovered as *different*. All the other kids had two parents; that was normal, and in the 1950s, normalcy was all. Though Joseph McCarthy was unknown to me, the atmosphere adhered to his law of conformity-as-the-highest-virtue. To be different, to transgress the norm in any way, was frowned upon, and in the world of children, laughed at. Not to have a father was the same as being weird, and I must protect my self-acknowledged failure dearly. Thus, did a great deal of my childhood energy go into concealing my "inadequacies"; at eight years old, I was guarding a checkered past. Inevitably, my preoccupation served to divide me from my peers, and it is fair to say that the loneliness I experienced as a child was largely of my own creation. I am sure that to me it seemed logical: since everyone else was loved by two parents, and I by only one, I must be less lovable.

But I didn't want anyone to feel sorry for me. My father had died when I was three years old, and throughout my childhood the response I had most often observed in people who knew or were told was one of maudlin sympathy. Neighbors and family had clucked over "poor Selma and the two girls" for as long as I could remember, fostering in me an early abhorrence for pity. Even genuine expressions of condolence did little to alleviate my feelings of inferiority but, rather, aggravated the conviction that my father's death set me apart. I was the victim of an awful circumstance—of that much I was sure—but lingering on it only magnified the aura of misfortune. My father's death became a subject to be staunchly avoided, and it was not until my college years that I could talk about it with any degree of ease. The confusion, the self-consciousness, the shame, had been that deeply imbedded.

I grew up in a female household. My mother, my sister, and me—a fragmented sentence. Mazie, the black housekeeper, was there too, in the daytime, and with my mother away at work, she was always waiting for us when we got home from school. Perpetually energetic and vigorous, Mazie would entertain my sister and me, tell us stories, listen to ours, treat us to sing-alongs and snacks. My mother was hardly in a position to afford her full-time services, but Mazie had sacrificed a higher-paying job so that she could take care of us. She felt it was her duty.

The night my father died, she had been baby-sitting for us, and—a religious woman—her experience of the event had struck her as a devout calling: "I knew I had to stay with my two girls until they were old enough to distinguish between good and bad." But beyond providing my family with a lasting and invaluable source of friendship and support, Mazie's impression of that night had an effect on how I was to think about my father; indeed, her story is one of the few indications that I was part of the drama that changed my life.

"Your parents were going out for the evening," she says. "Your father wasn't feeling very well, but he said he'd go anyway. He came into your room and kissed his babies good night. When he leaned over your sister's crib, he turns to me and asks, 'Mazie, you take care of my girls.' I felt a shiver go down my spine, and I said yes, I'll take good care of them.

"A few hours later, everything was very quiet in the house, you suddenly cries out in your sleep, 'Daddy, don't go. Don't leave me.' And then I heard footsteps, the floor creaked, and I knew he was passing away. A few seconds later, the phone rang and they told me your father was dead." Thus did Mazie link her life to ours, determined to educate us in the ways of discernment, fulfilling the task that, to her mind, my father had requested. When she first told me the story, I must have been about eleven, my eyes opened wide with its mystery. There was a very special bond between my father and me, I decided, and the seeds of a highly romanticized relationship were sown.

Completing the female tableau was my grandmother. A Russian immigrant with one of those lyrical Eastern European accents so quickly fading from the American scene, she never lived with us but was a constant presence in our house. She was a dynamic woman with fixed ideas, and the fact that her beautiful daughter, married only four years, was now a widow with two children to support was unthinkable. Devoted to her grandchildren, it was her daughter who forever remained her obsession. Without a second thought, she would trudge over to prepare our meals or medicate us with chicken soup or stay the weekend if it meant that her daughter could be freed from family pressures. If "Selma could have a good time," if "Selma would only meet a man," everything would be as it should. My father's death became the symbol for all the hardships my grandmother had ever experienced, and until the day she died, she could not speak of him without crying.

Not really wanting for adult care, or security, or love, I nevertheless grew up in a home shrouded by tragedy. We were three females, not a family, suspended in the constant expectation that one thing and one thing only might redeem us: a man. Our greatest sense of optimism came from my mother's occasional weekend trips to the mountains. Trying to resist the temptation of getting our hopes too high, my grandmother, my sister, and I would nevertheless wait eagerly as evening enfolded the Sunday of such a weekend, privately envisioning the wishful scenario while listening for her key in the door: *Maybe she met someone, a wonderful man whom she likes and who will marry her and make everything all right.* We waited for a prince who, with his kiss, would restore us.

While adolescence is widely regarded as one of the most painful phases of life, it was for me the dawning of self-esteem. Recognition by the male sex, important to all teenage girls, represented the key to my validation. Magically, as it seemed at first, boys, people of the male gender, actually liked me.

Indeed, my early teenage years were a boon. Teachers no longer asked embarrassing questions about parental occupations, and since half the student body of my junior high school commuted from Harlem, a two-parent household no longer stood as a prerequisite to normalcy. Priorities shifted from home life to street life, and hanging out at the corner candy store was the favored activity. Though hardly the belle of Washington Heights, I had a place with the neighborhood kids and, for the first time in my life, I moved with a crowd. With my mother at work (Mazie had left when I was twelve), I was at a distinct advantage in the hanging-out department, and made the best of those after-school hours, popping gum and flirting tirelessly. Yet, for all the acquired peer pleasure, my on-going lookout for male attention did not end at the corner candy store.

When I was fourteen, I started to attend Friday-night services at the temple across the street from our house. I went alone and I prayed. Lowering my head during the weekly prayer for the dead, I was transported by the solemnity and found comfort in the act of communing. The rabbi's unfailingly heated sermons would roar through the small synagogue, frightening me a little even as I accepted every word as truth. At the end of the service, I would wait patiently for my turn to shake the hands of the rabbi and cantor so that I could say, "Good Shabbos" and receive their approving smiles. They liked me, I thought, for coming to services on my own; they must consider me special; perhaps they even felt fatherly toward me.

Leaving the synagogue, I would walk along familiar streets, extending the ceremony with a private ritual. My destination, as surely as though it were written in the prayer book, was the bridge that links Manhattan to the Bronx. It was a dangerous route, but I felt protected. Arriving at a spot that overlooks the East River—an unlikely spot, perhaps, for a romantic vigil—I would continue the ceremony of communing. From photographs, I would picture my father's face and, choosing the brightest star in the sky, I would silently talk to him. I would let him know that I was OK and that I missed him; that had he lived, ours would have been the most perfect and close of relationships; that we would have understood each other in every way. I was sure of this, and just as sure that he was listening.

In my father's image, I created a god. He alone among adults remained wise and all-knowing even during that teenage time when no one over twenty-one could possibly understand anything of importance. Then, as my Friday nights were given to more secular activities, such as dating and parties and falling in love, romantic illusions similarly found satisfaction in flesh-and-blood objects of idealization.

To my first serious boyfriend, I brought expectations nothing short of omnipotence. He was four years older than I, and in college—not a boy, but a man, and being loved by a man meant total liberation from feelings of separateness. Beyond the unquestioned necessity of physical attraction, I bestowed on Eddie the power to see inside my being, to touch and anticipate my frailties and needs, and to love me for them. Nor were these unreasonable hopes met with utter frustration, for Eddie shared my exaggerated concept of what it must mean to be loved by someone of the opposite sex—his mother had died when he was very young.

Together we created a storybook bubble of a romance, the Catherine and Heathcliff of upper Manhattan. Doomed as were our counterparts to endure a relationship so heady—our years together were fraught with misunderstandings and reconciliations—we defended the turbulence by pointing to the bittersweet transience of love. "All things of beauty are fleeting," Eddie was fond of noting. The cause of our final rift, however, was grounded in far less mushy soil. Eddie was eager to settle down and start the family he had never had. Yet on the night he proposed, after four years of believing that that could be all I wanted from life, I turned him down. In fact, no sooner had he popped the question than the bubble burst: I literally felt myself fall out of love with him. The dramatic shift in my affections was unnerving.

In retrospect, it seems no small irony that the first man I loved —after my father—was as in need of a mother as I was of a father. But far from perceiving this common bond as further proof of our destined pairing, it seemed to me to be the major flaw in Eddie's appeal; his neediness made him imperfect, and in the end it was his neediness that induced my disenchantment. I would remain faithful to the man who was perfect.

At "sleep-away" college I was once again awkward and shy. Instead of the familiar New York City turf that had nurtured me, I opted for the foreign soil of Alfred, a village in upstate New York founded by Seventh-Day Adventists and now primarily populated by the students and faculty of the university that bears the village's name. For the first time, I realized that not all the world was Jewish or black, that in fact I was part of a minority. I also learned that there is a specific creature known as a "Jewish girl from New York," of whom intelligence, wit, and a certain amount of pushiness are to be expected. Though not totally without appeal, she is not likely to be voted Homecoming Queen. After several weeks on campus, during which this new information was assimilated, I became reasonably comfortable with my identity as outsider, for at Alfred University there was a clique for everyone—including outsiders. We were the beatniks, the intellectuals, the artist types—basically, we were the Jewish kids from New York. (It must be noted that New York City and upstate New York have nothing in common except a governor and, in the mid-sixties, Regents examinations.)

Drinking was an integral part of the social life, which routinely consisted of parties, dancing, and beer. Alcohol was new to me, as was its loosening effect on inhibitions, so along with

the intoxication of my three-point-two beers came the other
side of light-headedness: With increasing regularity, an evening
of rock 'n' roll and alcohol would lead to thoughts of my father.
At first sentimental, to the strains of "Daddy's Home," perhaps,
the feelings would gradually intensify and I would soon be in
the grip of a choking need to get away from the stale room of
merrymakers. Escaping into the crisp Alfred night, I would
allow the sorrow that filled me its release. Hot tears stung my
freezing face, but the sobs that shook me felt good. After so
many years of public evasion and private, sugar-coated fantasies, I was finally acknowledging the pain and the longing. I was
beginning to mourn.

One day, seated on a bus headed for NYU (I had transferred
there after my freshman year), I was struggling to understand
my irrational attachment to a man I was dating whose feelings
toward me were anything but constant, when I had the following insight: he seems to love me one minute and then, for no
reason at all, he's distant—just like my father! The realization
was staggering, the closest I have ever come to an epiphany. It
is perhaps only a coincidence that the bus was passing over the
Washington Bridge, the one I used to walk to after Friday-night
services, when the enlightening thought struck; what was not a
coincidence, I understood in that moment, was my pattern of
behavior with men. I fell in love too easily, as the song goes, and
once drawn to someone, any ensuing frustration or disappointment, rather than making me back off, fanned the flames of my
devotion. Truth to tell, the very cooling of the man attracted me
still further. Even Eddie, my high school romance of four years,
had been most exciting to me during his habitual periods of
deciding we weren't right for each other. The two or three men
I had focused on since then, in retrospect emerge as the classic
Don Juan types: dripping with charm and dry on sincerity. At
twenty-one, what I recognized was that by repeatedly getting
embroiled in the here-today, gone-tomorrow brand of affection,
I was grappling with the abandonment of my childhood. A
rejecting man was the only kind I was familiar with. Now that I
understood the beast, I would surely master it.

Of course, it wasn't that simple. Psychological insight may

lead to self-knowledge, but knowing why something hurts doesn't make the hurt go away. Understanding the basis of a neurotic attachment is no guarantee of disengagement. My infatuation with the man I had been thinking about on the bus continued, as did his ability to lead me on and let me down. When the intrigue at long last faded, it was as much from weariness as anything else. But I emerged from the fixation, which dragged on into my mid-twenties, with some important information about myself. My father's death was more than a poignant happenstance in my childhood; it was a fact in my life that affected everything I was and everything I did, as much a part of my present as my past.

I needed to be someone's "Daddy's girl," to luxuriate on his knee and bask in his approval. At the same time, I placed great value on my independence, resisting pressure from my family to settle down with one of the sensible young men who had proposed. Even as most of my friends got married, I, quite unconsciously, assured my "freedom" by remaining fixed on a man with no such intentions.

My fiercest desires were at odds: to be secure and protected in the love of a man, and to prove that I could succeed in the world on my own. Both of these needs, existing in contradiction, emanated from the unresolved impressions of my childhood. The little girl who looked on with envy as others climbed onto their daddies' laps, and the second-grader repelled by the kindness of strangers, waged war in my brain. I knew I must find a balance, become my own arbitrator instead of seeking relationships that reflected my ambivalence. To find peace as an adult, I must first make peace with the wounded child inside me.

I approached the quest for self-knowledge (it just so happens that I graduated college in 1969, on the brink of the "Me Decade") with varying degrees of single-mindedness. Certainly the women's movement, political activism, career choices, and marriage both contributed to and distracted me from a wholehearted pursuit of analyzing my psyche. That I had actually succeeded in meeting a man with whom I could share a fulfilling relationship seemed one of the miracles of our time. Yet his extraordinary reserve of warmth and patience, nurtured by the close-knit family in which he had grown up, had proved stronger than my resistance to reciprocal love. Indeed, becoming part of his life had seemed my entrée to normalcy.

For all the external satisfaction and involvement, however, the dull ache persisted. Marriage was not a panacea, but a placebo. After the initial belief in its curative effects had worn off, I found that I was embroiled in the very situation that frightened me most: I was living day to day with a man that I loved. Old doubts and sorrows, rather than being laid to rest through marriage, were reawakened by it.

One night, after returning from an evening with friends, Jeff and I were just outside our apartment when I felt him looking at me with unusual intensity. "What is it?" I asked. "You have so much sadness in your face," he told me.

Life, as is its wont, went on. Though I had always vowed never to be a teacher (it was *the* profession prescribed to all middle-class girls as a sensible supplement to marriage), it did in fact emerge as a sensible supplement for a novice writer. I enjoyed many aspects of teaching, including the education it afforded. I was continually disarmed, for instance, by the nonchalance with which children spoke of spending the weekend at the home of this or that parent. The family unit, no longer the sacrosanct symbol of infallibility, had ceased to be a measure of a child's claim to normalcy. "Father Knows Best" had been replaced by "One Day at a Time." Varying lifestyles were easily accepted, but the death of a parent remained an uncomfortable subject.

I continued to seek information, but the results of my search were discouraging. From Freud, I gleaned the significance of the father-daughter relationship, the sexual implications inherent in his theory that a girl's first romantic-love interest is her father. But what about the impact of a father's sudden disappearance? How did that affect sexuality, attitudes, self-image?

In vain, I sought the book, the treatise, the ultimate analysis that would satisfactorily, once and for all, shed light on this serious concern, a childhood trauma that certainly was experienced by a large segment of society. Especially in the seventies, there were a spate of books available to the general public aimed at explaining people to themselves: books on the family, children of divorced parents, mothers and daughters—the list is long and impressive. But even as the market swelled with this new genre dubbed "pop psychology," my quest went unfulfilled. Those rarefied studies I did find were highly clinical and, moreover, tended to focus on the death of the mother. The book I was searching for did not exist, and I continued to feel alone with my need for it.

Time and experience came to indicate otherwise. Though still somewhat uneasy about speaking of my father's death, whenever I did meet a woman who had grown up without a father—owing to death, divorce, or abandonment—and we felt comfortable enough to talk about it, eyes would lock in instant recognition; a sorrow buried deep was shared, and gradually, bashfully, we felt a bond in our deprivation.

Most women have a man that got away, a man that they have loved and lost. For us, that man was father, the first man that we had ever loved. With his presence, he had introduced us to the delight of being the female recipient of male love. With his disappearance, he had taught us the precariousness of love. Whether he died or abandoned us, we felt rejected. Despite, perhaps because of, this betrayal, he remained an indomitable force within us, an idealized standard against which all else would be measured, and found wanting. The man that got away was a constant presence in our private worlds; yet it was comforting, now that we could speak of it, to find others there.

After several encounters with women who had lost their fathers, the idea of joining occupation with preoccupation began to take form. I had been writing full time for a few years; inventing stories, reporting and interpreting facts, I was making a living telling about others. Yet the subject that permeated my consciousness remained a subject in search of an author. There were other fatherless daughters out there wondering what they had missed and clinging to idealized images that interfered with their ability to enjoy life. To make sense of my own unresolved conflicts, and to provide a resource for others, I would write the book for which I had always been looking.

What was the connection between father loss and the forces that motivate a woman? The question would take me back into regions I had wished never to revisit. But it would also lead me to understand a trauma whose impact had been felt from Washington Heights to the White House and was even now shaping the lives of over five and a half million girls in the United States alone.

Seeking personal experiences and professional expertise, conducting a nationwide study that would put me in touch with over five hundred of the countless adult women who had lost their fathers owing to death, divorce, or abandonment, I committed myself to a public exploration of the subject that for years I hadn't even been able to speak of.

TWO

A SUBJECT OF RESEARCH

The Father-Daughter Relationship

"You can have fun with a son,
But you got to be a father to a girl!"

In those two lines, Oscar Hammerstein presented me with the greatest enigma of my life: the inscrutability of the father-daughter relationship. A cover story in *Esquire,* an article about a father's love for his children, mocked my dilemma by observing, "Fathers and daughters are a deep and abiding mystery it would do no good to solve."

Is father-daughter love really so unknowable, so unexplainable, as to defy articulation? Is firsthand experience the only possible key to appreciation? Is my idealization of the man that got away matched in reality by a magical relationship that I will never have? What does it mean, "you got to be a father to a girl"?

I grew up looking for answers—in the occupied laps of other girls' fathers, in the satisfied smiles of those laps' inhabiters. I knew I was missing something cozy, something comforting, something protective and reassuring. TV persuaded me that Father knew best about his little Margie, while Nancy Drew and Scarlett O'Hara also enjoyed edifying relationships with their fathers. It was only later, much later, that I began to hear stirrings of discontent. Fathers weren't all wisdom and sympathy. To my amazement, they even began to emerge as antiheroes in the real-life stories of my friends. Perhaps I had main-

tained such a trusting relationship with my father by sheer
virtue of the fact that he, quite literally, didn't have to live up to
my confidence in him. I began to seek answers from more
realistic sources.

What is the father-daughter relationship? Recently, and be-
latedly, entire books have been given to the subject. And
throughout this book, the relationship is analyzed according to
the developmental stages of daughter. But we cannot embark
upon an investigation into the effects of father absence without
first exploring what is known about the influence of father's
presence. There are no such clear-cut answers as my childhood
fantasies provided. Instead, a survey of the literature reveals
traditional and modern views as various and controversial as
psychology itself.

When considering any aspect of the parent-child relationship, it behooves us to begin with Sigmund Freud. Though
many of his theories have fallen into disrepute, Freud did no
less than introduce to the study of personality development the
notion of the unconscious—a repository of unrecalled experiences hidden deep within our minds which motivate much of
our behavior. Primary among these experiences, Freud believed, was the inevitable sexual desire of a child for the parent
of the opposite sex. Taking his cue and terminology from classic
mythology, he dubbed this phenomenon the Oedipus complex.* The only way to resolve it was to repress it and thereby
achieve healthy identification with the parent of the same sex.
Thus, according to Freudian psychoanalysis, a girl's feminine
behavior is born through her sexual attraction to her father.

Initially, Freud assumed that sexual development was identi-
cal in boys and girls, but he later adapted his theory to acknowledge significant differences. Indeed, it is his very explanation of

---

* In Greek legend, Oedipus, not knowing the true identity of his parents,
married his mother and killed his father. A corresponding myth has a female
character, Electra, avenge her father's death by assisting in the murder of her
mother. Hence, the female form of the Oedipus complex is frequently referred
to as the Electra complex.

the differences which has aroused much of the criticism directed at him.

Breaking sexual development into distinct stages—the "psychosexual stages of development"—Freud cited first the oral and then the anal zones as the earliest sources of gratification, or pleasure. At the age of three or four, the child discovered the pleasure to be taken in the genitals, and thus began the *phallic* stage of development.† He felt that this stage was most important to personality development.

The phallus plays a key role during this stage. The boy gives up his rivalry with father for mother's attention because of guilt and the resulting stress of castration anxiety. He relinquishes Oedipal wishes for mother and identifies with father and masculinity.

The girl, on the other hand, enters the phallic stage upon observing the inadequacy she shares with mother: she doesn't have a penis. She has the more difficult task, therefore, of changing her primary love interest from mother to father. This transition completed, however, *she never has to totally relinquish her intense love for father because castration is not an issue.* She will come to identify with mother and femininity as a way of attracting father and other men, and indeed it is to this end that most of her energies will be expended. Whereas masculinity is attained through the demanding effort of repressing keen impulses, femininity is a learned method of gratifying those impulses. Of course, repression of her desire for father is necessary, but not nearly to the same extent. The girl will turn to men other than father when it becomes clear that he is not responding to her in a sexual way.‡

The objections to be taken with Freud's views of female development are glaringly obvious: Placing penis envy at the root of femininity, noting the lesser demands on female sexual development, imply a sexual bias that is immediately offensive. Moreover, since he believed that civilization itself was created

† Freud's male bias is apparent. The word "phallic" comes from the Greek *phallos,* or male genital organ.

‡ As we shall see in a later chapter, the girl who grows up without a male parent is particularly unsuccessful in abandoning father as a sexual object. In her fantasies, he remains the perfect, all-giving man.

through the repression of sexual instincts made necessary by castration anxiety, women were, by definition, less civilized creatures.

Freud, in fact, was the first to acknowledge the tentative nature of his theories on femininity. "[My opinions] can only be maintained if my findings, which are based on a handful of cases, turn out to have general validity and to be typical."

Psychoanalysts from Freud's day to this reconfirm the father's importance in shaping his daughter's feminine identity. While the role of penis envy is frequently played down, or even disputed, *father is credited as the major factor in his daughter's confidence in her femininity*. Recent studies in fact emphasize that one of the father's major contributions to his children's development is in the area of gender identity. He, more than mother, differentiates his expectations, attitudes, activities, and reactions to his children according to their sex, leading a professional review of these studies to conclude: "A fundamental part of the girl's sex-role development seems to be the positive acceptance of herself as a female. The father's particular relationship with his daughter seems very important to her sex-role development. He may foster the establishment of a positive feminine identity by treating her as a female and encouraging her to behave in ways which are considered to be feminine in society." Thus, according to this review, fathers saw their daughters as "more delicate and sensitive" than their sons, they rewarded their daughters for being "attractive" as well as "good," and it was observed that there was more "paternal stress on interest in persons for girls than for boys."

The image of female as soft, attractive, receptive, warm and understanding, supportive and helpful—an image created and sustained by patriarchal society—proves to be engendered, aptly, by our fathers. While mother may provide the model of femininity, it is father who motivates daughter to imitate feminine behavior. To please Daddy, the first man they love, girls take a profound interest in attaining and perfecting the societally approved notion of what it means to be female.

Father's encouragement of her feminine qualities will naturally influence daughter's confidence with men, or what Signe Hammer calls her "heterosexual femininity." His flirtatious, responsive, persuasive affirmation of her appeal will give her a sure sense of her progress in the female arena. Writes psychotherapist Marjorie Leonard, "It is not enough that the mother is available for identification. The girl also needs reassurance from her father that he sees her as a budding female, so that she can have confidence that males her own age will also accept it."

Psychoanalytic thought seems united in its belief that father is the instrumental force in shaping daughter's identity as a feminine person. As the first man to be attracted by her charms, his presence is decisive in her later confidence as a woman. "Crucial to the girl's development is whether or not her father was available to her as a love-object and whether or not he was capable of offering her affection . . . ," Leonard concludes, then adds the significant qualifier ". . . without being seduced by her fantasies, or seducing her with his counter-oedipal feelings."

The incest taboo—whether perceived as the triumph of reason over instinct, the Freudian view, or as itself an instinct, the view espoused by disciples of C. G. Jung—is a universal part of the human condition. Primitive societies had elaborate rituals ensuring against it, and the prohibition persists to modern-day families. Both Freud and Jung believed that repression of desires for the parent of the opposite sex gave birth to culture, civilization, and creativity, but the latter, identifying the taboo as a human instinct, didn't differentiate its influence according to gender. Indeed, most current professionals of either school have dispensed with making gender-related judgments, but the fact is that incest plays a far greater role in the lives of girls than of boys. As illustrated below, sexual activity between father and daughter occurs in more households than might have been expected.

In a recent study of 796 college students, researcher David Finklehor found that a little more than 1 percent of the women had been sexually victimized by their fathers or stepfathers. From these findings, Finklehor concluded, "Approximately three quarters of a million women eighteen and over in the general population have had such an experience, and another 16,000 cases are added each year from among the group of girls

aged five to seventeen." In contrast, none of the college men
Finklehor questioned reported incest with their mothers.

Though the numbers cited above represent only 1 percent of
the population studied, the father-daughter relationship seems
to be fraught with sexual tension, whether or not it is ever acted
upon. Is it because, as Freud would suggest, the young girl's
attraction to her father is never fully relinquished? Must he, for
the rest of his adult life, fend off the enticements of the young
temptress blossoming before his eyes? And sometimes—at least
1 percent of the time—is the come-hither glance of his daughter just too much for him to resist?

If, as most professionals believe, father is the determining
influence on his daughter's confidence in her sexual appeal, and
if it is his masculine approval that introduces her to the pleasure
to be taken in her femininity, then it is a precarious balance
indeed upon which they both tread.

There is daughter—young and adoring—how is father to control himself in the presence of such temptation? In their study
of incestuous fathers, Judith Herman and Lisa Hirschman
found, "[They] claim the sexual initiation of their daughters as a
patriarchal right." Dr. Holly Barrett, in a conversation with the
author, corroborated the finding. "It usually *is* the father who
sets up the seduction. Daughter goes along to gain his approval."

Obviously, and fortunately, father-daughter incest is not a
common occurrence. But there it lurks, just beyond manifestation, as a palpable facet of the relationship. Father—the older
man, mentor in the ways of femininity; daughter—the young
girl, eager to learn, eager to please; two players ripe for a sexual
experience, yet forbidden by a universally accepted taboo.

Many observers of the relationship theorize that it is the
conflict inculcated by this taboo that makes it so difficult for
women to associate love with sexual intimacy, that one glaring
legacy of the father-daughter relationship is a lifetime of confusion about mature sexual desire. This might lead us to conclude
that girls who grew up without fathers are at a distinct advantage. Yet, of course, father's role in the family goes beyond that
of sex object.

As we shall see in a subsequent chapter, father's emergence as a member of the family is a comparatively recent development in human history. In prerecorded time, a family consisted of a mother and her children, with the man's role in conception only minimally understood. The perception of father as an *active* member of the family is even more recent.

In 1954, Dr. O. Spurgeon English wrote, "A woman understands [the child's] rhythms of eating, sleeping, playing, and eliminating, as well as his emotional needs for touch, fondling, and companionship. It is probably within the potentialities of male psychology to perform these functions also, just as it has been possible for woman to enter the realm of man's activities. But the fact that anatomically and physiologically man does not function in such a way as to bring him into close contact with the infant has prevented him from even having been tested out in these areas. Moreover, it seems unlikely that he ever will perform these womanly duties in rearing the young."

English goes on to identify the father as the vehicle for introducing masculinity to his children, the all-important supporter of mother, and the parent who teaches his daughter that "the attention of men brings with it prestige and pleasure."

Though few professionals would dispute these latter roles, the father's contribution during infancy is now more fully understood. For in addition to supporting mother emotionally, the male parent is now recognized as possessing the key to one of the most important areas of the child's emotional development: her autonomy.

It is father who encourages the child to relinquish her symbiotic attachment to mother; he who reinforces her urgent yet tentative need for independence; he, in short, who imparts the inherent value of being a separate person.

Father comes to the baby from outside the profoundly intimate mother-infant connection. And if he is a loving, nurturing parent, his very presence illustrates the positive aspects of individuality. Through his attention and interest, the baby learns that she can be a secure and viable person, even as she ventures away from her mother.

Father comes to the baby from outside her most familiar setting as well. Allowing for the prevalence of his work outside

the home, he steps in to represent society at large and is hence
frequently credited with providing the bridge not only away
from mother, but toward the external world. It is through his
example that the possibility of success as a separate person is
initiated.

Thus, in her infancy, the daughter is rescued by her father
from her symbiotic attachment to her mother. As the girl enters
the Oedipal stage of development, her father's encouraging
signals and gestures educate her in the ways of femininity.
Then, throughout her childhood, her father comes home from
the outside world of work and society, representing adventure,
discipline, and responsibility—all of which, she knows, are
highly valued. During the pivotal period of her adolescent
years, her father becomes the mirror of her developing sexuality, and more often than not, she will see reflected in him a
keener approval of her softer, more pliable self.

From her very earliest days, a girl's attitudes and expectations
are being shaped by her father. Because of the powerful position he holds in her heart, in the family, in the world, he, more
than anyone, is subtly conveying to her knowledge of who she
will be. Yet at the same time, he conveys a double message: the
advantages of autonomy, and affection for her sweetest smile;
the pleasure of being separate from mother, and the pleasure in
being a female person, like mother. Should she identify with the
independence that father has taught her to value, or should she
shy away from independence, because Daddy likes her better
when she relies on him?

Many psychologists cite father's mixed message as the root of
female conflict: Is independence at odds with femininity? Can a
woman lead a productive, assertive life and still hope to enjoy a
love relationship with a man? Owing to the prominent influence the father wields in determining how his daughter will
integrate these dueling facets of herself, an expert in the study
of father-daughter relationships writes, ". . . Fathers have an
enormously important role to play in the socialization of 'liberated' daughters. . . . If the fathers of the future communicate
a belief that career commitment is not incompatible with femininity, we shall see many fewer women experiencing doubt

about the compatibility of their social and occupational aspirations."

It is not surprising that feminist thinkers have trouble with a lot of this. First of all, there is the problematic definition of femininity. Need it necessarily imply, as two respected scholars wrote: ". . . warmth and affection and sensitivity to the needs of others. Skill in understanding and communicating feelings and striving to be attractive in appearance . . . interests and preferences [that] tend to center around domestic, social and caretaking activities"?

There is nothing *inherently* feminine in any of this, feminists would assert. Yet these are the characteristics that we have come to associate with women in our society and, to a large extent, the characteristics that our fathers have traditionally and enthusiastically endorsed, from our infancy through adolescence.

Several feminist writers have also been offended by the idea of Father as Rescuer. For even as he introduces us to our independent identity, who is it that he is rescuing us from but mother? Implicit in this act of gallantry is the inferiority of our mothers—women—ourselves. Hence it follows that we, female persons, are inferior, and indeed, many would claim that that is precisely what patriarchal society would like women to recognize as yet another characteristic of femininity.

"My father always seemed superior to my mother," writes author Judith Arcana. "By the time I was an adolescent, and had begun to be severely critical of my mother, the difference between them was couched in intellectual and political terms. I thought my mother was empty-headed and boring; my father was well-read and always abreast of current happenings in the world . . . My father appeared to be always in command of his emotions. My mother and I were beneath him in this respect." In order to gain her father's approval, then, the girl is trying to take a role for which she has been taught to have contempt. To be feminine and desirable, she must also accept her natural inferiority.

"From fairy tales to contemporary T.V. programs," Arcana continues, ". . . all the daddies . . . are patriarchs just the same. Wise or foolish, they are the kings of their respective households. We see them as romantic figures, even in their negative aspects."

The father-daughter relationship would seem to be a bond of romantic undertones, and a hotbed of controversy. Had my father lived, would I be more or less than who I am? Would he have taught me? fought me? seduced me? used my adoration to ensure patriarchy? Or would his presence have instilled in me a surer sense of what it means to be a woman?

A review of the literature suggests all these possibilities, just as my fantasies remain fixed on the splendid love that might have been.

". . . Daddy's girl, who hung onto his belt and danced fox trots on the tops of his shoes, cannot accept that Daddy is not here anymore. How could Daddy, the smartest of men, who ought to have been elected President, how could my hero die? How could he not be here for me any-more . . . ?"

The author of the above is forty-five years old, lamenting her father's recent death.

What is it like for a *little girl* to lose her father, to be deprived of his love? How will the initial impact of loss and her ensuing childhood conspire to shape the woman she is to become? . . .

PART TWO

THE IMPACT OF
LOSS

THREE

I NEVER CRIED FOR MY FATHER

Children and Mourning

Before you can go through the mourning process, you have to know that someone has died. From this elementary fact I was protected. Like so many parents trying to shield their children from the darker realities, my mother told me, "Daddy has gone away." Specifically, I was told that he had gone on a boat ride.

The result of this deception was manifold, as I shall illustrate in a moment. But its immediate effect was to fill me with hope whenever in the vicinity of a large body of water. Wistfully, I would gaze out upon any lake, river, or ocean within view, waiting, as it were, for the ship to come in. The sight of her three-year-old so engaged undoubtedly saddened my mother, but she simply thought it wrong to encumber a child with the absolute finality of death. An extended boat ride seemed to her a positive alternative to the frightening specter inherent in the truth. I continued my vigil.

Other children, however, were better informed. This my mother learned when, one day during the first summer after my father's death, I refused to walk. Neither she, nor my grandmother, nor anyone else at the Catskills resort where we were spending a few weeks could do anything to persuade me. There, inside the stucco bungalow, I sat, resolute in my stand, immovable. After much hysteria, my mother was able to uncover the root of my tenacity: A girl a little older than I—she must have been five or six—told my mother that she had enlightened me as to the real whereabouts of my father. "Elyce thought he was on a boat," she said. "But everyone knows that he's under the ground."

To get me off the bed, and to quiet my apprehensions about *anyone* "walking on my father," my mother quickly discredited the little girl's assertion. "Daddy is not under the ground. He's gone away on a long trip." Would he ever come back? Where did he go? Why did he go? That I asked these questions can only be assumed; how they were answered remains unknown. I simply don't remember. Like so many other aspects of that crucial period in my life, I am dependent on the recollections of my mother.

Freud, addressing the subject of "childhood amnesia," wrote, ". . . [t]he child no less than the adult only retains in memory what is important; but what is important is represented in the memory by something apparently trivial. For this reason I have called these childhood recollections *screen-memories.*"

I am particularly struck by this idea of "screen-memories" because of the one clear image that I have retained from that time: *My father is holding my hand in the foyer of our apartment. We are saying good-bye to my mother, who is fussing with the baby (my sister). My father is taking me to Central Park to go on the pony rides, and I know that I am very pleased to be going out with him.* When people ask, which they often do, if I remember my father, it is that image which pops into my mind as I say yes. For years, however, my mother insisted that I couldn't possibly remember him or that excursion to the park, because I was just too young. Recently I brought it up again, asking, "Didn't he take me out for a pony ride?" "Yes," my mother said. "That was the day he died."

Somewhere between the Catskills and kindergarten, all pretense about boats and long trips was apparently dropped. Though neither my mother nor I can pinpoint the moment or conversation when the fact of death was revealed, it obviously was, because I do remember not wanting to tell anyone in school that my father was dead. But, aside from feelings of shame, the degree and manner of my early comprehension about death remain a mystery. The one thing that is clear is that, due to my mother's discomfort with addressing the subject of death, I did not begin to mourn for my father until fifteen years after he died. Mourning, repressed, became the undertow against which I struggled to become a woman.

Joseph Palombo, a highly respected authority on the effects of loss during childhood, has written: "[I]t may not be so much the death of a parent that ends up being traumatic but rather the surviving parent's response or failure in empathy in communicating the news to the child." In our study of the effects of father loss on women, 75 percent of those whose fathers died said that they were discouraged from expressing their feelings at the time of death. Repressed mourning, a harmful condition in anyone, is therefore a vital aspect of the fatherless daughter's mentality, one demanding particular attention when considering the woman she has become.

Throughout this volume we will encounter women in whom the absence of feeling at the time of loss contributed to the feeling of absence throughout their lives. Margaret, a thirty-seven-year-old therapist, is, by training and experience, acutely aware of this confounding aspect of losing one's father.*

"I felt left out when my father was taken to the hospital," she begins. "One minute I was told that he had to go to the hospital for routine surgery, and then he was gone. I was not allowed to visit him. I had no contact with him except on the phone." The operation, for perforated ulcers, was a success, but the patient developed peritonitis in the hospital, and died. Perhaps it was a dramatic imagination, or the abrupt way in which she was informed of his leaving, but at nine years old, Margaret had watched her father "being taken away" and known "somehow intuitively" that there was nothing routine about it.

Soft-spoken and given to reflection, a controlled and graceful figure, she is doggedly honest about herself and sensitive to others. Though the subject is painful, she wants to talk about it now, memories spilling to the surface in unself-consciously childlike images. "I have this scene that's imprinted in me of sitting by the dining room window on the floor and watching

* Unless otherwise indicated, names and identities of interview subjects have been changed to protect their privacy.

my mother drive him away, and he was the one who always drove. She turned the Studebaker around and I saw him sitting in the passenger seat. Somewhere in there I had—there was a very, very bad feeling about it. I had this feeling of weakness. He was a very stable figure and he wasn't in that role then. There wasn't the security . . . The last time I saw him was that scene."

Born in Poland, Margaret's father was the model of reliability, a watchmaker by trade. "His life was very ordered. He was very strong and quietly active. He was around on weekends and in the evenings, and had a lot of hobbies that he did at home. He liked classical music, refined things. I remember we used to have music nights, and we all four would be together, and we used to have chess nights." Quiet and strong, he was the center of his family, the foundation on which life at home was built.

Unable to visit her father in the hospital, Margaret gave in to feelings of helplessness. "It was a very strange time, very isolated. Not coincidentally, I got sick when he went into the hospital. My knees got swollen and I had a temperature, so I had to be in bed." She was still sick when, after about two weeks of daily trips to the hospital, Margaret's mother called her two children into her bed. (This is a common place for the widow to share her loss with the children.) "I figured that she'd gone to pick him up. That's my feeling, that they were going to be coming right home. The next thing I know, she calls my brother and me into bed with her. We all got under the covers and she had her arms around both of us and, in a very soothing voice she said, 'Your father has gone to heaven.' My brother, who is four years older than I am, started to sob. I don't think I felt anything at the moment. I had no desire to cry."

Margaret had adored her father, had looked to him for security, agonized over his sudden departure; but when told that he was dead, she "didn't feel anything." As a student of psychology and practicing therapist, she can recall with great clarity the mechanics of her denial.

"I remember going back to school about two weeks after my father died. I was walking in the schoolyard and a little schoolmate came up to me and said, 'Oh, I'm so sorry about what happened.' And I had no idea what she was talking about. So I asked her and she said, 'About your father.' And it's like some-where inside of me I recognized that it was locked away, that it was not appropriate to show my feelings to anyone.

"I used to dream about him. I would dream that he was coming home from work and I was running out to meet him. And then I would wake up and realize that it couldn't happen, and I would cry." She pauses. "I feel so sorry for myself when I think about that time . . .

"Life in the house changed a lot. There were three separate individuals. That's the real tragedy of his dying: it splintered us. From that point on, we were never open, and it was like the three of us were hiding our feelings from each other. The whole chess night and music night were stopped. For so much of my childhood, there was always this lovely classical music around me, and it stopped. Everything changed very abruptly.

"I responded to the situation by becoming very isolated. I feel like it was some kind of a switch, and I can remember it physi-cally happening that the only way I could live with it was to have certain times all by myself. I still find great comfort in privacy. I spend a lot of time inside myself, in a private world."

After their fathers died, most of the women in our study got the message that feelings were best reserved for private times. The extended hiding of emotions came to create a feeling of separateness from other family members, and continues, in adulthood, to impart a feeling of separateness from other peo-ple. Echoing Margaret's intense need for "a private world," 72 percent of the women in our study whose fathers died de-scribed themselves as being "introspective and really very pri-vate." Daughters of divorce and intact homes, and women who had mourned their fathers' death, were not nearly so invested in spending time by themselves.

In Margaret's case, as in many others, the need for privacy inhibited activity in the public world. Like the majority of fa-therless daughters, she did not shy away from working, but the prospect of committing herself to a profession made her uneasy. Nearly fifteen years after graduating from college, she finally decided upon a career, and entered a training program in coun-seling. Married to an old schoolmate—"I had always had a crush on him"—she was attracted also to the opportunity for personal communication afforded by the field of therapy. In fact, she notes as a paradox of her personality her burning need for privacy and her simultaneous penchant for honest, personal interaction. In pursuing her new career, "I found a world that fit my nature," and by listening to others, she became reacquainted with some of her own more troublesome secrets.

In their article entitled "The Fatherless Child," C. Janet Newman and Jeffrey S. Schwam explain the "paradox": A common result of loss, they say, ". . . may be the development of special empathy for other persons who have also sustained losses. Sometimes the motive is to associate with such fellow sufferers in order to share the fixation point." In the presence of other people's needs, Margaret found it easier to get close to her own.

"As part of an evaluation process at the Counseling Center," she recalls, "they had a group of us in a room and asked each of us to answer the question, 'Who am I?' The first thing I said was, 'My father died when I was nine years old.' It just came out! It was that much a part of me. I didn't even mention the fact that I was married . . . I think I'd answer differently today."

What transpired between that group session and our interview was that Margaret finally cried for her father. The process began during a four-week Reichian workshop that she was attending as part of her training. "The demanding exercises made me want to sob. I felt how much he was a part of me and how much of me had been locked up for so long. I realized that I had never grieved, really out-and-out grieved. I had never said good-bye. I needed help so I could let go of this private man that I had carried around since I was nine.

"When I said good-bye, it was a physical experience. I did it at home lying on the floor, crying and with words, and it's like my whole body went through such an upheaval that I had to run to the bathroom because I almost threw up."

More than two decades after she saw him driven away in the Studebaker, Margaret said good-bye to the first man she ever loved. No longer burdened by the weight of carrying him around, she is freer to love her husband and son. "I think that before I went through it, my capacity to live and to feel was diminished by many levels. There's an energy in the body that fizzes, keeping things down to a level it can handle, so you don't have the joy, you don't have the grief, and you don't have the fun. Now I spend much less time just getting by. I don't have near the depressions I've had behind me. I don't have to hide from the world any more. I still think about him a lot. But it's not as intense as it used to be."

Having mourned, Margaret experienced a liberation of sorts. She is freer to work, freer to love. Yet the psychological wound she sustained at her father's death, though healed, has left its scar. The little girl who heard the music stop remains wary of complacency in the face of contentment. "I always feel that I have to look at the negative possibilities of a situation before I can enjoy it. I look at what could be the worst that can happen, and if I feel that I have plans to deal with it, then I can move ahead.

"Sometimes when my husband is late getting home from work (he's generally very reliable), I am seized by panic, out of the blue, that he'll disappear. And what frightens me most is that the very thought of being without him is so devastating. Now, with the baby here, I sometimes get this stabbing fear that it's not just me that will be left alone."

Listening to Margaret speak of her irrational bouts of panic, I feel my stomach constrict. How often I have entertained similar fantasies! Particularly now that we have a child—and Jeff is a father—he is even more likely to be someone who dies.

Though reliable in many ways, Jeff would be the first to admit that promptness is not one of his strong suits. Having accepted this characteristic tardiness as a fact of life, I always add a half hour to whatever appointed time we have arranged to meet, either at home or out. But on those occasions when the clock starts ticking past the thirty-minute allowance, my thoughts invariably lead to what a part of me must await as *the* awful inevitability: "Well, he probably couldn't get away," . . . tick tock tick . . . "He must be held up at a meeting" . . . tick tock tick . . . "I hope everything's OK with the car" . . . tick tock tick . . . "Do the police call or come to the door when there's been an accident? . . . I wonder how they'll tell me."

These morbid scenarios are not limited to appearing when Jeff has not. Nor am I alone with them. Through the conversations and reading necessitated by this project, I have learned that daydreams of disaster are an integral part of the fatherless daughter's consciousness. In his excellent book *Your Inner Child of the Past,* Dr. W. Hugh Missildine emphasizes, "Your childhood affects everything you do, everything you feel." Regarding the child who has lost a parent, he suggests that such a loss may very well lead to a fear that all loved persons will die.

To be perpetually haunted by the threat of abandonment seems a condition inexorably attendant on early-childhood loss. In women who have not completed the mourning process, the threat is exacerbated, variously translating into apathy, depression, or anxiety in the face of love. As revealed in our study, women who had not mourned their fathers were more likely than women who had mourned to fear that their husbands would die. These findings, in conjunction with the emerging professional wisdom, indicate quite clearly that mourning at the time of loss alleviates a good deal of subsequent grief. "From the moment life begins . . ." writes social worker Lily Pincus, "human growth depends on accepting and mastering loss."

Thirty years ago, my mother told her three-year-old daughter that Daddy wouldn't be around for a while because he had gone on a long trip. She lied to me, and it is only within the past few years that I have begun to understand how that lie compounded feelings of parental deprivation. But though I speak openly of my mother's deception, it is not my purpose to accuse her, or cast her in the role of wrongdoer. Struggling with the traumatic devastation of her loss, at least as unschooled as were the professionals of that time in confronting the complex realities of death, she did the best she could.

Due to the avoidance generated by this most uncomfortable subject, death, it is only recently that the mental health community has addressed itself to the even more delicate issue of children and mourning. The causes and ramifications of repressed mourning are being articulated, and the importance of helping children to mourn has earned emphatic support.

*

There are many factors that contribute to an avoidance of mourning. First of all, there is the unspoken but agreed-upon standard that persists in this country which applauds stoicism in the face of death. Who among us does not remember the brave form of Jacqueline Kennedy publicly leading the nation and the world to the untimely burial of her husband? How greatly were her poise, her dignity, to be admired: this was class! Margaret, too, had learned the lesson of emotional restraint from a most persuasive teacher: her father. "I remember that he had a lot of kindness, but he was not affectionate. I knew he liked me a lot and I used to wish that he would show it. I would ask my mother, 'Why doesn't Daddy ever hug and kiss me?' And she'd say, 'It's not his way.' "

When asked about the nature of her childhood prior to her father's death, Margaret creates a vision filled with sunny images. She was a gregarious child, she says, spirited and fun-loving. Her early years were characterized by friendships and playfulness and doing well in school, the All-American, California-dreamin' childhood. Almost. For, lurking somewhere in the idyllic portrait, is the barely discernible shadow of a girl for whom all that sugar and spice did not add up to the proverbial apple pie. The missing ingredient would seem to be demonstrative affection from the parent she adored. "Something wasn't right," she tells me. "Because, contrary to that happy-go-lucky image, I have to tell you that I was overweight as a child."

The emerging picture of a little girl burdened in her otherwise carefree existence by the gnawing sense of emotional need relates directly to our immediate concern: Why didn't she feel anything when told of her father's death? Strong and stable as her father was, pillar of the family construct, and solid base of life at home, his reluctance to give his daughter tangible love in the way of physical affection played a major role in her subsequent inability to mourn his death.

Writes Lily Pincus, "The emotionally deprived . . . child may have learned to avoid the fear of abandonment and isolation by denying feelings and pain, and may thus have laid the foundation for defenses against feeling the agony of the final bereavement through death." While it is obviously hyperbolic to describe Margaret's childhood as "deprived," she interprets her former compulsive eating as a way of filling the void created by her father's withholding of affection.

Nor did her mother offer very much guidance in helping Margaret to cope with the much greater void created by her father's sudden and permanent departure. Following the tender morning in bed when the children were informed of the loss they now shared, all sharing of manifest sorrow ceased. The devastating reality of the family's new situation was to be suffered in privacy. Margaret never saw her mother cry, and from this she inferred that her own feelings were not to be acknowledged.

By maintaining a brave countenance, Margaret's mother was protecting herself at least as much as she was protecting her children. The heartrending sight of their grief would have made her feel that much more vulnerable.

In *Widow*, the personal account of what it is like for a woman to lose her husband, Lynn Caine addresses the subject of telling the children: "If I had been able to burst into wild tears . . . it would have done us all a lot of good. They probably would have cried, too, and we would all have been sobbing away . . . But all my energies, then and later, were exerted in holding myself together. I always had this Humpty Dumpty fantasy that if I were to allow myself to crack, no one, not 'all the King's men,' could ever put me back together again."

It was to lessen her own pain and to delay confronting her own uncertainties about death that my mother, too, attempted to mask not only her emotions, but the truth as well. Despite all good intentions, both disguises are impossible. In her book *A Child's Parent Dies*, Erna Furman writes, "Children are so observant of and sensitive to their parents' moods and nuances of behavior that, in our experience, it is impossible to spare them from knowing or to deceive them about the true nature of events."† As demanding as the truth might be, as heartbreaking as it is for a mother to see her child overcome by grief, the consequences of deception are more serious and long lasting. By withholding the truth from her child[ren], the widow is adding to their burden: Compounding the father's absence is the feeling of rejection, unexplained abandonment, and the

† This book is the result of a clinical study done with twenty-three children who lost a parent during early childhood.

frustration of knowing that mother, the only parent left, is hiding something. Anxiety is not decreased, it is multiplied. "For some reason, Daddy's gone, and for some reason, Mommy isn't telling me everything." Instead of one loss, the child must cope with two. She has been left *and* left out.

Margaret was left out not only by her mother, but by yet another signal coming from the people around her. "I remember that everyone acted as though it was my brother's loss." Absorbing the impression that "boys were more important," she doubted whether she even had the right to mourn.‡ With neighbors and relatives showering so much attention on her brother and his loss, it is not surprising that Margaret receded more and more into feelings of isolation. But, for the time being, her needs superseded her indignation.

"I made my brother into a father figure," she says. "And he performed like a father. For many years, he gave me a lot of comfort, he handled my discipline, and he was the person in the house I'd go to for advice. I didn't even admit the resentment and jealousy until recently.

"When I was in my twenties, a cousin of mine told me that she'd come across some old family pictures in a trunk. She'd found some of my father and thought that I should have them. I remember it made me feel good, because it was like she knew there was a loss for me. When I showed them to my mother, the first thing she said was, 'Your brother will be interested in these.' Once again, she was taking away my grief."

Margaret was nine years old when her father died, an age that made her particularly susceptible to the societal and maternal messages that discouraged manifest grief. According to the psychosexual stages of development posited by Freud, children between six and ten years old are in the "latency" phase, and as such are strenuously disinclined to show any signs of vulnerability. No longer dependent on their parents for all their needs, the overriding concern of latency children is the establishment of relationships outside the nuclear family. Gradually, they are separating from the objects of their previous idealization, strug-

‡ Children are denied the right to mourn for many reasons, and as we shall see in Chapter Twelve, the consequences can be highly injurious.

gling to achieve a balance between family and peers, self and others, reality and fantasy. When the latency child is confronted with a traumatic loss, she must reconcile her emerging independent image with the childish fears she is working so hard to suppress. Often, she conceals her more vulnerable feelings by day, choosing to save them for the private world of fantasy. Indeed, the fantasy life of children in this age group is particularly active, and Margaret's response to her father's death—her need for privacy, her recurring dreams of her father—is characteristic.

Over and over again, from the time she was nine years old, Margaret was denied, and denied herself, the healing release of mourning. Taking her cue from the restraint she had observed in both her parents, conflicted about appropriate behavior due to her age and gender, and subject to the restrictions imposed by societal standards, she entered adult life without ever having resolved the major crisis of her childhood. In this compounding of tragedy, she reflects most women whose fathers had died when the women were children.

The consequences of repressed mourning are numerous. As articulated in his essay entitled "The Child's Reaction to Death in the Family," Robert A. Furman writes: "When a person is unable to complete a mourning task in childhood [s]he . . . may be haunted constantly throughout [her] life with a sadness for which [s]he can never find an appropriate explanation."* Margaret validates Dr. Furman's assertion with her billowing laugh, and a jab at herself: "I feel like I have been such a sufferer."

More insidious than the free-floating depression described by Furman and experienced by Margaret, unacknowledged grief is frequently manifest as a chronic state of apathy. In extreme cases, the inability to mourn may very well evolve into the inability to love: "The death of a father may have a delayed effect on children if they are not helped to express their feelings about it. One effect may be that the child becomes afraid to

---

* The reader should be aware that, wherever necessary, and in the interest of consistency, I have taken the liberty of changing masculine pronouns to feminine in quoted material.

love. The youngster worries that if he or she dares to love another person, that person too may be taken away from them." A child who has suffered the death of one parent and the concomitant emotional neglect of the other, may remain fixed in a state of chronic detachment, unable to establish goals or relationships because of a compulsive fear of and distancing from commitment."

Paula, a twenty-five-year-old teacher's aide who participated in our study, wrote, "My father died when I was five years old, in a car accident involving the whole family. I don't remember any of it. My mother was very involved in her work both before and after the accident, and I was pretty much raised by my older brothers and sisters. I didn't start reacting to my father's death until I was a teenager, and I still don't think that I've accepted it. When I was twenty-three, I realized I had to do something about all the anger and feelings of helplessness, so I went into therapy. Then, two months ago, my therapist left the area, so although it wasn't my choice, the therapy was terminated. I have a very hard time trusting people, and that didn't help.

"I panic every time I allow myself to become at all dependent. It's a constant struggle. The person might leave, or die, and then I'd be hurting all over again. I'm at the point where I'm trying to convince myself that a certain amount of dependency isn't necessarily a bad thing. But I've never been able to imagine being in a relationship that *really* lasted, because I could never imagine trusting that much or committing myself that much. It's just too scary."

As Paula's self-imposed isolation reveals, the fear of commitment derives not only from the fear of being hurt again, but from the continuing need for parenting that dates back to her childhood crisis. Shame over this childish need, and a reluctance "to trust anyone, male or female," have led to a façade of aloofness which succeeds in keeping her at a distance from people and, the true object of her fear, her feelings.

Based on evidence that is just now emerging, and depending on a host of variables, it is clear that the ramifications of repressed mourning are profoundly far-reaching. Unresolved grief may result in unexplainable sadness, defenses against emotional commitment, or the very serious condition of denying feelings altogether.

Why, then, has the psychological community been so late in addressing itself to the trauma of childhood loss?

Freud said that the death of a father is the single greatest loss a man can experience, and undertook what many consider his greatest work, *The Interpretation of Dreams,* after his own father's death, in 1896. But while acknowledging the impact of the loss, his theories about the mourning process instilled a fervid belief that children simply could not mourn.

As with so many other taboo subjects, however, Freud led the way in addressing the very subject of death. In 1916, with the publication of his *Mourning and Melancholia,* the unconscious fears associated with death and "object loss" were examined for the first time.

According to the father of psychoanalysis, the mourning process is completed with "decathexis," or detachment from the love object, so that the survivor is free to "cathect," or attach, her love to someone else. In the case of an adult, this is certainly a realistic goal. But, as Freud's theory suggests, a little girl, upon losing her father, cannot one day emerge, as, say, a widow can, from the depth of despair, ready to meet another man to love. Since a child cannot realistically detach from her father in that way, she cannot mourn.

This theory was generally accepted in scientific quarters, and the subject of children and loss was for the most part avoided. It wasn't until the 1940s that children's reactions to death were finally addressed by the professional community. Initiated by Anna Freud's work in an English clinic for war orphans, progress in the field of children and mourning has been steady, and filled with controversy.

Many mental health professionals continue to feel that children simply cannot mourn, for the following two reasons: they are incapable of tolerating the pain; and, by way of avoiding the pain, they cling to an exaggerated attachment to the lost parent, which makes the completion of mourning, i.e., decathexis, impossible.

Other investigators strongly disagree. "The concept that children cannot long tolerate pain is simply inaccurate," state Newman and Schwam. In concert with the Furmans, they report that grief in even very young children is forthcoming if only encouraged. Further, the internalization of the deceased parent, if it develops along with the growth of the child,† may assist the child in coming to terms with his absence, and certainly needn't preclude the outward display of sorrow. Just as the adult disengages gradually from the love object, the child, too, must be allowed the necessary time for separation. Such a child, conclude Newman and Schwam, is ready to achieve decathexis in adolescence. Conversely, the child who has not expressed her grief, with or without the internalized father image, has not even begun to mourn, and as a consequence may carry grief and image inside her interminably—not unlike the man that Margaret "carried around."‡

Whether a girl can ever truly master the rejection implicit in her father's death, in his sudden disappearance, is questionable, but intelligent guidance through the mourning process will certainly help her to deal with the complexities awaiting her. Shame, confusion, denial, need not color an already darkened perspective.

And you asked where he went
And they said:
Heaven.
And they took you to a field of tombstones and columbine
They said:
This is where his perfect body lay.
And you were confused
now there were two of him
and none for you.

Most of the women in our study, like the poet quoted above, and myself, had to integrate their fathers' absence before being

---

† Newman and Schwam emphasize the importance of this developmental growth in calling forth the image of the deceased father. If recollections fixate on infantile need, separation is less easily accomplished.

‡ The Duchess of Windsor, whose father died when she was an infant, once described herself as "very much like a man in many ways." Additional impressions of her fatherless childhood may be found in Chapter Thirteen.

encouraged to feel the emotional impact of their fathers' death. We knew that Daddy was gone, but couldn't understand why he had *left us.* Nor were we encouraged to manifest our responses to the loss. It is only in the past few years that death has gotten off the boat; children have been granted permission to mourn.

"Blessed are they that mourn; for they shall be comforted." Modern psychologists unequivocally agree with this New Testament wisdom. Though it has been argued that mourning can follow the loss of any significant person or object, I will limit its definition to the one that Erna Furman uses in *A Child's Parent Dies:* ". . . [Mourning is] the mental work following the loss of a love object through death."

As early as the latter part of her first year, a child is capable of longing. Indeed, so much of the child's need to love and be loved is invested in her parents that any separation from one of them is likely to bring about very intense longing. The "mental work" of the mourning process, however, goes beyond longing, for, in addition to missing, or longing for, the absent person, the mourner must take on the painful task of separating from the loved one *forever.* For a child, this is an awesome demand. Says Furman, "Only in childhood can death deprive an individual of so much opportunity to love and be loved and face [her] with so difficult a task of adaptation."

Mourning, as analyzed by Furman, cannot begin without the *awareness* that there has been a death. The child must be told. Secondly, the child must have a basic *comprehension* of what death is. According to her study, ". . . [N]ormally developed children above the age of two years could achieve a basic understanding of 'dead' if they had been helped to utilize their daily experiences with this goal in mind."* The natural curiosity

* Though Erna Furman places two as the age at which children may achieve a basic understanding of what "dead" means, many experts prefer three years of age as the point at which comprehension begins. Joseph Palombo, former administrative director of the Barr-Harris Center for the Study of Separation and Loss During Childhood (at the Chicago Institute for Psychoanalysis), wrote that mother would do better to use words such as "gone" and "won't return" when explaining father's absence to the very young child. This explanation conveys the permanence of the situation, Palombo feels, without using terminology that might be beyond the child's comprehension. Since the concept of "perma-

roused by a dead insect, for example, can provide an excellent opportunity for an adult to introduce the concept of death, even to a very young child.

After awareness that there has been a death, and a basic comprehension of what that means, comes the most demanding prerequisite of the mourning process: *acceptance*. It is only when the finality of death has been accepted that a person can begin to grieve.

Grief: an agonizing, painful, draining activity, possibly the most demanding emotion known to the human experience. The person we have loved is no more, and the prospect of continuing life in the face of such a void looms intolerably cruel. Bereavement—sobbing yearning, damning the fates—is the instrument of our release; the alternative to feeling the loss in our gut is to risk irreversible damage to the life that remains, the life that is ours—the life awaiting the young child.

It is understandable that the impulse on the part of the surviving parent is to shield the child from such deeply felt emotions, to pretend tragedy out of existence. Yet who is more sensitive than a child to the ever changing nature of reality? Her very survival is intimately connected to the stability of her surroundings. Change, particularly a change in her immediate environment, cannot possibly be hidden from her. "This is exactly the message that fairy tales get across to the child," writes Bruno Bettelheim in his reverent ode to the fairy tale *The Uses of Enchantment*. "That a struggle against severe difficulties in life is unavoidable, is an intrinsic part of human existence—but that if one does not shy away, but steadfastly meets unexpected and often unjust hardships, one masters all obstacles and at the end emerges victorious."

While few of us can say with any certainty what has happened to the person who has died, we know what his death means to us: we have lost, forever, someone we love. And it is this fact, the fact of permanent loss, which must be honestly presented to

---

nence" is at least as unfathomable to a child as the concept of "death," I believe, with Furman, that it is more helpful to use the word "dead" from the very beginning.

the child. Only then will she be able to experience the depth of emotion evoked by her father's all-too-well-observed absence.

There will be countless occasions in the fatherless daughter's life when the void left by her faithless lover will be keenly felt. Yet if she has been allowed to experience the reality of his death, she at least embarks upon womanhood with a basic understanding of her loss, and the strength derived from the timely expression of emotions.

Naturally, the importance of mother's role cannot be overemphasized in this regard. For beyond presenting her child(ren) with the painful, permanent truth and encouraging the expression of grief, she must work to maintain the vital, developing image of father that will result in the child's later ability to detach from him. Infantile need and image are best discouraged.

Reflecting contemporary research, Newman and Schwam conclude, "[I]nternal fantasy can represent a form of ego strength, [providing] a source of internal growth in the absence of the lost object . . . For this to happen the surviving parent and others close to the family must bring a developmental perspective to the children and share detailed experiences and recollections, appropriate to the child's age, growth, and newfound capacities." They call this adult responsibility "assistance of mourning." Instead of being harmful to the child, this theory asserts, the internalized image of the father, developing simultaneously with the child, can provide a healthy inner resource that will, in fact, ensure later detachment.

The burden on the surviving parent becomes obvious. At a time of most profound trauma, with self-esteem and confidence predictably low, the widow(er) must call on strength and resilience as never before. And yet, as Erna Furman observed in her address to the 1980 American Psychoanalytic Association's workshop on Children's Reactions to Object Loss, "Helping the children adjust may be one of the most soothing activities for the young widow(er) to engage in."

*

As part of my investigation for this project, I had the opportunity to meet a family currently engaged in the task of mourning. I set out to talk to them with no small degree of eagerness. Having read what the experts had to say, and agreeing that children could be assisted through a realistic experience of loss, I would now discover if all the theory was practicable—if a woman my age who had been widowed, someone to whom psychology was no mystery, could in fact transcend the primal taboos about children and death.

My eagerness could be attributed to more than academic interest, however. For, beyond this opportunity to witness an informed approach to mourning, I was drawn to this particular family because of an almost bizarre set of coincidences: Here I was driving to meet a young woman whose husband had died, in May 1980, of heart disease; she was a widow at thirty-one, the mother of two little girls. At least in its external elements, it was not unlike catching a glimpse of my own mother's situation thirty years before. But this woman was my contemporary, and perhaps through her, and her fate which so mirrored my mother's, I would be able to discover some small understanding of my own experience. As if to highlight the hoped-for reflection, the woman's name is Elise.

I was greeted at the door of the stately suburban home by Sonia, the Spanish housekeeper, and two-and-a-half-year-old Diana. The little girl was playful and friendly (after the requisite looking over of the strange lady in her living room, me.) She seemed "normal" enough, shy and giggly by turns, showing off her dominance of the puppy that followed her around. "Her father died," I was thinking as I watched her. "Does she know or comprehend? It's so sad . . ." And then I realized, "Is this how ladies in my living room looked at me?" The pity that I had so abhorred, I was myself extending to this child. Conscientiously, I tried to retract the feeling, to look upon Diana as I would any other curly-haired toddler. But I was here specifically because her father had died, and I found myself searching her for the years I couldn't remember. Was there a sorrow lurking behind her shrieks of pleasure? Where was the sign that said, "Something missing"? I could discern none, of course, and could have spent hours watching her, when down the circular staircase came the sprightly step of her mother.

Elise is a warm and cheerful woman; attractively round and welcoming. Immediately, she apologized for the unfinished decor of the house—which I had noticed—explaining that she and Dave, her husband, had virtually "camped out here for four years," and that she intended to finish the house as they had planned it. I became aware of how suitably the house reflected the family: warm, opulent, incomplete. The place felt too big to embrace its residents, as though it were reaching out to hug from a distance.

Dave, an attorney, had died at the age of thirty-seven of a congenital disease called Marfan's syndrome. Elise had known, when they were dating, that his father had died of Marfan's at thirty-six. But when Dave was tested prior to their marriage, it was with a great sense of relief that he was found to be missing a characteristic of the disease.

Carried by a dominant gene, Marfan's characteristically causes an aneurysm, or bubble, to develop in the aortic route. A burst aneurysm usually means instant death, but its growth, if carefully monitored, can be contained surgically. On a Thursday in mid-April 1980, at one of his routine six-month checkups, Dave had been told that he had an aneurysm that had grown to the point where he should be seen more frequently. The following Tuesday, he had had to be rushed to the hospital. The aneurysm had grown markedly. "They couldn't operate," Elise explains, "because of a platelet problem. But they wouldn't let him leave the hospital. Those two weeks of waiting were very hard on him. It was very frightening, almost too cruel."

Unlike Margaret and so many others' experience of being excluded from the period of illness, Dave's daughters were, from the beginning, encouraged by doctors and family to visit their father in the hospital. He had a hard time dealing with twenty-one-month-old Diana's playfulness in the room and asked that Elise not bring her again. But he and his older daughter, Cecile, who was seven at the time, were just beginning to get close when he became ill, and it was important to both of them to see each other.

They had been spending increasing amounts of time together, "disappearing on Saturdays and Sundays," going to parks and museums. Dave was a source of information and comfort to his older daughter, a typical role for the father during that stage when a new baby is taking so much of mother's time. Indeed, my one recollection of my father is that picture of him taking me out while my mother "fussed with the baby."

"Cecile's last visit with Dave was not a pleasant one," Elise recalls. "It was two days before surgery and he was very frightened. He was irritated over all the delays and, though it wasn't directed at her, his anger, because he was such a big man, with a deep gravelly voice, was always very intimidating. She remembers her father being angry and, for a long while, she thought he was angry at her. They had had several nice visits before that, cuddling in bed and joking, but when that became her last memory of him, I knew we'd have to work it out. Even at the time, while it was happening, I knew it would be very important to talk it through."

So calm and controlled is Elise during our talk at her dining room table, that I comment on how prepared it seems she was for this singularly demanding situation. She is surprised at the suggestion. "Even when he went into surgery," she says, "there was never any doubt that he was going to come home. He was going to be fine. We'd get through this, and then go home and pick up our lives.

"I was so unprepared that when the doctors came out of surgery looking very grim (it had gone on for thirteen hours), I insisted, against the prodding of my parents, that I was fine, that no one had to stay with me. Obviously, they comprehended the gravity of the situation, but I kept assuring everyone, saying that Dave was going to be fine. It was like I knew somehow that I had to take control. They let me in to see him and it was horrid; he was like a machine.

"My mother convinced me that she should stay, and we found a place to sleep. The last thing I remember is that the nurse said she'd get me as soon as they got any sign of recognition. At about five in the morning, I awakened startled. I knew something was wrong, too much time had gone by. My mother found a nurse, who told us he had been beginning to awaken and she was coming to get me when things started to go haywire. His kidneys were failing and they were concerned about oxygen to his brain. Well, I knew. It was just a question of minutes, and then he died.

"People were calling the hospital, asking how he was, and all I could think of was that I had to get to Cecile. I had to be the one to tell her."

And so another young widow held her child close, in bed, to give the terrible news. "I told her, 'Your daddy died,' and she looked at me with such disbelief. And then we just fell apart, holding onto each other." Elise's already husky voice grows thicker, and some of the control wavers, reliving that highly charged moment. In all the hours we will spend together, talking of little other than her husband's death, this is clearly the memory that hurts her the most. After a brief pause, she is ready to continue.

"One of the first things Cecile said to me as we lay there hugging was, 'I need a stepfather.' She had spent the previous day with a friend of hers who has a stepfather. He's a darling guy, and it had been a fun experience for her. Obviously, what she was saying was, 'If you're going to take him away from me, replace him before I can feel the pain.' She was connecting with the immediate effect the loss would have on her: 'Who's gonna take me to the observatory?' "

After the initial shock, Cecile began to express concern that she might have some "powers." Her last meeting with her father had been an unpleasant one, and it is likely that one of the things that passed through her mind in her anger toward him was that he might die. She was perceptibly confused by the conflicting emotions of sorrow and anger, yet she needed to experience them both.

The psychoanalytic literature reveals that anger is one of the most common defenses against the helplessness that inevitably accompanies a loved one's death. Whereas sorrow represents passive resignation, a condition particularly uncomfortable for a seven-year-old, anger is active, participatory. Cecile was frightened by her "powers," but she probably needed to believe in them as well. Their existence was mentioned frequently those first days after Dave's death, with Elise repeatedly assuring her daughter that these powers didn't exist; that it was OK to feel angry, but that the anger, or any angry thoughts, did not cause Dave's death. Asked if she thinks Cecile is convinced, Elise smiles and says that yes, she believes the "powers" have been dispersed.

Elise's entire handling of this shattering event is in fact remarkable—for its sensitivity, its intuitive rightness. In no way concealing the depth of her sorrow—she cried openly and often —she yet had the presence of mind to include her seven-year-old daughter in all the manifestations of the tragic loss, knowing, somehow, that this was an experience of which Cecile must feel a part. Nowhere is this more evident than in the week immediately following the death.

"From the beginning, I thought it was essential to include Cecile's friends, and I think that has been one of the best things for her. Many mothers came to the funeral and made condolence calls, and I encouraged them always to bring the children. It was as important for those kids to see that we were all right, as it was for Cecile to see that we were all right. It would have been destructive to isolate her from her friends. Life goes on, and her friends were part of that.

"At first some of the kids were scared. So I would just say, 'We're OK. We miss Cecile's daddy, but we're OK.' Having the kids come was so good for Cecile. They really helped her through as much as anything I did. I think it also put their parents at ease."

Guided to some degree by psychological awareness, and by a healthy dose of natural empathy, Elise's "intuitive" decisions helped spare Cecile the additional pain of feeling different and isolated from her peers. She didn't have to sit in the classroom creating myths, or become shrouded in the mystery of some dreadful occurrence. Her friends were right there with her, asking the questions, sharing the fears. Even though some of them were children of divorced parents, Cecile's situation, they realized, was dramatically different from theirs: The separation imposed on her was, awesomely, irrevocable. Allowed to share in her loss, her friends became participants in the pain, and in the comforting.

The picture of this supportive group of friends conjures images from my own childhood: though I was only three when my father died, and not part of a social peer group as such, there must have been some constructive way to avoid the feelings of isolation engendered by my father's death, some way I might have been helped to assimilate the circumstance so that by the time I got to school, it didn't hang on my rounded shoulders like a book bag of ill-begotten secrets. Elise had certainly freed her daughter of such unnecessary baggage.

Then I remember Diana. So caught up have I been in the older daughter, the one who, like me, remembered her father (though I was never encouraged to do so), that her sister's loss has yet to be addressed, by me or her mother. Is that how it was in May 1980? I put the question to Elise.

"She kind of got lost in the shuffle," Diana's mother responds with characteristic directness. "I really did focus on Cecile. I think I made some mistakes with Diana. I didn't know what to say to her. At first, I told her that Daddy was 'bye-bye,' but I realized very quickly that I couldn't do that because not only was it not true, but 'bye-bye' would come to mean that anyone who said it wouldn't come back. Within a few days, I did tell her that Daddy had died, and that he would never come back. I don't think she knew what it meant at the time. But I'm trying to go over it a lot with her now."

I think about my younger sister, Caren, who feels she spent much of her life getting "lost in the shuffle." It was assumed that she just wouldn't notice her father was gone, because she was only fifteen months old when he died.

Yet their unabashed fascination with peek-a-boo games eloquently attests to the marked interest infants take in appearance and disappearance. However nonverbal, even a baby recognizes and deeply experiences the loss of a loved one.

Elise, who makes a point of encouraging her children to verbalize, admits being surprised at how much of her father Diana remembers. "When we were in Mexico this past Christmas—the whole family goes every year—Diana climbed into bed with me one morning and said, 'Hi, Boobie.' (That's what Dave sometimes called me.) I looked at her and smiled and asked, 'Who said that?' And she said, 'Daddy . . . I want my daddy to come back.' It's the first time she'd been so specific. She'd talked about him before, but in Mexico, he really started coming up a lot. Maybe it's because the only time he really gave her a lot of attention was last Christmas. Maybe she remembers that, somehow. He took her to the beach and played with her.

"I don't know if she understands what 'dead' is. I want her to remember her father, but she also has to accept the fact that he's gone, permanently. I think Sonia has told her some strange things. In Mexico, for instance, she pointed to the mountains and asked if her daddy was over there. That's why taking her to the cemetery, which I've done a couple of times, is so important. (I didn't take her to the funeral. I thought she was too young. I hope that wasn't a terrible mistake.) She calls the cemetery 'Daddy's park.' I think that's OK, but I also keep repeating that it's a cemetery, and when people die, they are taken to a cemetery.

"Lately, she's been asking over and over again, 'Are we alive?' I have this whole routine I go through: 'We are alive. I am alive, you are alive, Cecile is alive. We talk to each other, we blow on each other and laugh. We can do these things because we are alive.' Ever since Mexico, she's been talking about it so much that I think she's working a lot of it through. She keeps asking, 'I remember my daddy. Do you remember my daddy?' And I tell her that sometimes I feel very sad because I'll never see him again and I miss him.

"A few nights ago, when I was tucking her in, we were talking about it and I started to cry. I don't remember if she touched my cheek or if I wanted her to, but I told her I was crying and that I felt very sad. But then sometimes I worry that it might confuse her to see a parent cry. I think she should know what I'm feeling, though, and that it's OK to feel.

"Of course, she's obviously repeating a lot of what I'm feeding her. The other night, Dave's name came up and I was going through my thing about 'Sometimes we feel sad . . .' and she looked up at me with this mournful little look and said, 'Oh, yes.' But she's not merely mimicking. She's really trying to work it out. I've noticed that she brings up Dave when she's talking about things that frighten her. So, while she may not actually grasp the concept of death, she knows that this is a very complex thing that's happened."

Suddenly, Diana comes running into the room and announces that she has used the bathroom. Her mother beams with pride, hugs her little girl, shares the genuine excitement. The seriousness of our discussion has been dispelled by the other, "normal" things that are going on in this household: the satisfactions, rivalries, accomplishments, conflicts of growing up. All those "ordinary" things that every mother deals with. It's just that in addition to reinforcing her daughters' respective steps toward independence and personhood, this mother must also integrate for all of them the reality and emotions of deep personal loss. The enormity of her task is dizzying, yet here she is, all smiles, cheerfully cooing over Diana's use of the toilet. What is generally and rightfully considered an important achievement in the life of a child has, in the context of what is going on in their lives, provided a welcome bit of comic relief.

In the midst of the playful mother-daughter scene, a car pulls into the driveway. Diana's enthusiastic squeals announce a joyous daily ritual: Cecile is home from school. Elise bounces up to greet her older daughter at the door, and the recently quiet household is all activity.

Following instructions regarding piano lessons and pajama parties, Elise introduces me to Cecile. She tells her that I have her mother's name, and that my father died when I was a little girl too. Cecile flinches and I instantly understand her discomfort. Her situation, her pain, despite her mother's conscientious attention, are personal matters, certainly not to be acknowledged before a stranger. It is my turn to flinch when Elise continues, "Elyce is writing a book about girls who grow up without fathers. You can talk to her about it if you'd like. But only if you want to." The response is ready. "I don't want to." "Fine," says her mother; "now run upstairs and wash your hair." I attempt a casual smile, and Cecile is gone.

She had thrown me a meaningful glance, of reproach, I am sure, before disappearing upstairs. "What do you wanna go and do a thing like that for?" her look clearly implied, and I have to ward off a recurring occupational hazard of this project: the feeling that I am a spoiler—entering people's homes, encouraging them to call forth and talk about what is unarguably a tragic circumstance. Why not leave well enough alone? What's the good of asking people to drag out their demons?

My self-flagellation is interrupted by a quiet inquiry. "Can we meet again next week?" Elise is wondering. She's really enjoyed our talk, she says. It's helpful to share her doubts and decisions with someone who's been there. We set up an appointment, and my own doubts are calmed. In her soft-spoken fashion, this characteristically reassuring woman has reminded me that demons don't belong in dark, tucked-away places: a ghost has less power when there are other people in the room.

During our second meeting, Elise's readiness to meet all questions directly once again prevailed. She talked at length about her own adaptation to the loss (See Chapter Seven), admitting the pain, the conflicts with the children, the bouts of weariness that still take hold. No, of course it has not been easy. Yet with all the intensity that has become a daily part of her life, she acknowledges the fact that she has been fortunate in some ways. From a wealthy family, and widowed by an up-and-coming young attorney, she has been spared the strain of financial insecurity, a burden that has weighed heavily on many bereft young women.

Moreover, there is one area in which her recently father-absented home has been substantially blessed, and that is in the steadfast presence of her own father. "He's been incredible," she says. "He's even more there for us than Dave was, very involved in our lives. The girls certainly haven't wanted for a male figure."

Though it is widely believed that a father substitute can go a long way toward alleviating the absence of the biological father in a girl's life, the women in our study were surprisingly indifferent toward, and unaffected by, men who acted as surrogates—except in the case of grandfathers! Alone among surrogate fathers, these men were able to make a positive contribution to their father-absent granddaughters' lives, helping them to feel more confident and assertive than fatherless women whose grandfathers did not participate in their upbringing.

Elise elaborates on her father's contribution: "He's there every morning before Cecile goes to school, just to give her a morning kiss. And he takes her out, like Dave used to, on Saturdays. Diana has teased him a couple of times and called him

'Daddy,' but it's always with a grin in her eyes, like she knows better.

"I've been very lucky. I can't even say what my girls will miss by not having a father, because as long as my father is well, they have a very positive male figure around. In fact, I sometimes think it'll be harder for my kids and me when *my* father dies. I've thought about it and I pray that it doesn't happen for a long time. He's so energetic, so affectionate. All three of us are terribly dependent on him."

Elise goes on to describe her father, a highly successful businessman, using words like "aggressive," "bright," "generous," "creative"; a man whose public life, vigorous as it is, has never been so preoccupying as to take him from his first priority, his family. As his only child, Elise has benefited from the love and loyalty of this man consistently throughout her life, and listening to her speak of their strong attachment, and despite everything she's been through, incredibly, I find myself envying her.

It would be wonderfully satisfying to be able to predict that Cecile and Diana, thanks to their mother's sensitivity, will grow up having perfectly integrated the death of their father. According to the experts and all that is logical, Elise has done everything possible to provide both her daughters with a sound emotional framework in which to cope with their father's death. They've cried together, asked questions, verbalized the confusion, the anger, the grief. And without the slightest hint of morbidity, remembering the man that was their father has been vigorously reinforced.

It would be satisfying to predict a clean bill of mental health for these fatherless daughters, but of course such predictions are impossible. We have, however, had a glimpse into the present, if not the future, and can feel reassured that there are productive ways to help children with the mourning process; that the family in a state of loss can unite, rather than isolate, its members.

"Mourning never ends," says Erna Furman. That it begins is crucial. Since the early 1970s, there have appeared on the market scores of books intended to help children deal with death, and classes introducing the concept are also being offered in public schools around the country. Yet a mother attuned to her daughter's needs remains the single most important factor in the girl's subsequent adjustment to father absence.

When a girl's father dies, she is suddenly deprived of the first man she ever loved, and she will carry that rejection with her for the rest of her life. An early acceptance of her loss is invaluable, just as resonances in her adulthood are inevitable.

FOUR

A PARODY OF INCEST

Women Who Never Knew Their Fathers

As we have already seen, the nature of a child's reaction to her father's death hinges to a significant extent on her age at the time of loss. Margaret, at nine years old, was caught up in establishing an identity away from her parents; mourning the real, physical loss of her father would contradict keen impulses toward independence, so that society's push toward stoicism was innately reinforced. Cecile, at seven, was capable of understanding the concept of death, yet young enough to be especially receptive to her mother's sensitive "assistance of mourning."

Just as her stage of development will largely contribute to the child's reaction to death, there is one circumstance which, because of its timing, separates its victim from other fatherless daughters. The girl whose father died when she was an infant must struggle with the stultifying void of never having known him.* Try as she might to plumb the hidden corners of memory, there is no image for her to recapture, no man to claim as father. For her, there is only the fact of her own existence to attest to his. No wonder that I cling to the lone memory of my father as I did to his hand on that distant Sunday afternoon.

---

* I refer in this chapter to girls who were younger than two when their fathers died. And when speaking of women who never knew their fathers, I am including only those for whom the separation was irrevocable because of death. Where abandonment or divorce was the cause of absence, subsequent contact with the male parent was possible, providing a very different perspective of the loss—one that is discussed in Chapter Six.

Girls who were infants when their fathers died have no such connection. Photographs and mother's conscientious assistance in remembering—as so admirably displayed by Elise—certainly can be helpful, yet they are surprisingly rarely forthcoming. A syndrome dubbed "father hunger" by a researcher at the American Psychoanalytic Association (APA) is frequently the result of this early deprivation. Attempts to re-create the missing father become a persistent theme, if not the motivating force, in the child's life.

My sister, Caren, was fifteen months old when our father died, and through her, I have come to understand the particular trauma of never having known. Sitting in her comfortable country kitchen in upstate New York, she tells me, "There still hasn't been acceptance of the fact that I will never know him. I sometimes think that if I were hypnotized, I'd at least capture a memory of him. But there's nothing. As far back as I try to remember, there's just nothing there." She speaks on the edge of tears, and I realize just how much of her energy has gone into "trying to remember."

"I don't even remember ever crying about it," she continues, "as a child, that is. It never dawned on me that he didn't know me, and since everyone used to tell me that I looked a lot like him, I always assumed we'd get along. Mom used to say that he was living on a star, so I just figured he was up there watching me."

So that's why I spent all those Friday nights looking up at a star! This little sister of mine who doesn't remember yet provides me with a clue to my own behavior. In fact, I have frequently been surprised at the breadth of Caren's memory. In the course of our discussion, I come to appreciate it as her way of breathing life into the past, resuscitating the man that got away.

Just when does memory begin to function? There is no definitive way of knowing. Certainly, mastery of language helps us to retain our experiences through remarking on them, but remembering is not generally regarded as a particularly advanced aspect of mentality. Freud believed that even infantile memories, blocked by what he called "the amnesia of child-

hood," could be resurrected from the unconscious, sometimes
via hypnosis, and frequently in our dreams. But, for the person
trying to capture the image of a lost parent, dreams are, at best,
a substitute. In fact, when weighed against knowing that parent, just about everything and everyone in life may be perceived as a substitute.

A noted child psychologist writes, "It is not at all unusual for
the individual who has suffered loss of a parent . . . to create in
[her] childhood fantasies of a highly idealized parent. In [her]
imagination, the idealized and loving parent would correct all
the difficulties [she] encounters, would appreciate all [her] efforts, indulge [her] endlessly without ever setting limits or punishing . . . A girl who has lost her father may idealize him and
reject men . . . because she feels they are lacking."

Conjuring an image of her father, and his place in her world,
Caren corroborates the theory. "When you ask how I thought of
him," she says, "how I still think of him, the word that comes to
mind is 'perfect': understanding, funny, very loving and caring,
very gentle. I guess I always felt that if he had lived, *he* would
have loved me. No one else has ever loved me like he would
have."

Margaret, too, despite her reference to her father's withholding of affection, emphasized his admirable qualities, and retains
an image of a man who was quiet, strong, the foundation of the
family. Indeed, the women in our study whose fathers died
painted far more positive portraits of their male parent than
any other group.† And in those instances where daughter was
too young to remember her father, the idealized image was
frequently, if unintentionally, reinforced by mother and other
relatives who thought it best not to provide daughter with *any*
image of the deceased. For if most of us were protected from
acknowledging a death, many daughters who were very young
when their fathers died were discouraged from acknowledging
a life.

"The older I get, the more I think about him," Caren says,
"because I wasn't encouraged to do so as a child. People used to
say, 'Lucky for Caren, she never knew him; she doesn't know

† Please see Chapter Nine.

what she's missed.' Naturally, I created a father who was all out of proportion to reality. I don't even remember ever seeing a picture of him when we were kids."

I am reminded of something Barbra Streisand has said. Herself a fatherless daughter since infancy, she was describing the manner in which her father's absence was dealt with during her childhood. "My mother never mentioned him, never talked about him. I guess she thought if the subject wasn't brought up, I wouldn't notice that something was missing."

It is edifying for Caren to learn that her experience so precisely resembles that of an admired personality. Equally comforting is the opportunity to share impressions with a friend. Engrossed in our conversation, we are joined by one of her neighbors, a buddy, with whom good times and cups of coffee are the usual fare. Leslie is also an émigré from New York City, a distinctly urban thirty-year-old who, like my sister, resettled in this small rural community at the behest of her husband. Having found a common bond in poking fun at the small-town limitations of their new lives, the neighbors on occasion approach the more serious territory of their shared limitations from the past: Leslie's father died before she was a year old.

"The first tangible evidence I ever had that I really had a father was the first time I went to the cemetery," Leslie offers. "I was in junior high school. I can remember walking over and seeing the grave, and there were little rocks on top of the tombstone. I remember standing there and wondering what he looked like. I actually wanted to dig up his grave so I could see him. Then it dawned on me that it would just be bones.

"Afterwards, while my mother and I were waiting for the cab to pick us up—we must have been in the office, but I have a picture in my mind of a beautiful, open pavilion—I had this bizarre fantasy: The cemetery became very beautiful, and I saw myself dancing among the tombstones in a flowing white gown. Gracefully, I walked up to his grave and masturbated on the tombstone, the way I used to on the cupboard door at home. The image haunted me for years. I guess I married my father in that fantasy."

After a moment, Leslie, who has been married for eleven years, continues. "My husband's sexual needs drive me crazy.

That's the basis of all our fights, because he sometimes makes me feel like a whore. I wish so much that we would just cuddle so that the little girl in me could feel loved by a man. That's the part of a relationship I like most: the flirty, little-girl part. Sex is just a necessary result."

Leslie's ambivalence toward sex recalls an insight of Vladimir Nabokov's Humbert Humbert. Tortured over his inability to win the affections of his beloved "nymphet," he notices ". . . Lolita's smile lose all its light and become a frozen little shadow of itself" when she sees a father and daughter exchanging affection. And he realizes:

> It had become gradually clear to my conventional Lolita during our singular and bestial cohabitation that even the most miserable of family lives was better than the parody of incest which, in the long run, was the best I could offer the waif.

Cuddling, paternal affection—these are what the fatherless Lolita longs for. Sex with her older lover, as that for Leslie and many other women who never knew their fathers, is in fact a substitute, a parody, a "necessary result" of her quest for male approval.

As we saw in Chapter Two, a girl's confidence in her femininity depends to a great extent on the approval she received from her father. And that sexual self-image is derived from an overall physical self-image that father also had a hand in molding. If he wasn't there to encourage his toddler daughter's confidence in her physical self, doubts about her body integrity are not unusual. In fact, they precede and then become incorporated into her ambivalence toward men, sex, and her own femininity. This inferior physical self-image may be discerned in the image that the girl projects.

"When I was in junior high school," says Caren, "I turned into a monster. I would put on the 'scuzziest' clothes I could find, and hang around the streets. You know, I'd strut around in black stockings with purposely started runs, short skirts, a lot of makeup, teased hair. On a conscious level, I was doing it to be cool. But even then, I knew it was awful-looking.

"My best friend and I used to shoplift. It was our routine after-school activity. I guess I did it because I wanted things. I wanted everything. From my very earliest memories, I can always remember wanting, feeling that my clothes weren't nice enough and that I didn't have as much as the other kids. Even in fourth grade, I was stealing pencils and Magic Markers.

"I'm still very greedy," she continues, "but now it comes out in more socially acceptable ways. I'm in a local theater group, and I think I can honestly say that the only times I'm really happy are when I'm on stage and people are responding to me, laughing and applauding.

"Offstage I need applause too, but of a different kind. I want every man who meets me to find me beautiful and irresistible. First I want them to love me nonsexually, to find me the most enjoyable, intelligent, warm, beautiful woman. To love *me*. But then, if the man doesn't feel any sexual attraction, I feel like a failure.

"I guess you could say that I want to be seen as the perfect woman; first the little girl, and then the irresistible sex goddess. Not that I respond in any way! I'd never do that to Cliff" (her husband). "I just need to feel the approval."

According to our questionnaire, Caren is alone neither with her fantasy nor with the particularly intense need for approval the fantasy reflects. When asked whether they wanted to be seen as the "perfect woman," subjects who were under two when their fathers died answered in the affirmative more frequently than any other group.

"In my own defense," Caren continues, "I should mention that therapy has alleviated a lot of this. I mean, I don't think I'm so horrible any more, because I grew up thinking I was the pits. I'm also trying not to be so needy, so hungry for adoration. I work very hard on my appearance, but at least I'm beginning to believe that I am an attractive woman. (That last word is quite a sign of progress for me.) I'm also beginning to appreciate how much Cliff must approve of me, since he's the one who's had to put up with all this.

"I'm working on accepting myself as a worthwhile person despite the fact that I'm not gorgeous. I still have trouble seeing myself as thin, because I carry around this chubby, awkward image of myself. I know it's silly" (she does not weigh more than

105 pounds), "but that's still a trouble spot. Still, I know if I get to think more of myself, I won't have such ridiculous expectations of others. I guess I've always been compulsively needy, and I'm trying to get a handle on that."

After years of therapy, Caren has come to understand the connection between parental deprivation and neediness. And along the way, she turned her troublesome teens to advantage in her choice of profession: for the past eight years, she has been a probation officer, working primarily with delinquent adolescents.

*

While incomplete resolution of the Oedipal conflict may be the first thing that comes to mind when considering girls who never knew their fathers, this stage is yet preceded by others in which father plays a most significant role. For, as noted above, before she must grapple with sexual identity, the toddler looks to her father to reinforce her physical identity—which will in turn permeate every aspect of the way she feels about herself.

Until the age of three, love is acutely tied up with physical-need gratification (generally supplied by mother) and body development. Mobility, coordination, confidence in body integrity, all these are the accepted domain of father.‡ If he is not there to help the child overcome her natural fears of increased physical independence, anxiety about her physical viability may result. This is not to suggest that physical development will necessarily be retarded by the father's absence—in fact, this is one area of early-childhood growth that is not dependent on emotional attachment—but certainly the child's confidence in her physical abilities will be shakier without the encouraging support of a caring male figure; this anxiety is likely to continue into her overall feelings about herself. ". . . [T]he image of the self is derived first of all from the image of the body," notes child psychoanalyst Selma Fraiberg.

Lacking confidence in her physical self—which will soon tie into her sexual identification as a little girl—the toddler de-

‡ Most of the women included in this volume were raised prior to the introduction of alternative-lifestyle possibilities. Hence, unless otherwise indicated, the father's relationship to the family is being considered in light of traditional roles.

prived of her father's attention may, as a consequence, sustain "narcissistic injury," a disproportionate concern for self.* A certain amount of narcissism, characterized by self-respect and self-esteem—a caring for the self that is independent of external affirmation—is seen as a healthy element of personality. The small child deprived of early reinforcement for physical accomplishments may come to lack this inner source of confidence and find herself caught up in unhealthy narcissism, constantly in search of self-esteem through the admiration of others. Only people and things outside herself can assuage the persistent doubts and insecurities feeding into this glaring facet of "father hunger."

Even as a young child, Caren, characteristically, "wanted everything." Her kind of neediness, well documented by the professional literature, was temporarily fulfilled by stolen pencils and Magic Markers. As an adolescent, she turned to shoplifting, continuing to make external objects a source of narcissistic fulfillment.

Dr. Irving Kaufman, in a panel discussion at the 1975 Annual Meeting of the APA, reported," [There is] a cluster of traits typical of adolescents who have suffered repeated early object loss. They turn toward the external world in a greedy, grasping, destructive, and conscienceless way, and they manifest an overriding urge toward constant motoric activity as the means for releasing impulses . . . These patients cathect the environment as a source of needed supplies. They equate object loss with loss of care."

Why does father's absence create such far-reaching impact if mother is the traditionally acknowledged provider of infant care? The first and most obvious answer is that, as we shall see throughout, when father dies, mother frequently absents herself as well, either emotionally, or physically (she must go out to work), or both. Yet, as discovered by the invaluable work of Anna Freud, the father's role is the harder of the two to duplicate.

The Hampstead War Nursery, a colony of the American Fos-

* Narcissus was the youth of Greek mythology who, gazing at himself in a pool of water, fell in love with his own reflection.

ter Parents' Plan, was a residential center for children left homeless and/or parentless by the bombing of London during World War II. In addition to establishing a secure and healthful environment for the children, the nursery afforded Anna Freud a unique, and ground-breaking, opportunity to study the effects of parent loss—whether by absence, illness, desertion, or death —on children.

Prominent among her findings was the serious consequence to child development imposed by separation from the mother. "But even though the mother herself is lacking from the residential child's daily care, her functions are taken over by other 'motherly' people. The child who is not cared for, handled, fed, bathed, petted, and played with by his own mother is thus handled and taken care of by others whom he learns to accept as mother substitutes. But there is no one who, to the child's knowledge, takes over the functions which his own father, owing to absence, illness or death, cannot fulfill. Impersonal and invisible powers, i.e., the organization, the committee, the governors, a board, provide the material means for the child's upbringing and, by their decisions, determine the child's fate. These powers are beyond the range of the infant's comprehension and play no part in his actual life. *There is thus no father substitute who can fill the place which is left empty by the child's own father"* (italics mine).

In outlining her observations of father deprivation, Anna Freud went on to note that while the consequences may not be apparent in young children, ". . . with adolescents of both sexes juvenile courts frequently quote in their summing up of a case of delinquency the absence of the father as the determining factor in the child's dissocial development. It is a matter of common knowledge that one cause of the delinquency of adolescents and preadolescents in war and postwar periods is the incompleteness of the family setting owing to the father's absence in the Forces."

Again, according to traditional lifestyles, it has been the father's role to exemplify for the child the outside world; the world of opportunity and adventure, yes, but also the civilized world, where restrictions and the temperance of primitive instincts are a necessity. Mother may teach her child the social graces, but it is this force from the external world, the father, who represents the strict realities of social existence. His ability to pass easily into that outer world impresses the child, and as a way of both imitating and pleasing him, she comes to value discipline as well as grace.

Thus far, we have seen the connection between the mastery of physical skills and the development of self-esteem and discipline. By his example and encouragement, father plays a vital role in all these areas. Yet nowhere is his presence more valuable, or his absence more keenly felt, than in the psychological task upon which all childhood development rests: separation from mother. Self-esteem cannot evolve without the perception that there is a self.

The process by which the infant/toddler grows away from mother and toward selfhood is called "separation-individuation" by mental health professionals. For the first year of its life, the baby has been primarily involved with its female parent. Now, as stated by Dr. Margaret Mahler, a renowned pediatrician and psychoanalyst, ". . . the father image comes toward the child . . . 'from outer space' as it were . . . as something gloriously new and exciting, at just the time when the toddler is experiencing a feverish quest for expansion." The father, almost literally, becomes the "knight in shining armor," rescuer from the mother and the dependence she has represented. (Of particular note is the fact that girls, in comparison to boys, have been observed to attach themselves "earlier and more intensely to their fathers," preferring father to mother as early as seven months of age, the initial phase of separation-individuation.)

In his role as rescuer, then, the father is also helping the mother to separate from her child, and to grant the child the independence she simultaneously longs for and fears. The father thus acts as a wedge between mother and child, assisting his daughter in one of the most crucial steps of her development.

Very often, the widowed mother turns to her child for the support and companionship her husband might have provided. Rather than encouraging her child to feel comfortable with a separate identity, her needs communicate an intensified desire for closeness. To retain mother's love, the child has little choice

but to comply. At just the time when normal instincts are entic-
ing the child away from mother, maternal needs are seducing
her toward mutual dependence. The relationship becomes dis-
proportionately intense and the message mixed: on the one
hand, the child is being held back by an overprotective and
frightened mother; on the other, she is being handed emotional
responsibilities beyond her years.

The woman with no conscious recollection of her father is
someone who, by definition, spent her earliest years, her psychologically formative years, deprived. Lacking a male parent
to appreciate her physical accomplishments, the girl is likely to
have sustained an injured sense of self and a gnawing hunger for
affirmation. While perhaps imperceptible throughout her childhood, the neediness that compelled her might have manifested
itself first in her adolescent years; "wanting everything," and
missing the socialized representative of the outside world, father, combined in many of these situations to result in antisocial
behavior, an attitude toward external reality both grasping and
undisciplined. Often, the child never got to be a child, being
asked by mother to go from symbiosis to companionship without experiencing her own individuality.

The little girl with no father to admire her first steps toward
femininity approaches the development of her sexual identity
heavily encumbered. With self-esteem in all probability suffering, and being asked to play a role in the family for which she is
not ready, she has yet to tackle the complex issues of the Oedipal drama.

In its broadest terms, the Oedipal scenario unfolds as follows:
the child feels a strong attraction to the parent of the opposite
sex; the parent of the same sex becomes an obvious rival; the
child grows to recognize the impossibility of wish fulfillment,
and instead of striving *to be* the parent of the same sex, strives *to
become like* that parent. Thus do desire, aggression, frustration,
and disappointment contribute to the eventual sexual identity
of the child and to the fabric of a mature personality.

Resolution of the Oedipal conflict—seen by Freudians as the
stepping-stone to maturity—becomes nearly impossible for the
fatherless daughter for two reasons: With the father absent be-

fore the curtain even goes up on the drama, a fantastic idealization is likely to occur, and Oedipal longing, based on that idealization, intensifies rather than resolves. The girl is engulfed in a lifelong commitment to the perfect lover, a fierce dedication to the man that got away.

Secondly, the means by which daughter acknowledges the fact that father is not to become lover is found in an array of emotions directed toward mother: jealousy, rivalry, guilt, and finally, acceptance. But instead of competing with mother for father's affection, the fatherless daughter recognizes mother as the sole provider of love. She must repress all hostility and admit only positive feelings toward mother. She wants to please her only surviving parent and assure herself of the security of this all-important bond. By devoting herself to mother, she is also identifying with the last person to do so, father, and thus her much-needed relationship with him is, to her mind, maintained.

The dynamics by which the father-deprived daughter copes with the Oedipal drama—devotion to mother, identification with father—would seem to suggest a direct link between fatherlessness and homosexuality, and professional case material does in fact allude to this connection. Yet there is even stronger evidence that girls whose fathers died seek to be loved by men with far more urgency than they seek to imitate them. A good reason for this is that widows, in contrast to divorcées and single mothers, tend to substantiate their daughters' idealized images of men and the comfort they can provide. By presenting a portrait of a powerless woman who needs to be rescued by a man, the widow/mother becomes a role model, reinforcing the daughter's need for men and her later heterosexual choice.

In selecting her man, the young woman with no remembered father is operating under two major delusions, however. First, there is that perfect man that no mere mortal could ever live up to. And even more insidious, because less frequently understood, there is the assumption that she is in fact ready for a mature sexual relationship. For, buried deep within her is the repressed aggression against mother which has, until now, been directed toward the most available receptacle: herself. With the arrival of romantic interests, the parasite that has been feeding on her self-esteem may at long last be directed outward, and unfulfilled wishes directed against her mother may be transposed into sadistic relationships with men.

Whether or not we wholeheartedly subscribe to the Freudian schema of early-childhood development, the by-products of father loss in a very young girl are generally agreed upon. Evidence from a broad spectrum of philosophical leanings indicates a tendency toward low self-esteem, narcissism, and a conflicted relationship with mother—all of which conspire to create a shaky feminine identity. Denied the encouraging presence of a male parent as she tried to establish physical separation from her female parent, the girl whose father died before she was two is likely to be in a state of acute self-doubt. Grasping and needy, desperate for admiration, she vies for attention but will defy any man to love her. Like a toddler, she will step tentatively into the future, reaching out with one hand, pushing away with the other.

*

Corroborating the professional literature, our study revealed that women who did not remember their fathers were far more likely than any other group to have been involved in conflicted relationships with their mothers during childhood and that, in fact, the conflict continued to prevail.

My ongoing conversation with Caren and Leslie shed further light on this connection between early father loss and anger toward mother.

"I used to adore her," said Leslie. "I used to think she was the most untiring, dedicated, selfless mother in the world. I always wanted to please her, to make her happy. And I used to promise her that I'd never leave her alone.

"I think I believed that her lot in life was somehow caused by me, that the drudgery of going to work every day was my fault, so it was my responsibility to make things better. At the same time, I knew that was impossible. Because I wasn't a man.

"It seems sometimes as though she stressed her aloneness, that she didn't want anyone ever to forget it. I used to be embarrassed by the single bed she slept in. I always wished she'd have a double bed like everyone else's parents. And she'd always be asking relatives to drive us places. Like we couldn't get anywhere without a man and a car. I guess it never dawned on her to learn to drive."

The connection between repressed aggression toward mother and hostility toward men becomes apparent as Leslie continues. "I think part of me blamed my mother for never remarrying. As I got older, I became aware of all this anger that I felt for her, but I didn't know what to do with it. I guess I thought a man would make everything better, but I have to admit that I lose interest in a man the minute he shows a real interest in me. I've been shitty to every guy in my life. I get satisfaction out of having the last word.

"I use men a lot. Often, it's to drive me places. It's as though I'm saying, 'I really don't want you, but if you do a lot of really nice things for me, maybe I'll reconsider.'

"Sometimes I wonder if I'll ever be able to love a man totally. I think I'm not allowing myself to, because that would mean I don't love my father any more. You see, I've never relinquished him as a sexual object, and I don't think I want to say good-bye. So how can I possibly love a man in a sexual and adult way?"

Leslie's ingenuous question suggests the complexity of the fatherless girl's dilemma. But while the fantastic and harmful idealization of men is shared by most women whose fathers died, the girl who never knew her father clings with particular fervor to the image of perfection that he represents. When compared to this image, all subsequent relationships become inadequate substitutes. Simultaneously, hostility toward mother often translates into hostility toward men; and sometimes even morality itself serves as a symbol against which to unleash frustration, while father, the knight in shining armor, remains just beyond reach, the hero.

Caren, acknowledging the delusion, finds it preferable to the alternative that is the void. "I still have never said good-bye to him," my sister murmurs. "There have been times, when alone, that I have little conversations with him, and when I've even pretended that I'm saying good-bye. But they are really just trial runs, because I know that doing it makes me afraid, afraid of facing the reality that I will never know him, that he will never come back, that my life will never be changed."

A respected member of the community, wife and mother, admired for her quick mind and ready humor, Caren does not have a bad life. Yet, perhaps she, like many women who cannot remember their fathers, exercises all that energy, commitment, and involvement as a way of filling, day by day, the void left by father. If the rewards are perceived as merely a substitute, or at worst, a parody, they are yet replete with intrinsic and extrinsic value—to herself and the people around her.

As we shall see in Chapter Thirteen, the world itself has benefited to no small degree from the tireless efforts of women who sought to re-create in their work the longed-for image of father. "One of the most important things about directing *Yentl*," Barbra Streisand said of the film to which she devoted years of her life, "is that it gave me a chance to make a father." Indeed, she "made" him warm and kind, wise and compassionate, the type of father we would all like to have. But perhaps even more significant, Streisand chose this story because its action is precipitated by the death of the heroine's beloved father: To carry on the reverence for books and learning with which he had imbued her, and to thus keep him "alive" within her, she defies law, tradition, and even nature itself. She dares to pursue intellectual accomplishment in a time and place where it is forbidden to women.

The director and star of Yentl's story has frequently been accused of similar unnatural ambition, yet her hard work and dedication to achievement reflect the efforts of many women striving to fill the void bequeathed by a father who left no image. The image of a father who *chose* to die yields a far less productive effect: The daughter of suicide, another victim of serious loss, expends much of her psychic energy trying to erase, rather than create, an image.

FIVE

A FACE NOT EVEN A FATHER COULD LOVE

Daughters of Paternal Suicide

My father died after eating a pastrami sandwich. He had been warned not to by doctors even then aware of the causal relationship between cholesterol and heart attack. Though I cannot claim any deep-seated aversion to the fatty meat, I have wondered more than once what would have happened had he dined that night in November 1950 on less risky fare. Would he have lived, and be alive still? Would everything, my whole life, have been different? Furthermore, why did he eat what he had been specifically warned against? Did he care so little for life? For me?

There are those who, remarkably, believe that all deaths are self-willed, that people die when they are ready and not a moment before. My father's incautious attitude toward his diet notwithstanding, I consider such theories to be so much nonsense; yet one woman who was four when her father died of a heart attack told me, "I think he gave up. He had had enough of living and I don't think that's fair, because it wasn't enough for me."

In the case of suicide, of course, philosophical arguments are beside the point—there is no question about intent. (Though reasons may be open to dispute. A. Alvarez, however, in his ground-breaking book on the subject, points out, "One vital meaning of the act is . . . the suicide wishes to show those who survive him how bad things are.") While daughters whose fathers died can damn the fates that deprived them of their male parent, the child of suicide must carry the unique burden of *knowing that her father chose to die . . . leave her.* Nothing, not even his love for her, seemed reason enough to live. The most terrifying fantasies of childhood—rejection and abandonment—are for her realized, magnified and integrated into the way she will perceive herself and her world. Two noted professors of psychology describe parental suicide as an ". . . almost uniquely inexpressible tragedy, a tragedy reaching even beyond other childhood bereavements."

"It's really the ultimate rejection, isn't it?" Gena laughs nervously. A pretty young woman who dresses down her attractiveness, she talks to me from across her sister Lori's rather sparsely decorated living room. Thirty-two and thirty-four, respectively, they are willing to speak this evening on a subject that clearly evokes tension in an otherwise close and supportive relationship. They had warned me, on the phone, that they don't exactly see eye to eye on the event that fractured their lives twenty-eight years before. Only on its pervasive impact do they agree.

"See, I had always sort of, you know, cursed heaven that he was unmercifully taken away," Gena says. "Then, when I found out what really happened—"

Lori cuts in: "All of a sudden, it was like, 'the bastard.' " Gena leans back as she frequently will during our meeting, deferring to her older sister's more commanding recollections. Within only a few minutes of being with them, I am aware of their roles; roles, I will learn, that helped them to cope with the knowledge of their father's terrible choice.

Lori and Gena were brought up to believe that their father, a writer of minor renown, had died of the polio he contracted while doing public relations work for the government in Japan after World War II. "He couldn't handle it," Lori recalls (she was four at the time). "That's one of the few vivid memories I have of him. I remember he was in the bedroom, next to the bed, and he couldn't stand up. There he was on the floor and he just couldn't get up. It was real bad. He was a really active man. And then, there he was: wakes up one morning paralyzed."

The family returned to the States and moved in with the maternal grandparents, the children seeing their father on his weekend visits from the nearby hospital. "That's my only memory of him," offers Gena in her thin voice. "I remember him in the wheelchair drinking beer and me sitting on his lap. It's always been a very pleasurable image, you know, sitting on Daddy's lap . . . I think he was an alcoholic, though."

Lori jumps to his defense. "He wasn't really an alcoholic in the true sense of the word," she castigates her sister, and continues the story, the facts. "After two years between the hospital and the VA, he didn't regain the use of his arm or leg, so he went down to Florida *supposedly* to write a novel. But I think he knew what he was going to do. My grandmother says he gave himself two years to be able to walk.

"Anyway, I remember when the phone call came. I was only six, but I remember it so clearly. We were at my grandparents' house, and it was that time of day where it's just turning to dusk and you haven't turned the lights on yet. That's the feeling I have, of it being very gloomy."

"I remember everybody crying," says Gena. "I can't even remember if it was because of a death or because our mother had to go to Florida and we were sad because she was leaving us."

"I don't remember crying. I just remember it being gloomy," Lori corrects her sister. "In school, you know how they always make you write little essays about your family?" Her voice takes on a sarcastic edge. "Well, this one teacher said to me, 'Your father couldn't have died from polio, honey.' So I went home and asked, 'Mommy, you don't die of polio. What did he really die of?' 'Kidney disorder,' she tells me."

"Yeah, that's what I remember. That my father died of kidney failure," says Gena.

Recalling their misinformation, both sisters are bitter, resentful, almost adolescent in their anger toward their earlier naïveté. They have suffered a profound betrayal, and it is somehow easier to lash out at the withholding of the truth than at the truth itself.

"When I was sixteen, I was real mixed up, your typical rebellious teenager," says Lori. "I was confused about everything, and finding out about this was all I needed.

"One day I was going through some old things in my grandmother's garage (she had all this great stuff dating back to the twenties), and so I'm looking through all these papers and I find this death certificate—my father's death certificate. And it says, 'Gunshot wound inflicted by himself.' I freaked."

Lori told no one of her discovery. Not even Gena, with whom she was very close. "I didn't want to traumatize you," she explains to her younger sister.

"You held it over my head a lot, though," Gena says and turns to me. "When we would get into fights, she would say, 'There are things about this family that you don't know.' A couple of years went by, and then one day we were talking and—I don't know what made me say it, I mean I had never even *thought* it before—but I said, 'Nana told me he killed himself.' It's just like it entered my head and I threw it out. It was really weird. To this day, I don't understand exactly what made me think of that. It was like I actually surprised myself.

"Growing up, I had this whole fantasy image of him, this wonderful, loving father who loved us so much." She laughs sardonically. "I mean I used to constantly use him as a source of refuge. You know, if he hadn't been taken from us so unkindly, *he* would have loved me. And I'd think about sitting on his lap and him holding me and telling me how much he loved me." She laughs again.

"Then, finding out that he committed suicide, well it obviously shattered the fantasy a bit. Suddenly, he wasn't taken, he *left* me. I felt incredibly hurt, rejected. Obviously, I could no longer have this image of this wonderful father that loved me so much. It changed from 'Why were you taken from me?' to 'Why the hell did you do this to me?' And I still think about him all the time. He's a perfect image to conjure up when I'm feeling sorry for myself. Whenever I'm feeling incredibly pained or sad about something, I think about how much he loved me and the pain he must have felt to do that."

"It's really unfortunate, but my memories of my father, well, they're basically negative." Lori reasserts her more realistic perspective. "There's that morning when he woke up with polio, and then there's a time when he was drunk, saying nasty things to my mother, abusive things.

"But I must have had some positive emotional attachment to him, because I remember that while he was in the hospital, he made ceramic cups for all of us as part of the therapy program. Anyway, when I was about seven, I was sitting on my bed with my cousin and she bounced my cup off the bed and broke it. I was totally torn apart, like she had broken my link with my father.

"I do feel very connected to him. However emotionally unstable he was, there was something in him that was experimental, exploratory. I think he was driven by a quest to find out about larger things that are in existence, and I've always felt similarly driven.

"My mother is incredibly pragmatic. 'If you can't see it, it isn't there. What's important is money, security, power.' And my father was an artist, and he was driven by forces that drive people who are more intuitive and artistic. So I think a lot of my floundering would have been prevented if he had been around, because he would have admired my desire to paint instead of what I've heard from my mother all my life: 'So you paint, so big deal.' "

Both sisters feel a strong kinship with the intuitive forces that, thwarted, drove their thirty-one-year-old father to suicide. Implicit in their empathy is the culpability of their mother.

"I think I've always been angry with her for not being more supportive of him," Lori continues. "I don't really blame her, rationally, for what he did, but I can't help feeling that she deserted him emotionally. That when she married him, she saw him as a romantic figure, good-looking, dynamic. But the reality of what it meant to give support to this man was too much."

Their mother's second marriage, the sisters agree, was more suitable to her needs. "She married as soon as possible," Gena carps, "to a man we hated. He's aggressive, domineering, critical, a man who shouldn't have children. We cried when they got married.

"He moved us into this big, fancy house with a swimming pool, and the misery began. It was a wonderful house, but there was just no love. Slowly we retreated; Lori and I became each other's parents."

"I became really rebellious," says Lori. "By the time I was thirteen, my mother was chasing me around the table. I was constantly in trouble, staying out, doing drugs; it was a constant battle.

"I was a stringbean and a very late bloomer, and that added to my pain. I didn't feel that there was any love around the house, so it would have helped to receive it from an outside source. But it wasn't to be found. So when I learned the truth about my father, it was like I could officially become a beatnik. I was headed down that path anyway, and this just made me feel more alienated from the mainstream."

Despite her penchant for the unaccepted, Lori did go to college, only to drop out during her senior year. In the years that followed, she had "a million jobs," studied Buddhism, got married, divorced, remarried, and had a baby.

"I was always very unhappy in anything I pursued, because it was what I *should* do. That's why I had never seriously considered art as a profession, because I had been brainwashed to think of it as merely a hobby.

"But when Chris was born, everything fell into place. Her father and I weren't getting along and I was very adamant that either we see a therapist and work it out, or we're not going to live together. I would never want her to feel uncomfortable in her home, the way I did. So Tommy left and they see each other once a week, and I'm going to school full time, majoring in graphic design.

"Since I've had my daughter, I've never felt such a fierceness to live. I feel almost defiant in my will to be there for her, and I know it has a lot to do with losing my father."

Gena, just two years Lori's junior (there is also an older brother, who, as the sisters put it, "checked out and moved to Alaska"), has yet to accept herself as a grown-up. Unable to decide what she wants to do with her life, she's been working at home as a seamstress for several years, but "I don't consider it something I want to be doing."

She lives just a few blocks from Lori and Chris, and sees them often. Lori has been trying to persuade her to study graphic arts. "I've always been interested in art," she explains, almost as though in defense of her indecisiveness, "but am I interested enough to actually go back to school?" The question is rhetorical.

"I've dabbled in acting. I have a commercial agent, but nothing's come in yet. I guess I'm sort of a dilettante, and now I'm trying to focus on something as a career. I guess I'm going through some kind of crisis in terms of direction. But the problem is, I have no idea what I want to do."

Reminded by Lori several times during our interview that she was not even four when their father died—and therefore "too young to remember," "too young to have had a relationship with him"—Gena seems to function on an almost palpably shaky foundation, by turns describing herself as "incredibly shy," "withdrawn," "a creep in high school," "terrified of men." Describing her adolescence, she is even reluctant to use a word as definitive as "rebellious," settling on the softer, less daring "fresh."

"I had maybe four dates in high school. Boys were just out of the question. I mean I had little crushes, but they were secret. I was terrified. When I graduated, we moved to Europe, because my stepfather had some work there, and that was a relief because it disconnected me from the whole stigma of high school.

"But then, when I got back, I didn't have any friends, no one to talk to. I had lost contact with everyone. Gradually, I did start dating, but it was very superficial. It was really a number of years until I could actually relate to men."

When I ask Gena, who has never been married, if she's enjoying satisfactory relationships with men now, she becomes flustered, readily acknowledging her insecurity but unable to articulate its cause.

Finally, she ventures, "I think I have unrealistic expectations of what a relationship should be. I mean I've always been incredibly shy, even to this day. For a long time, I didn't allow men to come near me; I wouldn't even talk to them, I was so terrified. But even now that I've sort of developed more confidence, there are very few men I'm willing to have a relationship with."

Gena's reluctance to commit herself—to a man or a vocation —is not uncommon among daughters of paternal suicide, for it stems from her suspicion of culpability. Something she did or did not do may have precipitated the decision to die, so that, like many women with similar backgrounds, she equates involvement with risk.

As compared to 23 percent of women whose fathers died in other ways, 58 percent of those whose fathers killed themselves "felt responsible for the death." Our study further revealed that these daughters of paternal suicide have been divorced more often than any other group, and are more likely to "feel guilty a lot of the time." Interaction remains threatening to them because they have experienced its dire consequences.

"My whole approach to life is to hold back," Gena fairly confides. "I don't like to take chances, and getting involved with someone naturally means that you're taking a chance. I'm working hard at challenging this tendency in myself, because otherwise I'll never get anywhere.

"I think if you feel impoverished as a person, your expectations of men, women, even jobs, is that they will fill in all the emptiness. But because your expectations are so high, you back away."

Lori, who has been listening very seriously to her sister, becomes suddenly softer, almost wistful. "I remember when I was a kid, I had a girlfriend in the neighborhood whose father was like the father you always wanted, and I used to be so envious of her. I'd watch their relationship and it would make me feel more and more impoverished. It was so painful. It was like, 'Father Knows Best'; he even called her 'Princess.'

"It's so weird. Sometimes I think about all the people out there who've had a much harder time than I have. But just knowing that in this life, I just will never know that relationship, that father-daughter relationship, it just amazes me. It's like operating with a handicap," says the daughter of the polio victim.

*

The only way for a death to be assimilated and accepted is through the difficult, painful, necessary task of mourning. Yet, as we have already seen, children are usually "protected" from their grief. For the child survivor of parental suicide, the protective shield against grief is particularly intractable, for it is composed not only of mother's vagaries, but of age-old myths, societal prejudices, and fears of spiritual reprisal.

In his Introduction to *Survivors of Suicide,* Professor Edwin S. Shneidman writes, "It is probably not an oversimplification to say that in our culture there are essentially only two kinds of mourning and grief and reconstructive patterns: 1) those which accrue to deaths from heart attack, cancer, accident, disaster and the like and 2) those which relate to the stigmatizing death of a loved one by suicide."

Survivors, while perhaps no longer plagued by the repercussions of "mortal sin," are at the very least ashamed. They must learn to live not only with a death, but with a terrible secret that inevitably carries with it blame, guilt, profound confusion. In a state of religious and/or social disgrace, the usually formidable task of mourning is made doubly awesome by a society more apt to ostracize than lend support. Only in sweeping the cause of death under the carpet, and quickly, may the survivor hope for any sympathy at all. And the child, bereft of her father, becomes the unwitting victim of what has come to be known as "the family myth." This, compounded by further specific factors surrounding the loss of a parent through suicide, renders a healthy expression of mourning—and thus liberation from the suicide—almost impossible for the child.

We have, in previous chapters, seen the crucial role played by mother in helping her children to accept father's death. When she is open with her feelings and honest about the facts, the children will benefit. Given the stigma of suicide, maternal honesty regarding feelings and facts is rare.

It is the express purpose of the family myth to conceal the fact of the suicide. The act itself is seldom mentioned, and indeed, in most cases, even the man who died is obscured. Replacing the depressed, withdrawn and, in all likelihood, hostile person who killed himself—and whom daughter observed—is an idealized portrait of a man done in by fate. This idealized portrait does conform to the image that daughter would *like* to preserve. Yet

the contradictory pictures of the father she would like to remember, the father she is being encouraged to remember, and
the father she in fact does remember, only serve to further
confuse her.

Discouraged from even talking about her recollections, lest
the unmentionable truth be uttered, the child has little recourse but to withdraw into her own, isolated world of uncon-
firmed memories. There, alone, she endeavors to reconcile the
conflicting impressions presented to her by a world that, by
virtue of her very youth, she is working hard to understand. She
is grieving, to be sure, but for whom, thanks to the family myth,
she cannot be quite sure. Thus, the family myth begets isolation
and confusion, which in turn may render the girl markedly
insecure about all her perceptions.

As reported in the professional literature, many survivors of
parental suicide develop learning disabilities and conditions of
pseudostupidity as a result of questioning their capacity to learn
or to know—for "knowing" has become forbidden. Others, like
Gena, function under the debilitating state of painful shyness
and grow into adulthood with an overall distrust of their capacity to make decisions. How can they trust anything, even every-
day realities, when the seminal event of their childhood has
been so shrouded in mystery and misunderstanding?

"I don't know what I believe," a sixty-year-old woman wrote
in response to several items on our questionnaire. "One morning when I was seven years old, the house became engulfed in
hysteria, and no one told me what was going on. My father had
cut his throat and wrists with a butcher knife, but all anyone
could say to me was to be quiet and not create a bother.

"Several days afterwards, when I saw the flowers on the coffin, I realized Daddy was dead, that he would not be coming
back home with us. My father was gone forever, but no one ever
even tried to explain nor console me—not ever. All my life,
fifty-three years later, there is never a day free of the pain, or
the feeling of bitter helplessness. I've had many different jobs,
converted to several religious affiliations, been married, divorced, and had numerous lovers. At no time have I ever felt
that anything was right."

All the confusion and isolation as she struggles to understand what happened, inevitably lead to a diminishment of the girl's self-esteem. Then, as she comes to recognize all too well what happened, her doubts about her worthiness are cemented.* "He didn't love me enough to want to live." "He did not think I was worth living for." This is at the heart of what her father's suicide means to his daughter. The first man she ever loved chose to leave her. The implications about her viability as a lovable female are obvious, yet there are defense mechanisms, primarily two, that help her to integrate the profound sense of rejection.

The first defense, or coping strategy—documented in the professional literature and evident in our study—is guilt. As we saw in Chapter Three, it is not unusual for children whose parents have died for any reason to persuade themselves that they are somehow to blame. Cecile, we will recall, talked about her "powers"; taking responsibility for the loss helped to alleviate the feeling of helplessness and rejection after her father died. Similarly, in a study of forty-five survivors of parental suicide, Drs. Albert C. Cain and Irene Fast reported, "Coming home late from the playground, a bad report card, poor table manners . . . even 'getting another bad cold' were all stated as the cause of the parent's committing suicide." It is quite evident that, to the child's way of thinking, guilt removes some of the insult from the injury.

But even beyond the conviction of their own misbehavior or omnipotence, many survivors of parental suicide attribute the parent's act to their own sin of omission. Incredibly, they grow up believing that they not only caused the suicide, but that they could have prevented it. "If only I had listened to him, talked to him more, been there for him," repined one woman I interviewed. As heavy a burden as her "negligence" is, it yet lightens the greater strain of believing that she was deserted because of generalized unworthiness.

Guilt, of course, is a double-edged sword. It may help the child to ward off suspicions of unworthiness, but at the same

---

* Very few of the women I interviewed could remember the exact manner in which they learned that the cause of death was suicide. Perhaps the very secrecy after the death, feeding off observations made before the death, leads most children to "just figure it out."

time it pierces her self-esteem. If she caused her father to die, she is less a victim; but if she caused her father to die, how lovable can she be? In an effort to dull the sense of rejection and the guilt, she calls upon the second defense mechanism observed in children of suicides: identification.

Freud defined the successful completion of mourning as the ability to detach oneself from the deceased. But the girl whose father killed himself does not want to become detached from, or mourn, her father. For as long as he lives through her, there is less reason for guilt, less evidence of having been rejected.

Identification may first be observed as the girl strives to behave like an adult. "We became each other's parents," said Lori and Gena. "I became the little man of the house," another woman asserted.

But a more dangerous result of identification with the dead parent is manifest in a preoccupation with suicide itself. This preoccupation is not unfounded, since ". . . suicide survivors [children of victims] have a statistically greater risk of committing suicide than other people." Whether the chicken or the egg comes first is irrelevant; the point is that children of suicide are aware of this haunting correlation, so that what starts out as a way of defending against rejection may evolve into identifying with the ultimately self-destructive behavior of the parent. By identifying with the parent who killed himself, loss may initially be denied, but ultimately the identification turns in on itself and the child is trapped by the very suspicions she was trying to disavow: suspicions of her unworthiness, her overall badness, her father's rejection. Having come full circle to be confronted by what she perceives to be her unlovable self, now convinced of her similarity to her father, and aware of traditional family histories, the daughter of suicide may become obsessed with her own self-destruction, even to the point of suicide.

> I am unlovable.
> + I am like my suicidal father.
> I must destroy myself.

Given the pervasiveness of the family myth, and the lack of community support that evokes the isolation, disillusionment, and insecurity of which we spoke, adding to these the child's attempt to deny her feelings of rejection by first taking on the responsibility for the loss and then denying the responsibility *and* the loss through identification; given this superstructure of denial, confusion, and guilt, it is not surprising that the work of mourning is rarely completed in healthy fashion among children of parents who have killed themselves. For the daughter of paternal suicide—who has been willfully abandoned by the first man she ever loved—the need to deny the rejection may be so acute as to lead her to the ultimate denial of separation: she will reestablish her relationship with father and prove her love for him by joining him in death.

Fortunately, this outcome is more the exception than the rule, but the internal wound of paternal suicide may cause any number of psychological problems: from developmental arrest, to agonizing shyness, to neurotic inhibition regarding personal or professional commitment, to severe self-destructive behavior.

While Lori seems to be "holding it all together" through her "fierce desire to live" for her child's sake (and indeed by expressing it this way, she acknowledges her awareness of the statistical evidence), Gena, at thirty-two, continues to exist in a state of quest—for self-confidence and for a decision about what to do with her life.

Madeleine, a twenty-nine-year-old woman with whom I spent several days during the summer of 1981, embodies practically all of the documented reactions to parental suicide and lives in the constant shadow of the nature of her loss: its abruptness, its implicit accusation, its suggestion about her own worth, and its prognosis for her future.

*

The first of three children, Madeleine was born and raised in an exclusive area of Boston. Her father, gregarious and outgoing, was a doctor; her mother, a model of grace and efficiency, oversaw the household—husband, children, and staff of three— with quiet composure. Both parents came from wealthy backgrounds.

Madeleine paints a rosy picture of her early childhood: "close-knit family," "very happy and privileged," "country house in the summer, Bermuda during vacations, I didn't suffer for anything materially, and my parents were both pretty loving.

"I really don't remember anything unpleasant as a child. I was a happy, healthy, outgoing kid. I went to one of the finest schools in all the country, a private school for girls. As a student, I did well up to a point. Scholastics didn't come easily, but if I worked and studied, I did very well.

"I was very competitive athletically, always popular, president of my class, really the perfect girl; outgoing, pretty, had a cute figure, the all-around picture is one of a healthy, well-adjusted child. And as I said, life at home was always healthy and sober . . ." She corrects herself. "I mean somber.

"I was particularly close to my father. I think he and I were very much alike. Very compatible. There was an unspoken and unconditional bond between us because our characters were very similar. It was always a very secure feeling for me when he came in from work. It was like a routine: he'd shut the front door, hang his coat and hat in the hall closet—I thought about that closet a lot after he died—and I, very excited, would go to greet him.

"I can't really remember what we did in the evenings, except, well, I guess I recall several experiences of him being upset or angry with me. But it doesn't change the general color of my warm feelings about him.

"There were several times when he wanted me to stay up and talk with him, I must have been eight or nine, and I was too tired. He would scream at me, hit me, and my mother would act as a buffer. I mean he would get really angry and start yelling, 'She's too tired even to talk to me.' One time, he even ran after me with an andiron, but my mother calmed him down.

"See, I think I provoked him a lot. I was very mischievous. He would ask me not to do something, like kick the screen door at the country house, and I'd just keep doing it over and over, and then he'd get really angry and spank me. And, of course, I'd be shocked.

"One very vivid memory I have is when he came into my room late at night because I was having nightmares. He sat down on my bed very seriously and discussed the nightmare situation, very gentle, smiling at me, soothing me. And the thing is, I didn't really have any nightmares. I just wanted him to come in and talk to me."

These conflicting memories—of the harsh, punitive father pitted against the kind, comforting father—are common among daughters of paternal suicide.† Madeleine, for example, knows that her father was highly emotional and hot-tempered, but in defense, blames herself for the intensity of his anger. Maintaining an idealized portrait is less painful than confronting her own resentment and early sense of rejection.

In her summer frock and sandals, more reminiscent of a waif than a child of a wealthy family, Madeleine has been relating the memories of her childhood life with gusto. Even the negative incidents with her father are quickly covered by handy rationalizations. But the mood changes abruptly when the conversation turns to her father's death.

There is a long silence.

"I remember he hadn't been around for a while. It was anywhere between two days and two weeks. My mother kept saying he was working. But I knew something was wrong. A gloom had settled in the house. Something was off. I don't really know how much time elapsed between his death and my mother finding out about it."

In a barely audible voice, she explains, "He had checked himself into a hotel and took medication and alcohol.

"I remember, the night before she told me he had died I dreamed that he was walking around the kitchen and he was dead and I fried an egg and slapped it on his forehead to try to bring him back to life.

"The next day, all these people were gathered in our living room and I kept saying, 'Where's my father? Where's my father?' People just avoided the subject. Finally our family doctor and my mother took me into the bedroom and the doctor told me that my father had died. I turned to my mother and said,

† Of the women I interviewed whose fathers died, only daughters of suicide had strong negative memories of their male parent.

'What if when I'm older, I start to cry?' And she said, 'Well, that will be all right.'

"I don't know what gave me the idea that I had to wait, because my father had been very emotional. He cried a lot, hugged a lot, yelled a lot.

"Later that day, I called my best friend and said, 'My father died.' And she said, 'What?' And I screamed, 'You heard me. I said my father died,' and I slammed down the phone and threw myself on my parents' bed, kicking, screaming, and crying. And then that was it—the last time I cried.

"I was told that he had died because of some stomach trouble. But I specifically remember saying to a friend, 'Gee, I don't think he really died because of his stomach, because they have hospitals now and they can cure people. No, I don't think it was his stomach.' All along, I felt this confusion and ambiguity around what I had been told. It just didn't set right."

At ten years old, somehow determined not to cry, isolated by the family myth into suspicion and distrust over what she was being told, Madeleine also felt confused by the suddenness of her father's death. "I kept wondering why someone hadn't told me he was going to die, so that I could have done something about it.

"I didn't cry at the funeral. But I remember, driving back to the house, someone was asking me directions and I felt like a real hotshot. Then this other woman in the car started answering for me and I got furious. I just wanted to kick and scream and kill this person. There was all this displaced rage, and I still have it. I am just so furious at him for leaving us and not telling us he was going."

Adult explanations to the contrary notwithstanding, Madeleine intuited the deliberate desertion implicit in her father's death. The powerlessness of her situation, her inability either to prevent or talk about it, evoked years of socially unacceptable acting out.

Yet her initial reaction to the shattering of her "happy, privileged home life" was to deny it altogether. Like Lori and Gena and many others in her situation, she felt it incumbent upon her to behave like a parent. She, in a sense, gave up her childhood to become an adult.

"I became very aware of being the oldest in the house and helping my mother out. I remember feeling that I had to hold the household together, and that I needed to be stronger than my mother and take care of her. I was very concerned over her. She got even thinner than usual, and I wanted so much to please her, make her feel better. So I became the little man of the house. And I really do believe that my sturdy little attitude helped her out in a way.

"Of course, I was getting into a lot of trouble at school, always being called into the headmistress's office for this or that. I think I was trying to cause a commotion in the classroom so I could get sent to the headmistress's office and cry. But not about my father—I found lots of other things to cry about. See, I've always been very much like my father, very emotional."

Less than a year after her husband's death, Madeleine's mother remarried. "I adored him. The transition was pretty smooth and the household really altered for the better. He came along, my mother was happy, and we were a family again. There was a man in the house. It was like a weight had been taken off my shoulders."

But not really. Two months later, "The trouble began. As I think about it now, there may have been some competition between my mother and me for my stepfather's attention. And my role as mother's protector was eliminated. I sort of lost my mother to this man, 'to this *other* man,' I almost said."

Replaced in her role by a more appropriate player, Madeleine was finally alone with her feelings: her rage, her confusion, her rejection, her guilt. An imaginative child, she constructed an elaborate set of rituals to ensure her isolation.

"I wouldn't let anybody touch me. If they did, I would wipe it off. If my mother kissed me, I would wipe it off. This went on for years. And still, to this day, if a stranger on the street touches me, I wipe it off.

"Somebody in school once knew that I did this, and she chased me and put her hands all over me. I raced into the bathroom to get it off. I felt contaminated. I felt so hurt that I wanted to shut everybody out. I thought if anybody touched me, they'd get into me, and I didn't want anyone creeping into me.

"I also became very superstitious. I had these prayers that I would say every night, and in the elevator of my house, and on every street corner. I would stop and say a silent prayer for everybody living and dead. In the elevator, it involved standing in each corner of the elevator and then standing in the middle. My stepfather once took notice of this and tried to stop me. We got out of the elevator together, and then I raced back in and shut the door so I could finish the ritual. This must have gone on from the time I was eleven to fourteen or fifteen. But that was nothing compared to the other things I got into.

"I just felt so terrible that he had died. So uninformed: like if I could have only known how much he was suffering, *I could have kept him alive.* Maybe if I had spent more time with him, he wouldn't have killed himself. If only I hadn't kept kicking the screen door, he wouldn't have gotten so mad and slapped me and we would have gotten along better and he would have loved me and he wouldn't have killed himself.

"My mother always told me I was his favorite child. I think he loved me. Yet how could he have killed himself if he loved me?"

The revelations spill out in a torrent, leaving us both exhausted. Though I have done my research and am familiar with the symptoms, I am deeply moved by this confession of guilt; this conviction, held firmly still, that a ten-year-old's disobedience drove her father to such despair that he ended his life; and the associated belief that if only she "hadn't been too tired to talk to him," she could have prevented his dramatic act.

To further ensure her isolation, Madeleine initiated another ritual: overeating. The compulsive intake of food, which began when she was in the seventh grade, in fact served several purposes: it provided a protective pad between herself and others, it muffled her anger, and it ended any possibility of realistic competition with her slim, attractive, remarried mother.

Yet her female parent was concerned about Madeleine. In an attempt to help her daughter, and under the advice of the family physician, she obtained a prescription for diet pills. And thus began another insatiable appetite.

Before the decade of outright addiction to drugs, however—which would come in her twenties—Madeleine took to filling herself with equally punitive morsels. Like so many adolescents suffering under an intense feeling of deprivation (see Chapter Four), she went on a rampage of stealing. Certainly it wasn't for want of material things; what she needed was to grab, take, have.

"At the same time that I was president of the school, I would go into people's lockers during study hall and steal money from them. In fact, the headmistress once called a special assembly and said, 'There is this very sick person who has been doing these things. Please let us know who you are so that we can help you.'

"And I remember after the assembly, standing in the hall with all the girls and saying, 'I really hope whoever it is turns herself in.' And I knew it was me, and I would do it again and again and run with trembling hands into the bathroom and take the money out of their wallets. And I never got caught. I was never caught at all the terrible things that I've done, the lying, stealing, cheating . . ." (causing her father's death?) ". . . It's amazing."

Madeleine ran away from home one week before high school graduation. "I was supposed to give the graduation speech, and I knew I just couldn't go through with it. I weighed 116 pounds and I felt so fat and so ugly and so disgusting at 116 instead of 105 that I ran away. I left my parents a note saying I was going to Oregon. I had a boyfriend there.

"A few weeks later, I got a letter from my mother in which she said that there was something about my father that she felt I should know: he committed suicide. Can you believe that she had never even mentioned it to me until then? I was nineteen. Of course, I already knew at that point—I don't even remember how or when I found out, but I knew—and we had never even discussed it.

"I think my running away made her realize that I was lost, and she was trying to reach out. But it was too late. I had this thing inside me, and I wasn't able to change the way I felt about myself."

Despite the alleged ineffectiveness of her mother's letter, Madeleine did return home. But the suicide continued an unmentionable subject, and Madeleine's attempt at straightening out was quickly aborted.

"I lived at home and gave a crack at nursing school which lasted about four months. Again I was president of the class and doing very well academically. But I thought they were all such idiots. How could I be doing so well if I was really so dumb? So I left and got a job in a department store, where I worked myself up to manager of a department. I got into drugs, started drinking and stealing like crazy from the store. I was manager and stealing about a hundred dollars' worth of merchandise a day."

Still "uncaught," she left Boston for a year's stint at college—and more promiscuity, more drinking, more drugs. In fact, she was very much "caught"—in her identification with the man that got away. Alone with her tumultuous impressions of his death, and struggling over the degree to which she was responsible for it, she took a course of action designed to prove her loyalty: with drugs and alcohol, instability and self-destructiveness, she was emulating, and thus seeking to maintain a relationship with, her father.

"I was doing handfuls of reds and marveling at how many I could do in one night. Once, I concocted this experiment where I took one the first night, two the second, then three, four, five . . . nothing happened. Ironically, well not so ironically, I think my father died of a Seconal overdose."

The overtly self-destructive behavior was rounded out by binging on food, taking enough speed to throw up and thus lose weight, doing hallucinogens, and having ever more meaningless sex. "I think of myself as basically a sensuous, horny little woman. And at that time, I was really into flirtatiousness, so if I felt an instant attraction, I would just go to bed and not expect anything more than being held and being touched. I had a strong need to be held. And I always ate afterwards, always, always, always ate after sex."

Then she met Pedro, an exotic Latino who offered more than sex. Footloose and streetwise, he could supply her with drugs, a life of crime, and perhaps most important, the total alienation from her mother that resulted from taking up with him. Her guilt finally confirmed, she set out on a full-fledged mission to punish herself—and to join her father through the ultimate punishment.

"We hitched across the country, doing robberies, setting people up. Like I would get a job at a 7-Eleven-type store, and when the supervisor wasn't around, Pedro would come in and 'rob' me. I'd shut the place down, call the police, and then we'd head for the next place.

"I even broke into some friends' house once. I knew they'd be away, so when they were gone, we broke in, drank all the liquor, stole their camera, and left."

She recounts these escapades as though rattling off experiences that happened to somebody else. And it is with similar dispassion that she comes to the incident that finally ended her life of petty theft.

"Soon after we got back to New Haven, I jumped off a train. I was very drunk and very stoned, and at the hospital they sent in a woman psychiatrist to talk to me about it. She was chubby and young and I think I hated her because I was chubby and young too. She dared to imply that maybe jumping off the train was a suicide attempt. I told her to get the fuck out of my room.

"And then the doctor in charge of my case, who must have been very wise indeed, sent over a gentleman who had known my father: a psychiatrist. He looked a lot like my father, and he talked to me in such a nice way. I fell absolutely in love with this man. I continued to see him on and off for about three years, until he left the area.

"When he told me he was leaving, I cried for at least four hours. I couldn't even get from his office to my house. I had to just get off the bus, sit down, and cry. I'm sure I was crying for my father, but, at the time, I didn't realize it. I kept thinking to myself 'Why am I crying so much for this person? You'd think my father had died.'

"I still can't associate feelings of death with my father. I can't directly cry for him. But I can identify with what he must have been going through, the inner turmoil and confusion and self-hatred, and just being overwhelmed with the enormity of life."

Persisting in her unshakable conviction that she was just like her father, Madeleine couldn't mourn for him, because she wouldn't let him die. He continued to rage and rant and lash out at life's injustices through her. Only in her previous "on again, off again" relationship with the psychiatrist had she allowed

anyone to be kind to her. Yet she refused to see him regularly, as
he suggested, because "I wouldn't let myself have that.

"If I see a man who's white, educated, from a background
similar to mine, I immediately think, 'Fuck you.' I get hostile
and defensive, feeling coarse and ugly and vulgar. My only way
of dealing with men, of feeling good around men, is to go where
the 'street niggers' hang out, or the truck drivers, or construc-
tion workers, and go straight for them. I know just what to do
and how to get them and how to talk and how to walk. I guess
it's a certain bawdiness in me that I really enjoy. With men
closer to me in education and social background, I just get all
caught up in the anticipated rejection. I mean, there's this feeling that I don't deserve them, that I'm obviously unworthy of
love and permanence in any man. If I would seek out people
like my father, they would probably die, or leave like my therapist did."

Yet it is quite possible that through her attraction to exotic
men, Madeleine is in fact remaining faithful to her father. Because of a man's very foreignness, a temporary relationship is
ensured, and, as noted by one professional, "by being . . . very
exotic [he shares] her father's status—unavailability."

"I've always associated sex with feelings of shame. That's one
reason the guy in Oregon didn't work out. He was very poetic
and sweet, and I always felt very crude next to him. When we
made love, in order to get off, I'd have to close my eyes and
think of something disgusting. Like there was this revolting
garage mechanic I knew, so I'd think of him.

"But if I have sex with men who just give me what I want and
then walk out the door, the shame is built in. Of course, it always
hurts when they leave. So I start eating. There's this one guy I'm
seeing now who always responds when I go to see him, and then
he walks out of my life until I'm after him the next time. And I
know I should stay away, because I'll stay happier that way . . .
and thinner. The truth is, I've been hurt constantly by men, and
I'm sick of it."

The relationship with Pedro ended soon after their child was
born. "We had been in New Haven a few years and the shrink
was long gone. I was pregnant and on welfare, and Pedro
thought that was great, we had arrived. After I had the baby,

we'd get drunk and he'd beat me up, and I remember thinking, 'Is this what you want? You're as low as you can go, this is really what you've got now: a man slapping you all over the room.' And it could have gone on like that except I finally realized that, before long, he'd be beating up our child, and that was it. It enabled me to leave.

"I spent a long time after that believing that my legitimate escape from the pressures of being a single mother was to go out and get drunk and get laid. I must have slept with tons of men, all out of this predominantly black bar I know. But the pain was still there. And, I don't know, at some point I knew I had to do something."

What she did, about a year prior to this interview, was to join Alcoholics Anonymous and Overeaters Anonymous. And she attends meetings often, sometimes two a day. When asked to what extent membership has changed her life, she categorically states, "It hasn't changed my life. It's given me life.

"I know I've got some day-to-day struggles ahead, but I've reached a turning point in my life. Now that I'm on the program and not taking drugs or drinking or overeating, I see that there are certain issues with men that keep coming up and it's not enough to just not do drugs and not drink. I am going to have to resolve this thing with my father so I can get on with it.

"I need to remember him, and I need to go through whatever those steps are that you have to do to mourn a person properly. I need to feel the rage, the sorrow, and the real acceptance that he's dead."

Though she's finally committed to therapy, Madeleine's task is extremely difficult, because her mother, with whom she is slowly making peace, still doesn't want to address the circumstances of her first husband's death. "Every now and then I bring it up, but it's obvious she doesn't want to talk about it. I think my brother keeps a lot of her guilt alive. I mean, I ran away for ten years and, though I'm perceived as the black sheep of the family, at least I'm finally doing something for myself. But my brother, who is heavily into drugs, by the way, just hangs around her like a wound that doesn't heal."

Madeleine becomes agitated at this point. We have trespassed on forbidden territory: her mother's role in all this. She insists that we get back on the track of her own life. "I've resigned myself to the fact that she and I will never be able to talk about it. It's really taboo in our household, and even including her in our conversation makes me very uncomfortable."

She tells me about a dream she had recently. "It was in an old amphitheater for operating, and they brought him in to me on a stretcher. He was dead, wrapped up in gauze. Some of my fellows from OA were in the balcony, so I felt secure. I had a backpack on my shoulders, and I went up to him and started screaming at him and stomping my feet. 'You left me. I was a little girl just getting close to my father and you left me without warning and I'm furious with you.' I got so angry and so enraged that my shoulders were trembling and the backpack sprang off. So, that's what I remember. When I awakened, I was still pretty into it, the anger, but it felt good, about twenty years late in coming.

"See, I guess I've always thought my battles were with my mother. I had to punish her. That way I could maintain a very rosy relationship with him. And I didn't have to let go.

"Now that I am letting go, it hurts. Whenever I see a little girl with her father, I envy her because she has her daddy. I think a woman who grows up knowing how to handle herself with a man, and how to be loved by a man, has a definite edge on those of us who never had that. It's like part of us is missing.

But it's not only in relationships with men that I was affected. I see his death as a dab of ink on a piece of blotting paper. It just spread into every area of my life. From his death stemmed everything else. It's like B.C. and A.D."

The knowledge that the first man she ever loved chose to create an uncrossable chasm between them haunts and seriously diminishes the confidence of the daughter of paternal suicide. Of course, there is one way of getting back to father, but fortunately that final option is so unthinkable as to be rejected, if indeed flirted with, by most.

The daughter of a man who chose to leave but *not* to die is haunted by the absence of finality. She, too, was left fatherless by his choice, but her options are all too realistic, and therefore equally preoccupying.

SIX

NO DEATH TO MOURN, NO FATHER TO LOVE

Abandonment and Divorce

When a girl's father dies, she has irrevocably lost the first man she ever loved. Try as she might to keep him alive in her fantasies, the relationship is over, and much of her psychic energy will go into compensating for its absence.

A girl who has lost her father owing to abandonment or divorce confronts no such finality. She ruminates, rather than mourns. Her father is alive, and perhaps, if she tries very hard, he will come back. If not to mother, then at least to herself.*

The degree to which the hope for reconciliation exists—and it is ever present in daughters of absent *living* fathers—varies with the circumstances surrounding father's withdrawal. In girls who never met their fathers, for instance, need and curiosity generally don't surface until maturity. A girl who remembers enjoying an active relationship with her male parent, on the other hand, will seek reunion at a younger age.

Lee, a successful public relations executive in her thirties, is

* When speaking of "daughters of divorce" in this book, I am referring to those whose fathers absented themselves after the divorce. Obviously, women who chose to participate in this project perceive their childhoods as having been deprived of a male parent. For those who continued to enjoy an active relationship with their fathers after the divorce, reconciliation need not have been an issue. In fact, many women in this group enjoyed improved relations with their fathers once all the parental bickering was out of the way, so that marital reconciliation was the last thing they wanted.

representative of the former situation. "Do you ever go through life unaware?" she asked me. She went on to describe an incident, a year prior to our conversation, that had awakened a dormant sorrow she'd never even suspected.

Visiting with some friends who have two young daughters, she was relaxing at their pool when tones of the girls' high-pitched merriment struck a somber chord in her. "There they were playing with their father—happy, squealing for joy—and a wave of remorse came over me. Honestly, it was a revelation, the way it hit me, how very different those little girls' lives would be from mine. They will have known what it's like to be held, kissed, cuddled, and loved by a man. And of course, I had none of that. Talk about starving to death!"

Lee's parents met while her mother, past forty, was working in a hotel. They spent a night together—"My mother always says he put something in her drink"—and nine months later, Lee was born. A turbulent childhood, shuttled between mother, foster home, and back again, provided so much emotional baggage that questions regarding her biological father were but a peripheral concern. Not surprisingly, this is a frequent early result of father absence owing to prenatal abandonment. The girl born to an unwed mother is likely to spend her childhood in unstable conditions. It wasn't until Lee was ten years old that she accepted, reluctantly, the decision that she would be living full time with a mother she barely knew. Soon afterward, questions about her father set in.

"By the sixth grade, I knew that my parents hadn't been married, but it wasn't until a few years later that my mother actually told me anything about him. She said that he was a writer, and I thought that was very interesting, since I was already editor of the school paper and very fascinated by journalism.

"She took me to the library so that I could read some of his books, and I remember being very, very impressed, and thinking that he must be a marvelous man. I started to wonder what I had inherited from him—that's always been a question—and I began having fantasies about meeting him. For instance, I would think about going to a writer's convention and just walking up to him without letting him know who I was, just so I could see the man. Of course, there's no way you can just walk up to someone and say, 'Hi, I'm your daughter.' I don't even know how I would prove it.

"At one point, I looked him up under twentieth-century authors, and the description of his background explained why I look the way I do, where I got my green eyes.

"It wasn't until last year that I seriously tried to find him. I figured, 'What have I got to lose? He must be seventy-eight or seventy-nine years old. I don't even have to acknowledge who I am.' I was sincerely disappointed when I learned that it was too late. He had died."

Lee insists that her interest in meeting her father was purely intellectual. But her pattern of frustrated relationships with men—"I always go after what I can't have"—as interpreted by a therapist friend of hers, belies her attested disinterest. The green eyes inherited from her father grow defensive, then defiant as she describes her friend's concern. "She feels that I will never be happy with a man until I resolve this father . . . father thing. She says I'm constantly looking for approval because I didn't receive any from my father. Now, how could my father disapprove of me? He didn't even know I existed."

The reconciliation wish comes earlier when daughter is witness to the separation. Even if life at home was a constant barrage of behind-closed-doors fighting, the daughter of divorced parents dreams of the magical redemption of the love that surely united her parents in the first place: the love that flourished, she guiltily imagines, before *she* came along to ruin it all. When he leaves mother, father is also leaving her, and it is unthinkable that he will not come around to seeing the error of his ways. As revealed in our study, daughters of divorce tended to take at least one year before acknowledging that father was gone forever.

Megan, a forty-two-year-old psychologist who was seven when her parents divorced, spent much of her childhood denying her father's hurtful choice. Yes, she had heard the arguments and her mother's accusations about other women; indeed, her own early memories of her father were of a "mysterious, elusive" man. But when, one day, he was suddenly

gone—without any explanation—she entered a six-month period of "waiting for him" and "wondering where he was." Denial then took another form: Rather than dream of his return,
she would make it impossible for him to do so. At seven and a
half, Megan decided that her father was dead. That's what she
told her friends at school, and that's what she told herself.

I listen to Megan with incredulity and even a small measure
of resentment. While I was trying to grapple with the horrid
permanence of my father's absence, keeping it a dreadful secret
from classmates, she was creating a charade of permanence.
While my girlhood imagination fairly burst with visions of mys-
tical meetings, hers was nullifying hope. The luxury of her decision was striking. For, just as she buried her father, she could
resurrect him—and she did. Megan got to meet the man that
got away.

"There came a point in my late teens where I was frantically
unable to separate from men I was dating. I just couldn't say,
'Good night.' Literally, I would lock a guy in my apartment,
terrified that if he left, I wouldn't see him again. Naturally, this
was devastating to both parties, and I knew that my emotions
were way out of control. I had to do something about my fear,
my anger.

"I wasn't aware of what I was acting out, why I was inevitably
attracted to good-looking, noncommital men, why I was so terrified of any kind of separation, but I was in therapy at the time
and talking more and more about my father. It became clear
that he was very much alive, and so was my need to see him.

"I had no idea where he was; I really didn't have very many
facts. Finally, I asked my mother about him. She suggested he
may have gone to Chicago—he had family there—and she gave
me his sister's name. I called his sister, my aunt, and told her I
was coming. She told me nothing about my father and I had no
idea what to expect.

"I went on the train, and when it pulled into the station, there
he was, exactly as I'd remembered him: handsome, glamorous,
well-dressed, ageless. It was amazing to me that all this time had
gone by and yet he was the same, as though nothing had even
happened. It was a terrific shock.

"I got into his car and started driving to his house. Though I hadn't ever consciously thought about it, I just assumed that he was a single person and that he'd be totally available to me, that he would devote himself to me.

"So there I was in his new Cadillac—which fit in perfectly with my image of him—almost at his house, when he bluntly tells me that he's married and has two sons. It had never occurred to me that that was even a possibility, that he had gone on and made another life.

"Suddenly I was terrifically angry. This rage started pouring out of me—Why hadn't he called in all these years? . . . Not even a birthday card—When he showed me some photos of me that he'd been carrying since I was little, I just exploded. Big deal! He got me to calm down by saying how much he'd loved my mother, how he'd never had as many good times with any other woman. It was a wonderful thing for him to say, but naturally it also reactivated all the guilt I'd been suppressing. At one time my parents were in love, then they weren't. Did it have something to do with me? Perhaps if I had been a better daughter, a prettier daughter, it would have made me more valuable, more worth staying for." (In the course of many interviews with daughters of divorce, I was struck by the frequency with which I heard this lament: if only daughter had been prettier, father would have stayed.)

Megan was understandably ill at ease in the home of her father and his family. Her presence, far from symbolizing hope and reconciliation, seemed to be an intrusive reminder of failure. As if to underline her suspicion of her destructive power, her father and his wife began arguing.

"My first morning there, I awakened to violent screaming and yelling. My father came in to tell me we were leaving. Nothing was explained to me, but I was sure that I was the protagonist of their dispute. I had done it again.

"We went to a motel. It was very frightening. I mean, he wasn't seductive or anything, but he had no idea how to behave with a female other than flirtatiously. And I had never spent so much time alone with a man, no less this stranger who was my father. Fortunately, that only lasted for two days. Then he took me to stay at his sister's.

"I was there for two weeks, during which he'd spend a few

very caring, very involved days, then disappear, then come back; back and forth, being close, being apart, involvement followed by silence. I couldn't stand the closeness, I couldn't bear the separation. What it came down to was, I just couldn't trust him. He wasn't the man I wanted him to be, and he wasn't going to make up for all those years I didn't have a father.

"He took me to the airport, and I wept on the plane. I guess when I came back to L.A., I still had the hope that he would write, but he never did."

Just as the meeting with her father resembled nothing of a magical reunion, neither was it a magical cure. But somewhere in her mind, the part that perceives reality, Megan was letting go. The mysteries of her mystery man had proved all too unriddling up close, and gradually he lost his stature as a standard by which to compare all others (a stature, for want of testing, that most deceased fathers never lose).

Letting go of her fantasy, she found it easier to let go of men. She wasn't locking them in any more, nor was she single-mindedly attracted to those who were eager to leave. Two years after meeting her father, she met the man who would become her husband.

"He wasn't particularly good-looking, but he was very soft and sensitive, caring and constant about how he felt; not hot one day and cold the next.

"My father came for the wedding. He was out of work and unmarried. I felt by then that he really didn't have anything to offer, that he was a taker, always on the brink of disaster, and really something of a pain. In fact, he sort of disgusted me."

That was the last time Megan saw her father. Her marriage, which had been unconsciously intended to reproach his character, lasted only two and a half years. Megan had let go of her father, but not of her need to be fathered.

"When I had gone to Chicago, at nineteen, I had told myself that I just wanted to see him, but what I was really hoping was that he'd take care of all the areas that had never been nurtured by a man. By marrying Steve, I chose a person distinctly unlike my father. Maybe I thought that would ensure that he would behave like a father should.

"In addition to his sensitivity, I was attracted to the fact that his parents had been married for thirty-five years. I definitely wanted to marry someone from a strong, intact home. I had just taken my first psychology course and I had it all figured out. But of course, I was still struggling with this need to be taken care of. Steve was a good companion, a good person, but he wasn't terribly strong.

"Also, he didn't make much of a living. He was an artist, and though we always had enough to get by on, it was frightening to me to be living like that.

"On another level, I was also very angry with myself for being so needy. Just before I left him, I read *Sex and the Single Girl*, and it really had an influence on me.† It became terribly important for me to take care of myself, to be autonomous. It's awful to admit, but I think I also gained some satisfaction from being the one to leave instead of being left. I certainly wasn't conscious of trying to hurt him, but I think I needed to do that, to feel in control of the walking-out process."

After two years, Megan traded a shaky sense of independence for another marriage. Jack was several years her senior and, more significantly, a doctor. "There's no doubt in my mind that I saw him as a father figure. I felt safe with him. Here he was, older and a doctor, someone with all the trimmings of being able to take care of me." Fifteen years and two children later, they were divorced. Despite his M.D., Jack was merely human, his black bag containing a troubled childhood and insecurities of his own. He didn't have the antidote for Megan's pain.

Asked to describe her current relationship, Megan takes a deep breath. "The minute that I think that he's not as connected to me as I want him to be, the rage is incredible. You see, I gained understanding from accepting who my father really was, but I didn't lose the pain or the trauma of his absence. I sometimes think that taking care of me is an impossible task. I've been through nine years of therapy, but I'm afraid I'm always going to be struggling with these issues, wanting a man to take me over, yet backing away from too much closeness. It's

† For Helen Gurley Brown's reflections on the loss of *her* father, please see Chapter Thirteen.

disappointing to me that I'm not cured, that there's no such thing as cure.

"I guess that's what happens when the early trust and security of a child is disrupted. You spend the rest of your life looking for a safe situation, and of course, nothing in life can ever be 100 percent safe."

The possibility of reconciliation informs all other differences between daughters of divorced and daughters of dead fathers. While I deplore the fact that I never even had the chance to know my father, it is clear that false hope is equally as frustrating as absolute finality. A bitter pill is hard to digest whether taken in bits or swallowed whole. The daughter of a deceased father knows she has little choice but to cope with the acrid taste left in her mouth; the daughter of divorced parents keeps hoping the prescription will be changed.

Patty, a statuesque, Liv Ullman look-alike, still has that hope. It has been twenty-two years since her father drove off in his new T-bird convertible and, as he had so many times before, she was sure he'd be back.

> If I'd known that would be the last time I'd ever see my dad, I might have watched the car drive away at least. But I stood where he left me, in the living room, and he crossed the room and shut the screen door carefully, quietly, and passed through my life.‡

Mr. Stokes was a nightclub entertainer. As such, it is understandable that he worked odd hours. His wife and his children were used to that. In fact, to Patty it represented a bonus, because it meant that her father, the parent she felt close to, was home during the days.

"I always felt much more attached to him than to my mother. After I was born, he took care of me, because my mother had to stay in the hospital. He was the one who took me shopping— even for my first bra. He taught me how to play the piano; he took my little brother and me trick-or-treating, and he gave the best birthday parties on the block. Everyone wanted to come to

‡ From a story written by Patty.

our parties." She giggles past the tears perpetually glimmering in her eyes. An ornate, wood-inlaid upright piano dominates the otherwise sparsely decorated room in which we talk.

Odd hours are one thing, but the piano player's family had far more offbeat rhythms to respond to. For as long as she can remember, Patty's father would periodically disappear—sometimes for three days, sometimes for three months. Not, she was dimly aware, on work-related projects, but so that he could be with other women. "That's just the way he was," she explains. "He'd been running away from home since he was eight years old." Several times throughout the interview she will refer to him with hardly veiled admiration as "a gypsy."

"My very earliest memory is of my mother and me walking home and there are several crumpled-up dollar bills in the alley, like crumbs leading to the back door. That meant Daddy was home. He would traditionally do that, just show up with money or presents. My mother accepted it because she felt you hang in there no matter what. That's what *her* father had been like.

"I remember one evening (I must have been about six), my father was lying on the couch downstairs, and my mother was upstairs packing his bag. I knew what that meant: Daddy is going to disappear for a while and I'll be left with Mother, someone I don't feel very close to. I went downstairs and told my father, 'Daddy, I'm going with you.' He said that that would be difficult. But to get out of really answering, he said to go upstairs and ask my mother.

"She, of course, was in a terrible state, trying not to cry. I said, 'I want to go with Daddy.' And she said I couldn't, that he was going somewhere I couldn't go. I just kept running up and down those stairs, from one to the other and finally, I started crying and I wouldn't stop, I wouldn't stop. They were yelling at me and shaking me.

"The end result was that he didn't go that particular time. In the future, it was decided, he would just leave from work. So that's what he would do, finish work at two in the morning and just not come home.

"Of course, he was there most of the time. But there were always little signs telling us he was going to disappear again.

Like once he gave up smoking for my mother and so a few
months later when I saw him with a cigarette, I knew: 'Uh-oh,
it's coming again, so get ready.' "

How, I wonder aloud, does a little girl "get ready" for such
inevitably ill-timed disappearances? How does she prepare for
the implicit rejection by her father, her favorite parent? Her
answer comes in a childlike voice, reminiscent of a refrain delivered with practiced regularity, "It was just a part of life: Daddy
comes and Daddy goes.

"I remember one night when we were saying our prayers, my
mother said, 'And a hug for Daddy, wherever he is.' "

With disruption a customary part of her routine, Patty wasn't
particularly concerned when, soon after her fourteenth birthday, all the separations finally evolved into a divorce. "It just
seemed like a logical step. Nothing was ever discussed with us,
but I was aware of increasing fights, yelling fights, so I didn't
think the divorce would create a different situation from what I
was used to, except maybe a relief from all the tension when he
was there. I just assumed I'd still see him at least as often as I
always had. It never occurred to me that he was leaving forever.

"I only saw him twice after the divorce. Once, he came with
his new girlfriend and her two children, wrote me a check, and
left. The other time, he took me for a ride in his new convertible."

Though at thirty-eight she still has trouble accepting the permanence of her father's absence—"Daddy is gone, Daddy
comes back"—Patty has done little to try to find him. Instead,
she just assumes that he will return. "He always did." Only
once, when she was sixteen, did she actively seek him out.

"Whenever my father was gone, I was alone, I was just alone.
I didn't feel part of any family except when he was there. So
when it finally seemed apparent that this disappearance was
different from the others, I went to the police station to file a
missing persons report. The officer took down all the information, filling out a lot of forms, and then it came out that my
father probably wanted to be missing. Abruptly, the officer
ripped up all the papers and threw them away. 'We can't help
you if he doesn't want to be found,' he told me. And of course,
with bill collectors after him, he had covered his tracks well.

Nobody, not even my mother, knew where he went. When I'd tell her that I wished I could see him, talk to him, she'd tell me to have a dream about him. I heard through some cousins once that he was in Georgia, but how helpful is that? No, I never put any energy into finding him.

"Of course, I have my fantasies about it. One time, when he was kissing me good night, he said, 'Why can't you be pretty, like your mother?' *I never forgot that.* I always felt ugly. Still do. So I used to think, if only he could see me now, he'd see I didn't turn out so badly after all. I'd think about going into a bar where he was playing and he'd say, 'Who's that pretty woman?' And then he'd realize, 'Oh, it's my daughter!' And so maybe he'd see that I wasn't so bad that he had to leave.

"See, my coloring is all wrong," attests the striking redhead. "I'm so fair, and he's dark as a Mexican. But I look exactly like him, have all his features." With sudden enthusiasm, she takes out some photo albums so that she can prove the resemblance. Perusing the photographs, and momentarily forgetting the point she is trying to make, I somewhat thoughtlessly mention that she looks a great deal like her mother. "Don't say that! I have *his* features, don't you see?" I correct my blunder, and make careful note of said features, dismayed by her continuing dependence on approval from this singularly undependable man.

"Throughout my teens," she tells me later, "I had a very low self-image. I was truly a wallflower, and if I ever did date, it was with a palpable fear of being left. I'd hang on and throw hysterical fits if the end of the relationship was even hinted at.

"When I was eighteen, I was taking an acting class, and one of the assignments was that we were given two minutes of stage time and allowed one line of dialogue. I stood there and watched my invisible father cross the stage and stand at the door. My words were, 'Don't go.' I was so into it, I almost couldn't get out."

The anxiety over being trapped in her fears, of being "so into it [she] almost couldn't get out," eventually led Patty to a defensive course of action. By the time she was thirty-five, she had tried emotional commitment four times during her young life, and it never seemed to work: after her father, there had been two brief marriages—each with men she describes as "cold and elusive"—and a bitterly disappointing love affair. To ensure against subsequent ruptures, she would avoid involvement altogether.

"Following all three breakups, I got very ill. I lost a lot of weight, just couldn't eat, and I literally couldn't breathe. I guess it's pretty obvious; I just didn't want to breathe any more. I didn't want to live.

"Now, I just don't let anyone in. I'm dating eight men, because I have to keep lots of spares. Half of them are in their fifties; the other half are in their twenties. Older men and much younger ones give me the feeling that I'm in control. I was dating married men for a long time too, because then the end is built in and you don't have to worry about it.

"Of course, I still have this Prince Charming complex, that someone will love me enough to stay forever. I tell myself I'm waiting for that, and when I find *him*, I'll give up my wicked ways. I'll give in to love again.

"But first I want to be very, very strong. I want to be so firmly established in my career that my personal security is guaranteed. No one will be able to pull the rug out again. I'll never give that power to any man again. That's why I'm purposely choosing men who are unattractive to other people, so I don't have to think about all that now. I'm safe."

Perhaps what Patty is safe from is other men. Perhaps she will not allow anyone to love her until the man who always came back before does so again. Despite the marriages, she has reverted to her father's last name, "So I'll be easy to find"; and sometimes she imagines that he's watching out for her after all, "like in *Stella Dallas,* peeking through the window."

Recently, a cat she'd had for eleven years disappeared. "I went crazy, made posters, wrote to vets with lengthy descriptions and photographs. I really became obsessive about finding him. Someone suggested that maybe I was doing all this because I feel I didn't try hard enough to get my father back."

"It's not too late," I venture. "Why not reopen the search?"

"I don't know. I guess I don't want to find out that he's just not interested."

Soon after our interview, Patty reconsidered. She located and spoke to her father on the phone. Though "suspicious and reticent" throughout their conversation, he agreed to reciprocate if she wrote him a letter. "It's really weird," she said to me; "I have a father again."

Since their initial, and understandably awkward, telephone conversation, they have been enjoying an active correspondence and, as of this writing, they are even contemplating a meeting. Perhaps Patty will be reunited with the man that got away; perhaps she will even have the chance to hear her father say, "Look at that pretty woman!"

*

At the same time that the divorce rate is reaching staggering proportions, the importance of father's role in his children's development is being examined and emphasized. Given the ofttimes dramatic custody battles we hear about, a lot of men clearly want to play that active role, are even fighting for the chance. That wasn't the case a very few years ago. Usually divorce meant growing up without a male parent—yet knowing that he was alive and functioning, maybe even thriving.

When I told Patty that my father was dead, she blurted, "Oh, that's so much easier! If he had died, I wouldn't have felt so betrayed."

In the introduction to her book *Daughters of Divorce,* Deidre S. Laiken writes, "And although the death of a parent separates a child from her family in many ways, there is a time set aside for mourning—a ritual that makes the ensuing loss easier to accept. No traditional mourning period is afforded a child of divorce, and the inability that many of us have had in reconciling ourselves to a loss that may or may not be permanent makes coping that much more difficult and confusing."

It is unfortunately true that fewer than half the women in our divorce group were told immediately that their fathers were gone for good—as opposed to 77 percent whose fathers had died. But it is also true that the overwhelming majority of daughters of deceased fathers—75 percent—were never encouraged to mourn, were in fact, if implicitly, discouraged. Hence, neither circumstance is presented clearly and honestly to the child, nor is she in either case assisted in expressing her feelings.

One must therefore take issue with the assertion that this way or that is the more tolerable manner of losing one's father, that one loss is easier to integrate than the other. Neither is to be recommended, nor is either generally lightened by an appropriate response. What does distinguish the daughter of divorce from the girl whose father has died is the possibility that father will return. This possibility, given credence in reality by the occasional birthday card, the infrequent visit, stokes the girl's dearest fantasies and keeps her suspended in a lonely limbo.

Even in our pseudo-enlightened age, the young child will have trouble understanding the permanence of her loss without some very specific adult guidance. She is used to hearing her parents fight, perhaps even familiar with the idea that her father is sometimes gone. Especially if nothing is explained to her, which is unfortunately the rule, the legal finality of divorce is unclear to her and she is left to perceive this absence as just an unusually long one.

As we have seen, the resolution of grief requires the painstaking withdrawal of love from the lost person. Imagine expecting a child to detach from a parent who is very much alive! Even if life at home was torturous, the reconciliation wish implies restored harmony—Daddy will come home and he and Mommy will love each other again. Thus daughter will be exonerated from her loss and her guilt. It is no wonder that so much psychic energy goes into hoping for father's return (unless, like Megan, the girl eradicates the possibility through contriving his death, the very extremism of which underlines the difficulty of assimilating his continued vitality elsewhere).

The reconciliation wish is purposefully served by the otherwise harmful conviction of guilt. As illustrated in previous chapters, children, simultaneously self-centered and helpless in a world of whirling circumstances, often imagine themselves responsible for occurrences that are in fact beyond their control. By taking on responsibility for the divorce, so inherently undermining to self-worth, the child yet reasserts her shaky sense of power and sees precisely the way in which it can best be utilized: if she was powerful enough to cause the divorce, so too may she get her parents back together. Of course, rarely do things work out that way. But just as guilt reinforces the child's dubious sense of control, it ultimately exacts a very heavy price. If she feels responsible for his leaving, she must also accept that she wasn't good enough, wasn't worth his staying around for.

The relationship between loss of a loved one and self-esteem is rooted in our earliest days of life. We come into the world utterly dependent on another for our survival. That our needs be met is our foremost concern; who does the giving is comparatively irrelevant as long as we are satisfied. As the universe expands to include the providers of our needs, esteem for self is necessarily accompanied by esteem for others. The "I" that was the focus acknowledges its utter dependence on others, simultaneously recognizing the precariousness of existence without them. The child's confidence in her own worth therefore becomes inextricably bound to the constancy of her providers. If they disappear, she is worthless. The fear of abandonment, as part of the human condition, is a natural outcome, and from that comes the urgent need for restitution when abandonment does occur.

Where death is the cause of loss, the mourning process is meant to free the mourner from her attachment, so that she may love someone else—for always that love seeks an object—and thus achieve restitution. If, however, the object is known to be alive, separation sufficient to love another is continually frustrated, not only in fantasy but in reality. Father is there to be loved, and the force toward reconciliation is compelling; when he doesn't come back, when her attempts at restitution are frustrated, the girl's failure as daughter and female is complete. In desperation, she turns to her only remaining source of validation: mother—who is also unlovable.

A study of teenage girls by Dr. E. Mavis Hetherington revealed that daughters of divorced parents had lower self-esteem than those of intact or widowed families. By aligning with mother's anger, they may have blunted the reconciliation wish, but it was at the cost of their own self-image. Describing the self-defeating pattern, Deidre Laiken writes, "Being one with Mother means relinquishing our natural and necessary longings

for Father . . . [But] low self-esteem is a natural and very evident result of a merger with the . . . parent who was left . . ."

Identifying with the rejected female, as most daughters of
divorce do, has two other, far-reaching influences on the young
girl's developing attitudes. First, she may incorporate her mother's bitterness and distrust of men. And she is reluctant to succeed where her mother has failed. Having lost her father, she is
acutely dependent on her mother's continued affection, and to
surpass her in the romantic arena would be to risk separation
from her one remaining parent.

The girl who was abandoned by her father enters adulthood
in a pervasive state of doubt. Lacking the concrete finality of
death, she is left without a male parent or an appropriate response, straddling the fence between longing and rage. If she
allows herself to love another man—which is difficult, given her
learned hostility—she faces detachment from her first major
love interest, a terrifying prospect. Yet, until she can detach
from him, she is not free to love anyone else. She desperately
seeks safety, yet has had no firsthand evidence of its existence
and feels uncomfortable with it. She feels a strong need to
identify with her mother, yet to do so reinforces her own worthlessness and discourages her from trying to succeed where her
mother failed.

She longs for a man, distrusts all men; feels powerful enough
to have ended a marriage, utterly powerless to sustain a relationship. She strives to prove herself lovable, shies away from
intimacy. An internal battleground of contradictions, resem-
bling the external battleground that informed her childhood,
the girl whose father left home is sure of only one thing: the first
man she ever loved walked out on her.

*

It is understandably difficult for the abandoned daughter to
reconcile herself to the fact that there is no reconciliation.
Whether her father didn't even know of her existence, as in the
example of Lee, or didn't care enough about it to maintain a
relationship, as with Megan and Patty, it is unlikely that the
security she craves resides in him. Somehow she knows this,

even as she actively seeks him out or merely waits for his return. Yet, unable to let go of her attachment to him by committing herself to another man, she frequently directs her energies toward a more tolerable symbol of security: money. While loving someone else might mean accepting the permanence of father's absence, financial security is an impersonal yet significant enough area in which to take a stand; for there, without giving up father, she may pursue both the independence and the safety she is looking for.

Of the abandoned daughters in our study 42 percent (higher than any other group) listed financial security as the "major driving force" in their lives. This is the case not only because of their adult need for safety. In fact, it springs from one of the primary results of father loss in childhood: a drop in financial status. Except in those instances in which a family was independently wealthy, father deprivation usually meant financial deprivation. And where divorce was the cause of loss, the appearance or absence of monthly checks often translated into how much father really cared.

Indeed, one of the earliest impressions a child of divorce is left with is the all-encompassing power of money; often it was at the core of family arguments; it could placate rejection; open or close wounds; and reassure the abandoned child that, really, she was loved. "Money is not all it appears to be," writes Deidre S. Laiken. "It is much, much more."

While the feminist movement is often credited (or blamed) for having awakened women to their potential earning power, the group of women under discussion required no formalized movement to motivate them. (Most of the women in our study grew up before the '60s.) Very early in life, they became sensitive to the power of money and resentful of a rejecting father's key to that power. In an economic world traditionally dominated by men, these women predated the feminist movement in their resolve to achieve independent financial security. Otherwise characterized by contradiction and turmoil, they were singularly decisive in their determination never to find themselves, as their mothers had, unqualified to fill a well-paying job.

"I never wanted to get married young," said Lee, who at thirty-eight owns a thriving public relations business and is single. "All my life, while I was living with my mother, I had total responsibility for the house. I cleaned, did the ironing, the grocery shopping, the cooking, everything. By the time I was eighteen and had moved out, I honestly felt I had been a wife! I've worked hard to accomplish what I have, and the idea of getting married and becoming dependent on a man is absolutely terrifying."

Patty, after three disappointing relationships, bluntly asserts, "I won't even consider love until I'm financially secure."

Their sentiments reflect the adamant position taken repeatedly in interviews and questionnaires. Only 20 percent of the abandoned daughters in our study received continuing financial support from their fathers, and trying to win that support often entailed humiliating appearances in court or demeaning pleas made by mother. The impact of these scenes of neediness frequently built to a fierce drive to attain security independent of a relationship with a man. Usually this security was sought through money. Sometimes, as in the case of forty-nine-year-old Bernice, money itself became demeaning, and security was sought in places more exalted than the marketplace.

"When I was eighteen, I converted to the Roman Catholic Church," she wrote in an answer to the questionnaire. "I did this because I liked calling intelligent, kindly, nonthreatening men, 'Father.' I liked the Italian name for the Pope, 'Il Papa.' I liked the words of Jesus whenever he made reference to, 'Your Father in Heaven.' As a Catholic, I felt less fatherless."

Bernice never met her father, nor did she know anything about him. He left when she was an infant, and her mother refused to answer any of her questions about him. He was not to be spoken of or even acknowledged as part of his daughter's life. Only one "fact" was allowed: "My mother told me that he left because he was disappointed that I was a girl. He was intensely interested in genealogy, and had wanted a boy to carry on his name . . ."

Despite the elusiveness of the man, Bernice grew up hoping that someday her father would make himself known to her. When she was thirty-one, she learned of his recent death, and only then did she begin to accept the finality of his absence. "But I'm still reacting to it—I've cried several times filling out this questionnaire.—The worst part is that I could have met him because after he died I found out that he lived within driving distance of my home."

Bernice has compensated for her loss by keeping her father alive within herself. In addition to her conversion to Catholicism, with its emphasis on "the Father," she frequently identified her interests—such as reading and photography—as being "like my father." Thus, as is often the case, she lessens the pain of her loss by incorporating some of her father's characteristics into her own identity. Given the sparsity of her information, it is not surprising that she has found in the New Testament yet another link with her male parent. "When Christ comes to this world for the second time, we will all be given new names. Girls will no longer fail their fathers' lineage label."

Rejecting ambitious career goals, perhaps because that's what her mother had in mind for her, Bernice has sought security through religious beliefs. Yet despite her emphasis on spiritual teachings, her tone became decidedly down-to-earth when asked, "What is your worst fear about your mate?"

"I am sometimes afraid," she wrote, "that my husband won't realize how important a father is to a girl. He should be the one man in the world that she can respect, admire, and believe in.

"There should be a hero's medal for good fathers. They should be honored by our government as much as soldiers. Nurturing a child is at least as much of a patriotic act as killing an enemy."

When a girl's father leaves home, at whatever time in her life and for whatever reasons, he sends the message, loud and clear, that she is not worth staying for. Particularly if he makes no attempt to continue their relationship, his daughter must embark on the complex journey to womanhood accompanied by the taunting shadows of rejection and guilt.

The man and woman who are her parents once loved each other and no longer do. Instead, they have fought, hurt each other, played out vicious scenes of bitterness. The question of blame, even as it echoes through the household, is a moot point —the verdict, as surely as the divorce papers, condemns *her*. She was bad, not pretty enough, demanded too much, destroyed by mere virtue of her existence. What more airtight evidence than the door her father slammed behind him?

To atone for her guilt, she entertains thoughts of reconciliation. It is unthinkable that her powers to destroy can't be put to more constructive use. Her appeals ignored, restitution denied, she aligns herself with mother. Their pact provides her single source of validation, even as it lends credence to her diminished self-esteem. By siding with mother, she is protected from the reconciliation wish and confirmed in her anger toward men, and herself.

The hostility seething in abandoned daughters is only barely muted. Ignited by the rejection of childhood, propelled by the very private but forceful hope of reconciliation, the anger frequently surfaces as determination. She *will* succeed; she *will* be safe; she will not need. If the girl whose father died harbors constant sorrow, the girl whose father left is anchored by her pain.

Whether fostered by the absolute finality of death or the false hope following divorce, the womanhood of fatherless daughters was given shape by the loss of love. Perhaps it was possible he'd come back; perhaps there was no possibility at all: Father was gone, the initial impact of loss was felt, and the continuing business of growing up without him beckoned.

PART THREE

LIFE WITHOUT
FATHER

SEVEN

MY MOTHER—THE WIDOW, THE DIVORCÉE—MYSELF

Mother as Head of the Household

The term for it now is "latchkey kids." We would come home from school, my sister and I, watch TV for a while, maybe do some homework, and then prepare dinner. Mom would be home around six-thirty, drained from a full day of typing and dictation, irritable with the press of subway rush-hour crowds. She would be hungry and want her dinner ready.

We feared her a little as we heard her key in the door, and hoped that her mood would not be too harsh. Sometimes, like a gift, she would be full of smiles and softness, but usually there was an edge to her arrival, vaguely accusatory—weren't we the reason that she had to go out and work, fight for a seat, push her way through the masses home?—so on those evenings when the lamb chops were cooked to perfection, still warm yet unburnt even as she entered the kitchen, it was with a special sense of well-being that we went to greet her with the ritualistic kiss.

We were keenly aware, my sister and I, of the "hard life" that was my mother's lot, and aware too of our role in it. So while other kids had mommies with scallop-hemmed aprons waiting with milk and cookies after school, it would be ungrateful for us to even wish for such a scene. Our mother worked hard to support us, and the truth of the matter is, I never could picture her in any kind of apron.

From the time I was twelve, when Mazie left and my grand-mother came over only once or twice weekly, it fell to me, the older daughter, to be in charge of the household chores. As I mentioned earlier, being on my own was to have some advantages in the "hanging out" department, but the overall picture of my late childhood and teenage years is one of responsibility—both in the sense of culpability and in the sense of duty. Certainly the former was never articulated as such; it was never said, that I can recall, "If it weren't for you kids, your mother's life would be easier." No, it was more subtle, discerned in the passing remarks "Be patient with her, she has to be mother and father to you" and "You know how it is; the minute a man hears that you've got two children, he loses interest."

We didn't have to be hit over the head to get the picture: we were the cause of the five-day workweek, the ones who had to be fed and clothed, the ones whose existence disenchanted potential husbands. No wonder she was nervous and excitable, and wasn't it our duty to endure her bursts of anger, anticipate and fulfill demands, try, try, try to please her?

"One of my earliest memories," writes a woman whose father was killed in action when she was three months old, "is lying in a crib and hearing Mama crying in the dark bedroom. Then, as her mourning began to pass, she became driven. I was her beloved's child, so I had to be perfect in every possible respect —pretty, clean, perfectly obedient and intelligent. I spent the first eighteen years of my life feeling like a souvenir and nothing more. If I failed at anything, she would use phrases like, 'What would your poor father think?' I felt constantly measured against an impossible standard because I was a child expected to live up to her memory of a grown man."

We were children of whom a lot was expected. Losing our fathers to death or divorce, many of us lost our mothers to grief, work, disappointment, frustration, and bitterness. And one day, while innocently immersed in the business of growing up, we lost our childhoods as well.

Yet, *what was it like for our mothers?* Or for the more than five million women in the United States today raising children without male support? Even as I return to the anxiety that permeated my youth, the anger and the desperate eagerness to please, I acknowledge, at last, *her* struggle, *her* constant sorrow. And I realize that we cannot attempt to understand the nature of the fatherless childhood from the daughter's perspective before first considering the perspective of its other major player: the woman on whom it fell to be in charge.

My mother was a child during the roaring twenties, a teenager during the Depression, and a young woman during World War II. She helped out at her immigrant parents' New York candy store, was admired as the beauty of the family, did well in school, and had a crush on Ronald Colman. College, though feasible for a girl of her intelligence, was quickly dismissed for lack of funds. And it wasn't that important anyway, for a girl with her looks would have no trouble finding a "professional" man who would rightfully provide her with all that she could wish: a home, a family, a social life. Her children, of course, would go to college, and she would live happily ever after in suburbia.

Being of a somewhat more impetuous nature than was expected of a young, Jewish, working-class girl, however, Selma continually disappointed her parents by spurning suitors left and right. This optometrist was too short, that lawyer crude of speech—no one was good enough for her. She knew what she wanted in a man, and would settle for nothing less. Bridesmaid at her younger sister's wedding, and then her younger brother's, guest at the nuptials of numerous cousins, she remained, remarkably, single.

As she approached the landmark age of thirty, with no prospects, she stood firm in her obstinacy and faith that her "very particular" expectations would be met. But then the war came, and with it the undeniable thinning out of the ranks at home. So when a Polish owner of a fruit and vegetable market, several years her senior, courted her with resolve at least as determined as her own, she was won. He wasn't Ronald Colman, nor a doctor or even an American, but he was strong, confident, surprising in the ways that he delighted her. To the joy—and relief —of everyone, Selma was married.

Four years and two daughters later, her husband was dead. A massive coronary left Selma with a toddler of fifteen months and a three-year-old.

I have heard the story many times, know the names and shortcomings of every suitor and the qualities that endeared my father, an unlikely candidate, to my mother's heart. But it is only recently that I have begun to appreciate the fear that must have accompanied her loss. Now that I am thirty-five and mother of a small child, I understand that thirty-five is far younger than I had perceived it to be, and she was even more unprepared for single motherhood than we who today see it headlined in every other periodical. Women did not expect to have to support a family in 1950; they weren't trained for it, and they didn't want it. What they did expect was to be married and provided for. "I was determined not to get involved with a soldier," says my mother, "because I didn't want to be a widow."

There is little question that my mother's bitterness has long been fed by irony. But there were many questions that I did wish to put to her, questions that could no longer be avoided in light of the inquiry at hand: what was it like for her?

For most of my life, I hadn't wanted to know about her suffering, or whether she might have borne the death more easily had it not been for the burden of two small children. I'd always suspected that, had it not been for us, she might have gotten over the grief and then gone on to a whole new husband, family, life—free of the two dependent little beings intensifying and reminding her of her loss. I had never asked her to confirm these suspicions, however, or allowed myself to dwell on them with any regularity—until the matter of her perspective revealed itself as a key to my own.

Settling opposite her at a small table laden with coffee and cigarettes, as I have so many times before, I valiantly begin: "How old were you when my father died?" The question erupts tentative, shaky. (Why can't I call him "Daddy"? Why does the word get stuck in my throat?)

"Let's see." She puffs on a cigarette. "It was November 1950 . . . two days after my thirty-fifth birthday. We had gone to the movies to celebrate that weekend. We went to see *Sunset Bou-levard,* and I remember I cried like a baby."

As she backtracks to recount the events leading up to his death, I discover that my father had been aware of his fragile condition during most of their marriage, in fact had suffered his first heart attack just a week after I was born. (My mother tries not to draw too strong a connection between the illness and his disappointment at not having a son, but she does mention it.) Against doctor's warnings, however, he continued to work long hours in the fruit stores (he had acquired a second store during their marriage), lifting crates, overseeing every aspect of his growing business. On Sundays, the one day he allowed for rec-reation, he would take me to the park. He was, I am assured, very devoted to me. And, a comparatively young man—my mother isn't sure of his exact age!—he was unconcerned with the repeated medical advice to take it easy.

Yet "He went to temple for the Jewish holidays like always that year, but he didn't come home from Yom Kippur services until very late, which was unusual. It had been fifteen hours since he had eaten. So I asked him why he stayed so late, and he said, 'Well, God puts in his book who should live for another year, so I decided to stay for the entire service.'"

My father was living with a subtle anticipation of his immi-nent death. He knew, despite his defiance of doctor's orders, the gravity of his condition. But lifted the crates anyway. Ate the pastrami sandwich anyway.

"I yelled at him something awful when I saw him eating that sandwich," my mother recalls. "And then he didn't feel up to going out with me that night, so I went to the party we were invited to with my sister, and Daddy went over to spend the evening with Norman [my uncle].

"We didn't even have our coats off when I got paged to the phone. It was Norman saying that I should come home immedi-ately, that Hy doesn't feel well, his stomach hurts. I couldn't believe he was telling me to come home just because of a stom-ach ache, but he was adamant. Of course, I left the party and headed to the house, but I had no understanding of how serious it was.

"When I got there, the doctor was with him and he was laying

down, obviously in a lot of pain. (Why they didn't get him to a
hospital immediately, I'll never know.) Anyway, I still had no
idea, it didn't even dawn on me, that he was dying. I was
holding his hand, telling him everything would be all right . . .
By the time the oxygen came, he was gone."

I had never known that she held his hand as he died. The hazy
images that have always been an implicit part of my mother's
hardship are coming into sharper focus. And I am struck by the
fact that, of course, like so many other young women confronted with widowhood, *she had no idea that this could happen.* "I was in a more or less hysterical state for the rest of the
night. Then, for a period of three or four months, I guess I was
pretty numbed up.

"My mother stayed with me during the *shiva* week, and, of
course, everyone was very sympathetic. My main concern was
to move out of the apartment and closer to my sister so that
you'd be near family and I could go to one of the stores, which I
was determined, despite a lot of legal advice, to maintain. I
knew absolutely nothing about how to run a store; the only
work I had ever done was secretarial. But I thought I knew what
I was doing. I had helped out at my parents' store.

"I can't say that there was any real financial panic—your
father had left two insurance policies and the two stores—but I
became aware that there were debts I hadn't known about. I
did sell one store, but insisted on keeping the other one. Like I
said, there wasn't any panic, but there wasn't any doubt either
that I had to work to support us, and managing your father's
business was what I wanted to do. So about a month after he
died, we moved and I started working at the store."

I am surprised at her pragmatism, with the apparent swift-
ness of her attention to practical matters. The devastation of her
loss seems to have been less paralyzing than I had suspected.

"I started getting chest pains," she continues, "and was told to
stay in bed. The doctor thought it was my heart. But that soon
passed, and I just went about my business, going to the store and
taking care of the children. Friends we used to socialize with
dwindled away, and I just became very wrapped up in the
children and thought nothing about my personal life. My children became my life. My children and making money. My

children were my whole life, but I don't have to tell you that."
No.

I ask the obvious next question: "Did you resent us?" Without
missing a beat, she answers in the negative. "Do you feel you
sacrificed a lot for us?" Again, without hesitation, "Yes."

She tells me of the various men who would have married her
"immediately" if not for the children. And of the several sug-
gestions that she give up the children so that she could have a
social life. The very idea is clearly unthinkable, yet I can't help
feeling that she wants me to appreciate the fact that she kept us.
No, she didn't resent us, but yes, of course, there were sacrifices.

"After a while, it became apparent that the boys in the store
were robbing me blind, falsifying receipts, lying about deliv-
eries. The store was open twenty-four hours a day and, of
course, I couldn't be there all the time. So, finally, I had to sell,
and find work as a secretary. Between my salary and government aid to widows with dependent children, we did all right. I
wanted you and Caren to have the best: piano lessons, dancing
lessons. I couldn't afford Hebrew school, but I worked out an
agreement with the temple of paying for your lessons by giving
my time as dramatics director."

Since I've been old enough to understand, I've respected this
particularly creative approach my mother took so that we could
go to Hebrew school. I look back on those weekend rehearsals—
the kids gathered around my mother, the director—with fondness and no small degree of delight that I always somehow
managed to be cast in a leading role in the Purim and Chanukah
plays.

Indeed, she did consistently and determinedly pursue the
best for us. While other working-class kids of single mothers
might have been sent to Y camps, we went to private sleep-
away camp; instead of tuition-free city colleges, we attended
expensive universities. Admittedly, we wanted those things,
and by putting herself into debt, she gave them to us.

As the interview progresses, I repeatedly try to turn the conversation to *her* perspective, *her* feelings, *her* experience. Not
the mother, but the woman. Yet, inevitably, her recollections
center on us: our lessons, our schooling, our needs. Indeed, we
were her perspective and the core of her experience. I have

been looking for the woman, but the woman is the mother. She cannot bring herself to acknowledge resentment, for that word, that emotion, is discordant with her very understanding of what motherhood is. She can talk about sacrifice, because that is something that mothers do.

"Of course I would have had an easier time getting married without the children. You'd have to be an awful dope not to realize that. I might have married very well . . . Not that I ever resented it."

"How about immediately after he died?" I take another tack, this one pricking a mite much. "Were you glad you had the children? Did they give you a reason to wake up in the morning, something to live for?" Elise, the young widow whom we met earlier, had said so, as have several professionals who have studied widowhood.

"Well, yes, I suppose so," my mother hesitantly replies, as though she had never before looked at it that way. "I was glad I had something to live for. But it's been very lonely, being father and mother to you. Put that in the book, that the hardest part of being a single mother is not having a companion."

I have been frustrated by my mother's confusion over details, and her inability to describe the personal side of her tragedy. But I recognize too that the man about whom I want to know so much is a man she knew for barely five years, a man she has not known for thirty-two years. The death, the mourning, the agony, the immediate rush of sensation in the face of life without him—all these are for her a part of the very distant past. What is real for her is the struggle, the lessons, the loneliness.

For Elise, a woman whose husband had died only months before our meeting, the transition between shock and acceptance has just recently taken hold. The reality of widowhood and single motherhood is, for her, still new. During one of our conversations (segments of which are included in Chapter Three), she talked about what it was like for her to adapt to widowhood.

"Dinnertime was the hardest thing at first. That was the time when we always used to be together. We'd listen for his car—he drove a Porsche, so it was a very specific sound—and Diana [her

two-year-old] would get all excited that Daddy was :.
he died, she'd hear other sports cars, and we'd both, almo..
reflex, expect him to walk in the door.

"Eating alone with the children was very painful. So I began
to avoid it. Very early. I also was not willing to cook. Anytime I
was asked out, I would go. I don't think I ever refused an
invitation. It's only recently that I'm beginning to cook meals
again and sit down to dinner with the girls.

"Weekends have been tough too. Remember, Cecile's first
question when I told her that Dave had died was about who
would take her out on Saturdays. I've been trying to plan activities with my parents or friends, because it was really wrenching
at first.

"Still, certain things touch it off. Something will happen and
I'll think, 'I can't wait to tell Dave . . .' When I was feeling my
saddest, I would feel him holding me and patting me on the
back with his big hand. I could feel it so distinctly. He was such a
big man. No one could hug like Dave.

"Of course, intellectually, I know he'll never be back. In a
way, I want to continue to miss him. Not so much that it keeps
me from living, though.

"I think having the children has helped me. At first there
were times when I wished I could just stay in bed. But because
of the children, I didn't have that luxury. I had to get out of bed
and live. I had to help them, and that helped me."

> Thou art a widow; yet thou art a
>   mother,
> And hast the comfort of thy children
>   left thee.

*

When I was growing up, there was something freakish about
the all-female household I called home. Everyone else had a
father who worked and a mother at home. One could perhaps
find solace in the merry escapades of Alcott's father-absent *Little Women,* but even they could gather mistily at mother's knee
to listen to father's letters home. Escape entertainment offered
little escape, for there was no Daddy to make room for, and
there were no letters home. Permeating every aspect of life was

the inescapable fact of being different, incomplete. As a family, we were castrated.

Recalls my sister, Caren, "Without a man, we never felt like a real, self-sufficient family. In fact, there was something odd about us, a family of women. I remember how I always wished I had a brother. Just having a male in the family would change everything. We wouldn't have seemed so separate from the rest of the world." Indeed, as revealed in our study, fatherless girls who had brothers were more likely than girls from households with no male at all to feel that they came from a "real family."

"There was a girl in our neighborhood," Caren continues, "whose mother was dead. I sometimes envied her because at least she had a father and that was more socially acceptable somehow."

Feelings of difference and inadequacy are a common childhood recollection among women who grew up without fathers. To a large extent this comes from the fact that men, in our society, are more valued than women. A household without a male at its head is looked upon as an aberration. Even in the eighties, when nearly 17 percent of all American families are headed by women, this very statistic is cited as evidence of the breakdown of the family. It is therefore enlightening, to those of us who grew up under the stigma of fatherlessness, to learn that father's participation as a member of the family is a relatively recent phenomenon in historical time.

"The fact is that the earliest human family consisted of a woman and her children," writes Elizabeth Gould Davis in *The First Sex*. "Fatherhood and the idea of permanent mating were very late comers in human history . . . [T]he word for father does not even exist in the original Indo-European language . . ." In fact, there is a great body of research to support the idea that even the father's physiological role in conception was for a long time misunderstood. Females were regarded as not only the caretakers, but the sole creators of offspring—a belief that persists in several primitive cultures to this day.*

---

* As an extension of what she perceives to be this basic human heritage, Davis includes American blacks among those in whom ". . . full responsibility for the children [falls] to the mother." Indeed, in 1980, 42 percent of black families were headed by women.

Though the precise details of the man's entry into the family unit vary according to author and philosophy, it is generally agreed that his earliest role was that of provider and protector. As such, he went from nonparticipation to leadership in comparatively little time. And with the exclusion of women from the workplace, he became the very backbone of the family, the difference between economic well-being and impoverishment. But what of his role in nurturing the children? Elizabeth Gould Davis takes a most extreme position when she writes:

> . . . [T]he only thing wrong with fatherless families . . . is not that they are fatherless, but that the mothers do not have the support and approval of society. In a normal, well-regulated, woman-centered society, this would not be the case. *The father is not at all necessary to a child's happiness and development†* . . . But in our patriarchal society a manless woman is an object of scorn and her children are either pitied or frowned upon. Thus it is our patriarchal mores alone that demand a father in the home—not nature or the well-being of the child.

For Davis, father as head of the household is a "perversion of the natural order of things," his participation in the upbringing of his children "unnecessary."

Collective modern thought is to the contrary. And most feminists would encourage, rather than discourage, father's participation, for, as evidenced throughout this volume, he does play a vital role in the psychological development of his children. He is necessary to a child's well-rounded view of herself and her world. Moreover, there are indications that men's initial interest in joining the family sprang from an innate desire ". . . to join in the tender and loving relations they observed between women and their children." Their desire to become part of the family came from a need to nurture.

Whether or not fathers are a natural part of the human family becomes, in the present day, a moot point. That they are necessary, that it felt positively unnatural not to have one, is a sure thing.

†Emphasis added.

Central to our acceptance of our fatherless state was the attitude and fortitude of mother. She, and her manner of adjustment to her fate, determined ours. "Whether paternal loss occurs by death or by divorce or whether there is no known father . . . the mother's relationship to the child is usually the decisive factor in the degree of normality or pathology of the child's future development." Echoing this professional observation, the women I spoke to repeatedly confessed uncertainty when describing feelings of childhood deprivation: Was it father's absence or mother's response to it that shaped their early impressions of incompleteness? Obviously, it is impossible to separate the two.

What are the elements of success in a father-absent home? Studies indicate that an active mother, an energetic woman who imparts strength, stability, and continuity, is more likely to provide her children with a sense of well-being than is a more passively accepting woman. Maintaining a financially and emotionally secure home life is of the essence.

Mother Hubbard, you see, was old: there being no mention of others, we may presume she was alone; a widow—a friendless, old, solitary widow. Yet did she despair? Did she sit down and weep, or read a novel, or wring her hands? No! She went to the cupboard.

Most of our mothers, neither old nor solitary, were hard-pressed to go directly to the cupboard. My own mother's swift attention to practical matters notwithstanding, there is first the period of grief, or anger, redefinition as a single mother. There are those three or four months of being "numbed up," as my mother described it. And even then there are the children.

The newly husband-deprived mother has lost a lover, an ally, a friend. Even where divorce is the cause of absence, she more often than not must confront isolation and change in social status. The friendships she enjoyed as part of a couple alter and often evaporate. She is a single, available woman now, not always welcome at intimate dinner parties. Losing her husband, she has also lost her previous standing in the social world. Unless and until she creates a new role for herself in the social scene, she will probably feel terribly alone. And even then there are the children.

Thus, in the midst of her consuming adjustment to her loss, whether mourning her husband or hating him, the new single mother must deal with the dual issue of support: She, unsupported by her husband and, frequently, friends, must find a way of supporting her family. Just when her self-esteem has been lowered, the demands on her have been raised. Probably in need of parenting herself, she must instead take on the role of mother and father.

While 80 percent of the mothers in our fatherless group worked after the death or divorce, only 37 percent of the mothers from the intact families worked. Thus, according to traditional roles, mothers did take on the responsibilities of both parents. And by going out to work, by becoming the "breadwinners," they necessarily had to forfeit some of the more commonly accepted facets of motherhood. Objective standards might deem our households "successful;" yet the price of that success was mother's reassuring presence.

Our mothers weren't there with milk and cookies after school, or medicating measles with chicken soup. They didn't have as much time as other mothers did to soothe us, comfort us, play, and help us with our homework. Someone else—a grandmother or a housekeeper—usually did that. And when our mothers got home from work, they were hungry and tired.

Several professional case studies suggest that mother is more lenient when father is away. But if his absence is permanent, if mother sees her children only after a hard day at the office, the leniency is likely born of fatigue, and the need is for a friend, rather than a child. Mother isn't being lenient, she is responding to her children as though they were adults. For us, her daughters, that is a far more exacting demand. ". . . [T]he mother trying to be father had trouble being mother," Bernard Malamud writes.

As reflected in our study, fatherless daughters spent less time alone with their mothers than did other girls. They received much less affection, while at the same time felt that "too much" was expected of them. They grew up feeling that, because their mothers worked so hard, they didn't have enough time for them. Given their mothers' previous unavailability, it is not surprising that, as adults, fatherless daughters are far less likely than other women to feel that they enjoy a good relationship with their female parent.

But what is the immediate effect of a mother's new status as a single woman? How is our development influenced by, and how do we accommodate ourselves to, this new person in the family: mother, head of the household?

On the one hand, we cling to her, literally, for our lives. Yet, in a psychoanalytic study of girls who lost their fathers, it was observed that "The counterpart of father-idealization was depreciation of the remaining parent . . . Devaluation of the mother following the death or departure of the father was present, to varying degrees, in all [cases]." Thus, we desperately need someone toward whom we feel "varying degrees" of hostility.

We are angry with mother for a number of reasons. The feeling of helplessness that accompanies grief, so intolerable for a child, is assuaged to some extent by anger. We can't be angry at father, for he is gone and it is our tendency to idealize him. Mother, therefore, becomes the obvious target, the culprit in this painful turn of events. She is at least as guilty as we are. Perhaps even more unforgivable, and igniting our anger further, is the fact that mother has proved herself to be powerless. She could neither prevent father's departure, nor soothe our pain or her own. She is at least as powerless as we are.

For our very survival, however, we must mute the anger. Mother is all we have left. To combat our fears and hostilities, we create an intense partnership with her. We will be good, we will be helpful, we will do anything to silence this anger that may provoke *her* to leave us too.

Variously dubbed "pseudo-independence" and "pseudo-maturity," growing up before one's time seems to go with the territory of fatherlessness. ". . . [I]t seems that the loss of a spouse . . . rouses the need to regress," writes Lily Pincus, "while the loss of a parent rouses the need to progress, to mature, to be potent." Particularly if she is an only child or the eldest sibling, the daughter of a single mother appoints herself, as Madeleine put it, "the little man of the house." If she is a good and helpful girl, her one remaining parent won't leave her.

Then, with the passage of time and mother's growing dissatisfaction, daughter's little-grown-up behavior comes to reflect a deeper determination: not to be like mother.

Mother is someone who was left. She is someone who is vulnerable and unhappy a lot of the time. In all likelihood, she is a woman whose self-esteem has diminished as a result of her loss. Daughter does not want to be like that. Yet, as a daughter, she naturally looks to her mother as a role model. Thus, the person with whom she most closely identifies, a widow or a divorcée, is someone who has been stricken by grief or by failure. Resolved not to meet the same fate, the fatherless girl learns to value control over emotionalism, bravery over vulnerability.

The early adoption of adult behavior thus serves two very definite functions for her. By being good and helpful, she ensures mother's continued acceptance and presence. And by being strong, she tries to resist identification with someone whose low self-esteem is threatening to her own.

Despite the obvious drawbacks of this artificial maturity, countless students of female psychology, from Alfred Adler to Gail Sheehy, have observed benefits to be gleaned from early appropriation of adult behavior—among them, the early development of competency and leadership. And seeing mother in the role of breadwinner reinforces the girl's sense that women can succeed in the outside world. Perhaps, as one author suggests, ". . . divorce or death could give a daughter the chance to grow up."

There does seem to be a strong correlation between father absence and achievement orientation.‡ But the cost of all the repression and posturing is high: the child's vulnerability and a lingering resentment toward a mother whose neediness forced her to deny that vulnerability.

Daughter is, of course, painfully vulnerable. She has no father, owing to all kinds of faults of which she imagines herself possessed. And by virtue of her very existence, she has intensified mother's hardship, both financial and social. She is, most

‡ This correlation will be fully explored in Chapter Thirteen.

agonizing of all to a child, different from the other kids. Of course, it is her primary desire to grow up, and fast; where is self-esteem to be garnered in childhood?

Owing to mother's expectations and daughter's urgent willingness to fulfill them, the single-mother / daughter relationship is hardly that of parent and child. Each, for her respective reasons, requires that daughter assume the behavior of an adult. Obviously, this defiance of nature will have a singular impact on the nature of their relationship.

About this relationship, much has recently been written.* If we are to believe what we read, daughters grow up loathing their mothers. Whether weak and ineffectual, or demanding and shrill, they impart a perception of womanhood fiercely to be shunned. We turn away from them so that, through some miracle, we can disassociate ourselves from their implicit definition of femaleness.

Our disrespect for our mothers comes primarily, we are told, from the role that has been delegated to them by our fathers. Father is the creator; mother, the vehicle. He is the boss; she, the selfless instrument of his will. Strive as we do to disavow her as role model, we are, after all, like her: female. From Freud to Friday, the message is clear: our mothers, subservient, become ourselves. For that, we hate them, ourselves. And thus is female self-loathing perpetuated and inevitable.

When mother is head of the household, however, she is neither passive nor ineffectual. She may not butter our bread, but it is through her efforts that it is on the table. A participant in the work force, she is a viable member of society, a shining example of what a woman can be. Yet, do we, her daughters, derive strength from her example? Only indirectly. Is our image of women exalted? No. For while we are exposed to the possibility of female potential, what we are most acutely aware of is that this newfound independence is not her choice. She'd rather be married. And as revealed in our study, the image of her defeat carries over: the fatherless daughters we questioned

---

* The most popular book on the subject, *My Mother, Myself,* was written by Nancy Friday, herself a fatherless daughter!

had decidedly lower expectations of women than did the
daughters in intact homes.

"My mother just crumbled," was the repeated lament of
many women I interviewed. "Without a man, we never felt like
a real family," my sister, Caren, said. While father, out of reach,
remained untarnished, mother's daily struggle conveyed a lasting impression about the comparative inadequacy of all females, an impression clearly illustrated in the following table:

	FATHERLESS GROUP	CONTROL GROUP
Mother worked so hard, she didn't have time for me	32%	6%
She gave me a lot of affection	41%	67%
Close friendships with women are really important to me	69%	90%
I have very high expectations of women	39%	53%
I have very high expectations of men	53%	53%

In an effort to compensate for our mothers' unavailability and
neediness, many of us aspired to become "the little man of the
house." By assuming the characteristics of adults, we convinced
ourselves that we were in charge and, perhaps most important,
warded off any possible similarities between ourselves and our
mothers: we were not weak, not needy, not to be thwarted by
typical female shortcomings.

It was only when we finally reached biological adulthood that
we began to understand how disfiguring was our masquerade.
The repressed child who had no part in the single-mother /
daughter relationship groped awkwardly for recognition, even
as she continued to fear the cost of exposure. The confused

female groped awkwardly too, seeking, yet dubious of, her identity as a woman.

*

At the same time that the fatherless daughter fulfills her role as mother's primary source of companionship, she is polishing the veneer that protects her from intimacy. Both to ensure mother's continued presence and to keep herself from identifying with mother's vulnerability, she creates a persona of independence on which rests no less than her self-esteem. As we saw in Chapter Six, the result of identifying with mother is a reduction in self-esteem. Hence, the daughter of divorce comes to deny vulnerability with particular urgency, observable in her later determination to succeed.

Yet neediness tugs at the fatherless daughter like a disconsolate child. As strikingly revealed in our study, she feels less "dependent" than the woman who grew up with a father, but she is also less likely to describe herself as "independent." Though daughters of divorce were a bit more likely than daughters of widows to describe themselves as "confident," women who grew up *with* fathers were more likely than either fatherless group to attribute that quality to themselves.

The dependence-independence conflict that has come to afflict so many modern women is particularly acute in those who grew up without fathers. For they have been engaged in this internal battle since childhood, and have firsthand experience of reluctant independence—in the persons of their mothers.

Reflecting on what it was like to grow up in a household headed by mother, the women I spoke to repeatedly referred to the issues of difference and pseudo-independence. Barely audible in the remarks below can be discerned the muffled voice of the unyielding child.

Hillary, the woman who remembers being in the crib and hearing her mother cry, was three months old when her father died. Now thirty-eight, she was a heavy drug user until "Six years of therapy saved my life." She grew up under the shroud of a hero whom she'd never met but was expected to live up to.

"Mine was a very large, close-knit family of recent immigrants to this country. My mother and father were the first generation of children born here. Father was very popular with my mother's people as well as his own, and his death left all of them wounded for years.

"He was part of the Allied landing in Normandy. As far as I've been able to discover, his tank was hit directly by a shell during the Battle of the Bulge.

"Both my grandfathers doted on me and I honestly wasn't aware of being deprived of something until I was about three. Occasionally, when I was very small, a relative would say something about 'your father,' but the idea meant very little to me.

"Once I started to play with children outside the family, everything changed. They'd always ask that basic kids' question, 'What does your father do?' When I'd say that he was killed in the war, I remember very well how different they'd make me feel. They'd tease me with that unconscious cruelty of children. 'You don't *have* a father? Well, look at you—how weird.'

"Just at that same time, when I was three or four, my mother finally managed to get my father's body shipped home from his military grave overseas. I still remember being dressed in a special new dress and black patent-leather shoes, and being taken to the train station to meet the coffin: a long black box, an American flag, trains whistling, the indifferent men unloading the 'remains,' as they called them, and my mother and grandmothers weeping as though they were terrified.

"My grandfather picked me up and said, 'That's your father's body.' My father—in a box.

"From then on, I had nightmares two or three times a week, mostly of being shut into boxes where I couldn't breathe, or of seeing this man I didn't know climb out of the box and try to catch me. When I tried to tell my mother of these dreams, she would grow angry and say that my father would never have hurt me.

"Maybe my father's death would have had a less significant impact if my mother had been a different kind of person. Various relatives have told me that even as a young girl, she was oddly brittle and liked things just so and very well structured. One reason she loved my father so much was that he took charge of her entire life for her. For the two years of their marriage, before he went to the front, her entire life revolved around him. When he was killed, she was shattered.

"For a good ten years, she was very bitter about losing him. Emotionally she was lost, and she hated having to go out to work. I remember her and my grandmother getting together for years and bemoaning the fact that my father had been killed so young. They would talk in an almost vicious tone of voice. They were very angry that he was gone, but they would never call it anger. When pressed, they would come out with patriotic formulas about a man's duty to his country and tell me that they were sure God had given him a special place in heaven.

"Whenever I asked anything about my father, all I'd hear was that he was the most wonderful man in the world, and I'd always wonder: if he was so wonderful, why did the Germans kill him?

"My mother was driven where I was concerned. I had to be perfect in every way. I also felt that she wished I'd been a boy so that I'd be more like my father. To her, 'You're just like your father when you do that' was the highest praise. Even to this day, she still talks about him as if he'd just gone off for a weekend and was coming right back.

"As a result of all her pressure, I grew up with a pretty standard case of lack of self-worth, or of self, period. Trying to live up to a grown man was unbearably difficult, so I began to have fantasies that maybe there'd been a mistake. I fantasized that my father was still alive, that some mysterious 'they' had put the wrong man in that long box. Especially when I started school and the other kids would tease me about not having a father, the fantasy became very important. It wasn't until I was ten that I let go of the hope that he'd return.

"I had a white toy horse, about a foot high, that had been my favorite toy since I was five. It was rather ratty, and my mother was always trying to throw it away. I decided that, rather than let her get rid of the horse, I'd bury it properly. I dug a hole in the backyard and put the horse inside a shoe-box coffin with an American flag over it and one of Dad's bits of insignia inside it. From that day on, I knew that he was really dead and wasn't coming home. I guess that's when the nightmares stopped.

"What replaced my longing for his return was a passion for

military history. I studied every book in the library on old battles—carefully avoiding World War II. I think this unusual interest made me seem like something of a rebel. In my small-town
high school, girls didn't like such things.

"In college, I wrote numbers of papers on obscure aspects of
military history, although my professors tried to discourage me
from going into the field professionally (at which they were
successful; I dropped out of Stanford to marry).

"When the antiwar movement flared up, I was right in the
thick of it. All my memories of missing my father came back,
and I was determined to do something to prevent other women
from grieving the way my mother had. Everytime I marched, I
was marching for Dad, quite consciously. Yet it wasn't until I
was undergoing psychotherapy, in my mid-twenties, that I finally wept for him, this dead hero I'd never even known."

Hillary spent much of her childhood trying to resurrect a
dead man. At the same time that her mother was demanding
perfection, her peers were reminding her of her imperfection;
and trying to get her father back, or at least be just like him,
seemed her only avenue of recourse. From mother and schoolmates the message was really the same: you're not good enough.

After years of nearly suicidal depression, she has emerged
from the war. Yet the subject remains a preoccupation. Married
for the second time, and tired of being "just a housewife," she
has begun work on a novel "addressed to problems like why
men kill and women mourn. I am trying to get some gold out of
a large heap of dross."

Across the Atlantic, in Germany, at just about the time that
Hillary was going to school, another fatherless girl was being
chided for her difference. Olga, also an only child, lost her
father to divorce. After an initial period of weekly visits, she
rarely saw him.

"At that time, parents being divorced still had a black
mark. It wasn't anything that was very common, and being the
only child made it even harder.

"All my classmates were always talking about their fathers,
what they were doing, bragging about new cars and successes.
So I told them that my father was a really successful business-

man, and that he had a big American car, which was a status symbol then. I just went on and on, making up stories about how great he was.

"One day, out of the blue, he was waiting for me after school in an old, beat-up Volkswagen. I purposely walked right by. I was with a whole group of my classmates, and I tried to totally ignore him. He had never picked me up from school before.

"To my horror, he came after me. He thought I hadn't seen him. I was teased about it a lot at school after that. Kids called me a liar; some of them wouldn't even talk to me.

"I really adored my father and was always hoping that my parents would get back together. There was a time when he wanted to come back, but my mother wouldn't go for it. He always made a lot of promises and I always believed him, but she never did. There was a big conflict between my mother and myself, because I had so much confidence in him.

"One year he told me he was going to get me skis for Christmas and I was all set. I had the ski trip planned and everything ready and my mother said, 'Don't you believe him until you see it,' and I jumped on her, saying that she didn't know anything and if he said he will get me this, I will get it, and of course, it never came through.

"Then, when I was thirteen, he remarried and moved away, and I've hardly seen him at all since then. Whenever I do see him, it's because I made the effort, and he's always rather indifferent, like I was just an obligation he had, a reminder of his failure.

"My mother didn't like to talk about him, and when she did, it was always pretty negative. She didn't have a whole lot of respect for him. I always thought, if she'd only give him a chance . . .

"When I was sixteen, I fell in love with a guy and waited eight years until he asked me to marry him. It was a disaster; the marriage only lasted for a year. He really hated everything about me and wanted me to change completely, which I tried to do. Being a good wife and mother was for me *the* thing. I'd do anything for him. So when he insisted on two beds instead of one, I went for it. And he insisted that we only have sex once a week, so every Sunday morning we had sex. It's almost like sex was demeaning to him, but anything he wanted, I tried to agree. I didn't want to be a failure. Finally, everyone I knew, including *his* psychiatrist, told me to get out of the marriage. But even though I realized they were right, I just didn't want to get divorced. I would have hung in there until the bitter end. Eventually I realized there really wasn't any choice, but it took me a while to get over the trauma.

"In the meantime, my mother had moved to America, and so I did too. I got a job as a secretary at a hotel and very quickly worked my way up to a managerial position. It was a very prestigious, high-paying job.

"I'm very insecure emotionally, but I am a survivor. The fact that my parents were divorced made me in a lot of ways strong, because I was on my own. My mother worked, and so I had to deal with my problems by myself. She didn't have time to listen to my little concerns. I was on my own very young, and that made me kind of a strong person in some ways. I started working jobs from the age of thirteen, making money and wheeling and dealing. Financially, I always know I can survive, but I am very insecure when it comes to relationships. And having a man in my life is much more important to me than having a job. I never was a career woman by choice."

We talked in the luxurious home of the man with whom Olga is now living. She willingly gave up her job when she realized how serious she was about him.

"Whatever I'm involved in, I have to give 100 percent. I feel that I have to be perfect, whether it's a career or a relationship, so I obviously can't do both, because then one or the other is suffering. And having a relationship is much more important.

"I am just so afraid of being hurt or rejected. Maybe he's getting bored with me soon and maybe he's finding somebody younger. I have a very negative attitude. It's like I'm trying to prepare myself for something bad to happen so when it happens it won't hurt that much."

As Olga says these words, other voices ring in my head: "I always feel that I have to look at the negative possibilities of a situation before I can enjoy it," Margaret had said (Chapter Three).

"One effect of [father loss] may be that the child becomes

afraid to love," Dr. Gilbert Kliman was quoted as saying. "[She] worries that if . . . she dares to love another person, that person too may be taken away."

The shock of paternal loss reverberates as surely as the voices do, frequently, as in Olga's case, tolling the reminder that men do not stay.

"I guess because my mother never wanted to talk about my father, I don't really know much about men. I was always defending him, so I have a tendency to idolize all men. I want to marry Jim and I'm doing anything I can to make this relationship successful."

Olga's fierce commitment to relationships can be seen as a direct result of what she perceives as her mother's lack of commitment to her marriage. Where Hillary's mother created an image impossible to emulate, Olga's mother created a void that her daughter still desperately needs to fill. In both cases, mother's response to father's absence was the key element in shaping daughter's attitude toward herself.

Cindy, neither suicidal nor fearful of not having a man, is perhaps a more typical example of the single mother's daughter. A poised and attractive young businesswoman, she reflects the subtle yet marked ways in which our unmarried mothers influenced us.

Her father died suddenly, in a car accident, when Cindy was seven years old. He had been a teacher, a kind, patient, learned man with whom his older daughter had spent many contented hours reading and listening.

"After his death, my mother became a walking ghost. It was very hard for her to take. She had always been very gentle when he was alive, and their marriage was a good one. She was very much in love with him, and apparently very dependent on him. For about the first two years after he died, she really wasn't there for my [younger] sister and me. As a result, I became the strong one in the family. By the time I was eight, I was making a lot of the family decisions.

"My mother became very short-tempered and distant. She had to go out and work right away, and she'd come home tired and grouchy. I remember, when I was nine years old, I kissed her good night one night and she told me not to kiss her like that. Ever since then, there was nothing physical between us except when she would hit me. Now sometimes she wants to hug and kiss me on the cheek and I just stand there like a wooden person.

"Even when we were still small children, she'd become frustrated very easily and slap us. When she remarried, the belts and coat hangers started, thanks to my stepfather.

"I was ten years old. My sister and I were very open to him at first, but he was a very difficult man to be around. He was a workaholic and he worked sixteen, eighteen hours a day. And he did not understand children.

"He had been brought up by the rod, by a strict midwestern Methodist family, and he didn't relate to us very well at all. We were to be seen and not heard. We did not eat meals with him, we were just kind of shunted off to the side, and my mother did nothing about it.

"During the two years that they were married, they had a son. My stepfather loved him dearly and showered him with attention and gifts.

"He and my mother had physical fights where they would actually be hitting each other, mostly him hitting her. Occasionally, she would call for me to come help her. In the middle of the night, I'd be awakened with her screaming for me: 'He's breaking my arm. Come help me.' So even though she was married, I still felt like I had to be her parent.

"Anyway, that only lasted two years, because he died. He worked so hard that he just wore out his heart. I remember the night that I was told that he died, I cried because you do attach yourself to a parent whether you like the person or not. But even though I was crying, I was pleased. I felt slightly guilty for feeling that way, but there was no denying it.

"So now my mother had to go out and work to support three children, and because of the authority I had developed in the family, there was a lot of conflict. As a growing teenager, you do a lot of crazy things and parents have to discipline you, but I just didn't respect her at all.

"I remember we went out to look for a new house and buy a new car and I decided which house we bought and I decided which car we bought. I wished I had a strong, supportive parent to look up to, but I just couldn't feel that way toward my mother.

"I couldn't confide in her, because I was always afraid that she'd get angry. Pretty soon it got so that adults were not people that I wanted to be close to. I became alienated from all authority figures. If there was an adult in the room, I just kind of acted like they weren't there. I would only relate to people my own age.

"I'm not saying that I became terribly rebellious. There were other kids much more rebellious than I was. But when I was fifteen, it was the sixties, the Hippie Era, and I did get caught up with a looser crowd. But it was still Main Street. At school, I still followed the rules and all that.

"But there was a kind of duality within myself that's still there: the child and the authority figure. I needed a parent to tell me what to do, but I didn't have one, so I would expect a lot of myself. Yet always having to be in control inhibits the child side of me. I sometimes wish I could let go of that need to be in charge, but I seem always to carry that load of having to be the responsible one.

"By the end of high school, I knew that I couldn't depend on anyone else to take care of me and that I would have to enter a profession where I could support myself. Art was the thing I was best at, and so after college, I worked staff jobs for record companies, and then a few years ago, I had enough contacts to open my own graphic design company.

"I want certain comforts in life, and I'm quite ambitious. I'm willing to provide the kind of lifestyle I want for myself, which is a good thing, because for some reason, I'm always attracted to very unambitious men; artistic, sensitive types with no particular drive. I try to nudge them a little bit and get them into a little better shape than when I first met them, give them a few ideas about how to further themselves professionally. But it never really works out.

"I think, if my father had lived, I'd be able to give my love more easily. I think I'd be softer and more feminine. But I've really had to develop this inner strength that makes me more aggressive, more masculine, really, than I'd like to be. I sometimes see this love radiating from my friends, a soft aspect of their nature that I know I just don't have. I think I'd love myself more if I had received more love from my father, but of course, he's gone. My mother loved me, I know, but she was having such a hard life."

When a girl loses her father, she loses her mother, too. And the normal role of child, in which she has appropriately been embroiled, must be dramatically revised to accommodate age-inappropriate maturity. As noted above, there are advantages to be gleaned from early appropriation of independence and competence, but what is lost is the confidence to be vulnerable. We must be strong, good, even perfect, if we are to lighten the load implied by our existence.

What can a single mother do to lighten our load? She can assure us of her love and our worth. She can, by instilling a positive attitude toward women, make us feel less handicapped for want of a man in the house. Yet if father is a recent comer to the family unit in historical time, woman's value as a contributing member of the family is even now still evolving.

Respect and regard for the fatherless household is intimately connected to the successful and ongoing ascension of women in society. Unless and until we are recognized, *and recognize ourselves,* as equally worthwhile citizens, mother will feel uneasy in her role as head of the household, victimized not only by the loss of her husband, but by responsibilities she neither wants nor feels capable of fulfilling. To make us feel like a "real family," therefore, it is not surprising that many widowed and divorced mothers sought remarriage as a source of restoration. Only by providing us with a "father," they believed, could they reestablish themselves as mother. The introduction of a new man on the scene, however, would redefine the daughter's role, as well.

EIGHT

MAKE ROOM
FOR THE NEW DADDY

Stepfathers

Once upon a time there was a stepmother. She led a very hectic life running around from fairy tale to fairy tale being wicked. The best that can be said of her is that she was merely vain, but toward her unfortunate stepdaughter she was frequently merciless: competitive, demanding, sadistic and, on occasion, even murderous. We all grew up knowing of and fearing her. But, as recent testimony attests, the lady might have been the progenitor of a bad rap.

Investigations into stepparents have shown stepmothers to be only slightly less successful than stepfathers in establishing satisfactory relationships with the children. And one of the reasons given for the lower success rate is ". . . the myth in our culture which denigrates the stepmother." Still famous for her role in the realm of fairy tale and myth, the stepmother is yet trying to establish herself in the less magical kingdom of "the reconstituted family." And with the soaring divorce rate and the concomitant possibility of remarriage, she and her rather less well-defined male counterpart have become a very real feature of society, and the subjects of a good amount of sociological investigation.

According to the U.S. Bureau of the Census, roughly six million children—three million girls—were living with a stepparent in 1980. Since men are more likely than women to remarry, we can estimate that a little less than half of these stepparents were men. And about these men, professional research is also encouraging. Concluded one study: ". . .[T]he findings indicate that stepfathers are more apt to achieve excellent relations with their stepchildren than stepmothers. This is in accord with the findings of all other investigators in the field."

Stepfathers would seem to have an advantage in that they don't have a reputation to live down. Yet, as we will see below, that may turn out to be a disadvantage. For the results of our inquiry were anything but encouraging. Regarding interaction between stepfather and stepdaughter, relations are, according to our sample, far from "excellent." Perhaps the contradiction emanates from our choice of subject. Unlike the author quoted above, we explored not the stepfathers', but the stepdaughters', perspective. And of the 38 percent of women in our study whose mothers remarried, 61 percent reported strong negative relationships with their stepfathers.

The high incidence of dissatisfaction was striking, as was the fact that most stepdaughters' responses to our questionnaire corresponded to those of women who had never had stepfathers. Hence, their overall perceptions would seem to have been informed not by stepfather's presence, but by the biological father's absence. Throughout this volume, therefore, they are included in the category of "fatherless daughters." Yet there are some specific attitudes and behavior patterns that do distinguish these women from those whose mothers never remarried, attitudes suggesting that, if anything, stepfather's arrival on the scene intensified their sense of loss.

It is true that many of us were pleased when mother started to date. Her resumption of a social life was both reassuring and a blessed relief. Some of the heat was off us, and maybe, just maybe, she'd "meet somebody," "somebody" meaning specifically a man who would marry her, father us, and restore the family. Maybe we'd get to be normal again. Yet, when mother one day announced that she was taking a new husband, it was rarely perceived as good news.

Daughter's ambivalence toward her new "father" is attributable to several factors, each of which will be elaborated in this chapter. Perhaps the initial rub is promoted by the fact that, once again, she is being asked to passively accept an event that will dramatically change her life. Antagonisms fester as the new head of household tries to establish himself, and mother, grateful for his presence, bows willingly to his often ill-conceived command.

Cindy's remarks about her stepfather in the previous chapter —"he did not understand children," "he didn't relate to us very well"—accurately anticipate the overall perception voiced again and again by women I interviewed. Often, as in Cindy's case, the perception was verified by equally negative experiences.

"We cried when they got married," Lori and Gena offer practically in unison. Barely three years after their father's self-inflicted death, the sisters were given a way out of the symptomatic confusion that follows parental suicide. They had something about which to feel adamant: Though their prospective stepfather showered them with gifts and then moved them from a tract house onto an estate, "We saw through him immediately. We didn't like him."

Gena elaborates: "When I think back on that whole period in that lovely house (and it was a wonderful house), I have not one warm memory. There was nothing but tension, uptightness, dark shadows. There was just no love. We were constantly being reprimanded, punished, criticized. I wouldn't call it child abuse exactly, but he did love to whack.

"I remember one time he was slamming me around the room, and I was scared. I said, 'What are you trying to do, kill me?' And he said, 'You'd be surprised at how much the human body can endure.' He was an incredibly aggressive person."

The sisters' initial suspicions were certainly borne out in fact. As I had with Cindy, I wondered aloud where their mother was during their stepfather's abuse. The answer, if more vehement than Cindy's, is similar.

"Our mother had been working full time, strapped down with three kids, and having no fun. Then, all of a sudden, she finds a wealthy man who is willing to marry her and can really provide for her. He was very different from our real father in that respect, and much more her type. So she was attracted to the glamour, the big house, and the fact that she wouldn't have to work.

"But just because she didn't work didn't mean she was there for us. I mean, she made dinner, she fulfilled her obligations, but she never stuck up for us when Harvey was on a tirade. I don't think she ever really enjoyed her children, and she'd go along with anything to maintain the grand new lifestyle.

"As bad as it was to lose our father, I think the relationship—or nonrelationship—with our stepfather was far more damaging. I don't know what Lori and I would have done if we hadn't had each other. It would have been so much better to just live in a cheap little tiny place with our mother. I really don't know if such a negative relationship is better than no relationship at all."

As we saw in Chapter Five, many of Gena's inhibitions were formulated as a result of her father's suicide. Yet, in answer to her query, our study revealed that women whose mothers remarried do have a tendency to view life more skeptically than other women. They were more likely to have undergone psychotherapy than women whose mothers remained single, and they also found therapy less helpful than any other group.

Girls who had stepfathers began dating and began having sex earlier than other girls, even reported "falling in love" at a younger age,* yet are less likely as adults to describe themselves as "trusting." Clearly, they needed to disassociate themselves from home before other girls; yet, because they were not ready for relationships, they were only disillusioned further.

June, an eighteen-year-old girl who operates from a decidedly skeptical vantage point, illustrates how early the disillusionment can set in. Even in describing her single memory of her biological father, she conveys a suggestion of suspiciousness: "My image of him, my first impression and the one that I am left with, is that he looked foreign," she says.

"My mother, who is Japanese, and my father, an American, were divorced when I was two years old. We were living in the United States, but because my mother couldn't afford to keep me, she sent me to live with my aunt and uncle in Japan. Of course, I can remember very little from that time, but one day, I

* Please see table on page 164.

remember, a foreign man came to see me. I was very scared of him, because he looked different from anyone I had ever seen. I was about four when this happened, and I remember he brought me a big doll. I was so small that the doll was bigger than I was. I got scared and started crying, so he had to leave. So that's the only thing I remember about him. I'm not even sure if they told me he was my father.

"When I was seven, my mother came to Japan to take me with her to New York. I was so excited. I remember it was a big deal to go to America.

"I think my mother tried hard to explain to me about the divorce, but I don't think I really understood. Anyhow, we got into New York real late, and we were both very, very tired from the trip, so we slept through the morning. My mother was still deep in sleep, and I woke up because I heard sounds coming in from the living room. Then I saw a man. I thought, 'Wow, there's a robber in the house.' So I started to wake up my mother, saying, 'Mom, there's a robber in here!' And she just goes, 'Silly, that's your new father,' and went back to sleep. So that was my introduction to my stepfather.

"See, it was really very strange. To me, my mother and my father, they were my fantasies while I was living in Japan. I never felt like I was motherless or fatherless, because I always had my aunts and uncles and they were like my mothers and fathers. I mean, I knew there was the big M and the big F. Somewhere. But everything was very hush-hush in Japan. They talked about my mother, now that I think of it, but not that much about my father. Divorce in Japan is considered very heavy.

"So when I was 'introduced' to Ray, I guess I just thought of him as my new father, rather than as a stepfather. I was only seven years old.

"He doesn't like kids. Neither he nor my mother like kids, and it was very hard for them. They didn't have any kids and then suddenly there was this seven-year-old in their life. I think it freaked them out. So our communication wasn't really that great. And it was very hard for him to take on the responsibility of a child. So I really didn't get close with either of them. Whereas, I have a feeling that Gary [her father] would have been very easy to get along with. He's somewhere in Europe now and someday I'm sure I'll get to meet him.

"Sometimes, I fantasize that typical meeting, with strings in the background and daughter and father run into each other's arms, crying, and instantly loving each other. I mean, that would be nice, but it's not real. There's a very good chance he doesn't even want to meet me, because of guilt, or not wanting to be reminded of the past. And I don't want to lay that trip on him. Maybe I'll try to get to know him without ever disclosing who I am.

"But I'm very glad about the way I've turned out, and it has a lot to do with the fact that I haven't had a close relationship with my parents. I've had to look into myself for answers, instead of depending on anyone else. I think if my father had been around, he would have been warmer than Ray or my mother, so I wouldn't have had the chance to develop my independence.

"Of course, when I was younger, there were a lot of times when I wanted somebody, and because I'm an only child, with no sisters or brothers and only a dog . . . well, you know, you can't talk to a dog. So I reach out to friends.

"But, at the same time, I've always considered myself a loner. I'm afraid of leaving myself open and vulnerable. I don't like getting hurt, and I'm so sensitive in my head. I think I'm really scared of rejection. I'm really insecure. I'm not sure why.

"I guess the fact that it was so hard for me to get close to my parents helped—or rather, hurt—the situation. So there was this constant need for approval and friendships, and yet when I got it, it was as though I didn't want it any more. Part of me wants to believe that it's from my wanting to be strong and on my own, independent. But maybe I turn away from friendships because I'm afraid of making myself vulnerable, opening myself up to rejection. Whenever I tried to say something personal about myself to my parents, maybe ask them something or mention a crush, they always sort of put me down for it. Like they'd say, 'Oh, that's so dumb.' "

Nurtured by a rejecting mother, an absent father, and an indifferent stepfather, June's wariness of people's intentions is not hard to appreciate. Nor is her guardedness uncommon among women whose mothers remarried. According to our study, 47 percent of the women who had stepfathers found it difficult to trust men—as compared to 38 percent of those whose mothers remained single or who had fathers at home. Furthermore, these daughters with stepfathers were twice as likely as other women to feel intimidated by people of their own sex. Regarding this last point, daughters of remarried divorcées were particularly adamant.

It would seem that the divorced mother's "failure" to hold father, followed by her lack of interest in smoothing daughter's troubled relationship with stepfather (if this was in fact the case), begets an acutely troubled mother-daughter relationship, which in turn translates into an overall disenchantment with females. As illustrated by June's remarks, this disenchantment is nowhere more evident than in the conflict that the girl brings to her own feminine identity.

"I don't think of myself as being a female," June states flatly. "I mean, I don't deny that I am a woman, but I don't like to think I am *a female*. I think more of myself being a person. Because if I label myself as a girl, I would feel like I'm limiting myself.

"Women are such funny creatures. Always competing for who's got the man, who's got the better figure, the better tan. In this society, women are brought up to be like vicious cats, always out on the prowl for a man. To me, women are competitive bullshitters. They're out for one thing: to beat the next woman.

"My relationships with men are much better than my relationships with women. I get along with men better. I prefer having men as friends much more than women. Of course, it's a big deal for me to be accepted by men, so I guess I have that competitive thing too, but it comes from my insecurities.

"But I'll tell you, the truth is I don't really care about anyone else. My goal in life is to be happy. I'm one of those 'me' types: if I'm happy, everything is cool. It's sort of a selfish way to go, but . . . it keeps me out of trouble."

The young woman's pronouncement of self-reliance punctuated with parentheses of "insecure," "vulnerable," "afraid," belies itself. Indeed, while women with stepfathers felt so little trust, they were also least likely to enjoy spending time alone.

Because she is only eighteen, June's bitterness is particularly disturbing, and her carefully conjured allure discernibly strains from all the hostility just below the surface. Of course, her youth may partially explain her stridency; that, and the fact that she is still living with her mother and stepfather—who are, during our conversation, as so often, out of town. Her experience of her childhood's household is closer, more immediate, than that of most of the women who have participated in this project. Age notwithstanding, however, no single inquiry aroused as much consistent ire among my subjects as did the one about stepfather. Whether abusive or merely indifferent, his presence in their lives had a greater negative impact than the biological father's absence had. None of the women I interviewed, and very few of those in the study, felt that they gained a father when mother remarried.

Once upon a time there was a stepfather. Because he didn't make the fairy-tale circuit, no one really knew what to expect of him . . . least of all, himself.

*

The stepfather's, like the father's, role in this society is ambiguous. Yet it may be easily understood that because of the very situation that has provided a place for him, ambiguity is even less acceptable.

Despite our ongoing allegedly liberating times, biological fathers can still get away with a minimum of actual interaction with their children. Father, let's face it, spends less time child rearing than bread winning. Indeed, it is his role as breadwinner that has fashioned his primary paternal function, namely to facilitate the child's separation from mother. Coming from outside this symbiotic relationship, he acts as a wedge between them and stands as an example of success outside the home.

The stepfather's "outsideness" has no such benefits. Stepping into the already existing family, he is often made to feel as though he were a trespasser, violating the status quo, with no sure idea of how to make himself welcome. At least the stepmother begins her tenure with an image, the disavowal of which provides her with a very specific opening task. "The stepfather operates against an absence of myth," one book asserts, "an unspoken assumption that his role is to play no role. Yet he does have a definite role to play . . . The difficulty lies in establishing the position."

The house is bereft of its leader, the children engaged in the myriad implications of parental loss, the daughter abandoned by the first man she ever loved. Into this scene comes the newly married man. Worse than an outsider, as far as the children are concerned, he is an interloper.

How does stepfather respond to the uncomfortable position in which he finds himself? Because of the high incidence of "reconstituted families" in our society, several professional studies have attempted to find out. From these, and from books for popular consumption, we learn that the overall picture is better than was anticipated. Yet stepfamilies as a whole do harbor considerably more strain than do "normal homes." And the stepfather, while he rates slightly higher than does his female counterpart, seems to enter the new family less prepared, more confused, and with a greater degree of resentment toward the children than does the stepmother.

If he has been married before and is separated from his biological children, his resentment toward his stepchildren may be readily understood. In fact, investigations show that the husband who has never before been married makes the best stepfather. Yet, "[t]he intrusion of the children, stated one way or another, is a recurring theme when stepfathers talk. Almost all . . . had underestimated the size of the undertaking, the magnitude of the problems."

Women, even the most career-oriented, enter a new family with at least some reasonable expectation of what it means to take on the children. Men, because of the continued ambiguity of the father's role, usually do not. When they decide to marry a woman with children, especially if they have never been fathers, they simply don't know what they're getting into. Hence, whether or not he has children of his own, the stepfather approaches his new position with at least some awkwardness. Superimposed over his fear of the unknown, on the one hand, or guilt about his own children, on the other, is the lack of clarity about what a stepfather is supposed to be.

Some men overreact to the nebulousness of their role by

immediately imposing their authority. Confused about what is expected of them, likely confronted by testing, and testy, children, they adopt a commanding, domineering stance. They foolishly assert what they perceive to be a much-needed macho hand, doing damage not only to the potential relationship, but often to the child as well. Certainly this kind of aggressiveness characterized many of the stepfathers described in our study.

The other common way of dealing with his dubious role is to ignore it altogether. He married a women he loves, and if she has children, he'll just passively try to put up with them for a few years, and then they'll be grown and gone. As June's childhood illustrated, however, an empty hand can be just as harmful to the child as a heavy hand. Either way, she feels unloved.

Of course, the disharmony between stepfather and stepdaughter is not all his fault. According to *Living in Step,* "Many stepfathers [felt] that they [were] prevented by their stepchildren from getting close to them . . . the children set up roadblocks to intimacy and warmth." Our study corroborated this sentiment. Despite the presumed confidence imparted by mother's renewed social life, her marriage was not welcomed by daughter. Thus, even before stepfather had a chance to demonstrate what kind of a parent he'd be, less than half of our subjects were glad of his arrival on the scene. Where does this disinclination come from? It could be, as with Lori and Gena, and Cindy, that the guy just wasn't very nice—elaborate gifts or no. But there are exacerbating reasons for a girl's prejudice against a "new father." His presence, uninvited by her, irritates, moreover, because of its inherent confirmation of another's absence. Like a variation on an old cliché: She's not gaining a stepfather, she's losing her real father . . . again. And this time, she may also be losing her mother in the bargain.

As had been repeatedly stated, a major facet of father loss is mother loss. Even if the mother manages to maintain an active, thriving relationship with her children, the desperate fear of losing her is ever present. When she becomes seriously involved with a man, tells her child that she loves this man, and that he is going to become part of the family, it is only natural for the child to feel threatened. She is losing some of Mommy's time, attention, love—things she is clinging to so fervently for her very survival.

When a child gains a stepfather, therefore, loss is the primary emotion she is experiencing. First and foremost, she is losing her mother. She is also losing control. Just as she was accommodating herself to the new family constellation—in which she probably enjoyed a leadership position—she is once again asked to adjust to a dramatic change over which she has no power. She had no control over Daddy's leaving, and she has no control over this latest decision that is going to change her life.

"Mourning is revived when new relationships are forming," stated Erna Furman at the 1980 American Psychoanalytic Association's Workshop on Loss. In subsequent chapters, we shall see the truth of this principle—how marriage and motherhood revive the pain of father loss. Surely the acquisition of a stepfather stirs up those old feelings most poignantly.

Mother's marriage emphatically declares that father is gone for good. Fantasies of reconciliation in the case of divorce, or magical resurrection if father died, must be forced even further from mind. Yet what of the love daughter feels for the man that got away? If she accepts this new man as "Daddy," is it not a stark betrayal of her real father? How can she possibly join her mother in this implicit act of disloyalty? The pain of loss is not abetted with the arrival of stepfather; rather, it is stirred and rekindled. Acknowledging the new man means that the main man is never coming back.

There are marked differences of opinion regarding how the prior marital status of mother affects stepfather's acceptance into the family. Those studies that have found widows' remarriages more successful cite the following explanations: lack of the distracting intrusion of the real father, and mother's more positive attitude toward men, which transfers to daughter's positive attitude toward stepfather.

On the other hand, those studies that have found divorcées' children more amenable to stepfather suggest that negative memories of real father promote rejection of him and the concomitant acceptance of the new and (it is hoped) better parent. Hence, whether death or divorce renders the child more open to stepfather remains an undecided question among experts.

According to our study, negative feelings were slightly higher in girls whose fathers had died.

(It may also be noted that there were far fewer remarried widows represented in our study than remarried divorcées: out of 269 daughters of divorce, 125 had at one time had stepfathers; only 88 of the 288 women whose fathers had died had mothers who remarried.)

The little girl at her mother's wedding, whether she's four or fourteen, is someone who carries a legacy of shattered trust. For reasons she can't understand, or chooses not to, the first man she ever loved is out of her life. Someone she really counted on is gone. As she watches mother kiss the groom, she wants to believe they'll all live happily ever after, but the pain and insecurity bequeathed her at an early age belie happy endings.

Mother and stepfather, smiling, arms entwined, glide up the aisle toward the future. Perhaps the newlyweds wave to daughter, gesture for her to come and join them. Tentatively, she makes her way, not even for a moment letting go of the past.

*

My mother remarried when I was five. The marriage lasted for seven months. I called him "Daddy," enjoyed the feeling of his big hand holding mine crossing streets, shuddered when he yelled at me, and doubted that he'd be around for long. Yes, we had a new last name, a new apartment, even two new brothers, but everything about all this newness felt wrong, temporary. Abe and my mother fought a lot, mostly about the children, maybe about money, too, but mostly about the children. One night I overheard them arguing about a "new lease" and silently trembled with fear that I was to be exchanged.

It was nice to go on outings, take rides in the family car, see them kissing—like they do in the movies—every now and then. But somehow, I don't remember being terribly invested in the new setup. In fact, I actually believe that I perceived it merely as "an experience." If I floated passively through it, behaved myself so as to avoid his wrath, went about my business very quietly, it would expire of its own fragility.

The scenes leading to the final curtain were hardly low-key.

Tears, accusations, hysterical shouting matches, viewed from
the farthest seat I could find, built to the eventual denouement.
And expire it did.

The boys and Abe moved out; I fumbled through embarrassing explanations throughout first grade about why my last name
was different from what it had been in kindergarten; and my
mother, emotionally battered, settled with renewed bitterness
into her role as provider.

Thinking back on that episode of my life, I am somewhat
surprised by my five-year-old's lack of hope. I don't think I liked
Abe very much, and I'm quite sure he regarded me as little
more than a burden. I don't remember actively wishing for the
marriage to end—I wanted Mommy to be happy, and I guess I
liked taking rides in a family car—but any attempts to ingratiate
myself with my stepfather were cursory at best. I didn't expect
him to love me: toleration would do, and a minimum of angry
outbursts directed my way.

During our interview, my mother told me that she had really
loved him, that she had tried very hard to make the marriage
work, and that the divorce left her disappointed and afraid of
relationships. Though I have managed not to give much
thought to the Abe portion of my childhood, I realize now what
a relief it was when it was over, how glad I was that I hadn't
invested any hope in him, and how a stepdaughter's needs are
so very different from her mother's.

Terry, born to an affluent southern family ten years after the
other children, was her father's favorite. She was a special surprise for him, if not for her mother—with whom she would be at
cross-purposes for the duration of her childhood.

"He was just tickled to death to have another baby," Terry
bubbles. "He spent an incredible amount of time with me that
he hadn't spent with my brothers and sister, because he had
been working. By the time I came along, he was very successful,
doing very well for a man his age—he was forty years old—
owned his own business, great big house, beautiful wife, everything was terrific.

"My mother was very occupied with the older kids, and I had
a nurse who was with me all day long, every day. So when she

left, I just died waiting for my father to get home. I can remember him walking in the door at night and I'd grab him around the knees. I had to be just a toddler then.

"After dinner, he'd carry me on his shoulders to the beach. He'd buy me an ice-cream cone and a book. And he used to read stories to me every night before I went to sleep. I was definitely Daddy's little girl."

There is nothing tentative about Terry. Even her southern drawl is pumped by rapid-fire delivery. She is a stunningly attractive woman, vivacious, and bright. At twenty-nine, she is president of a clothing manufacturing company in a major city.

"What kind of man was your father?" I ask her.

"Very determined, very strong, very masculine, very jovial. Everyone says he had a good sense of humor. He was very caring, very warm, very intelligent, very quick-witted. He was definitely the pillar of the family. He held everyone together."

When Terry was four and a half, her father died suddenly, of a heart attack. "And my whole family just fell apart. My older brother got married, my sister got married, my other brother joined the Coast Guard, and the youngest one, who was fourteen, started getting into all kinds of trouble.

"My mother didn't have a clue on how to be responsible for five children. She had never worked, never even written out a check. She was really beautiful, a real southern-belle type. I mean, she's the kind who saves the drapes to make dresses. You never know when you're going to need a ball gown. My mother never gave me any direction in life except on how to arrange flowers.

"I remember being five years old and my mother was going to the doctor all the time, and I didn't understand why my mother was going to the doctor all the time, and she was going to the doctor all the time because she was having a nervous breakdown. And everybody else was gone and I was left at home with my nurse.

"One day I was playing on the front porch of this playhouse my father had built for me, and I knelt down on a stone and it went the whole way into my knee. And I saw it there and I looked at it and I thought, 'My God, there's nobody here to help me.' My nurse was way on the other side of the house, and my mother was at the doctor's. And I pulled out the stone and I looked at it, and I remember saying to myself, 'If I ever want to remember what it was like to be five years old, this is it.' Very lonely. I was very lonely. Because my mother was not really there for me.

"Everyone tells me that after my father died, I cried nonstop for six months. I don't remember any of that, but they say they just couldn't stop me from crying. My mother has always said that the only reason she remarried was so that I would have a father.

"I was about six and a half when she married Louis. He was a really, really good man, a very nice guy. He had a normal, average job, he made whatever the normal, average amount of money was, nothing like my father, but he was a really good man. I called him 'Daddy' immediately, and it seemed like, by my mother marrying, things were going to be OK.

"He really tried to be a good father to me. He came to my dance recitals, when my mother never did, and he took me back and forth to lessons and classes, or whatever I had going on. He was always there, very steady, very dependable. But my mother wouldn't let me accept him. She was unhappy in the marriage, so she wasn't going to let me be happy in the marriage.

"I think she had just wanted to get married again, didn't know how to get along by herself, and so this guy came along, wanted to get married, so she said OK. Obviously, he was not at all like my father."

Obviously.

"They stayed married for twelve years, but they were very unhappy together. They used to fight a lot, and they didn't sleep together, and I was aware of that at seven years old. Every single day, I heard about how my stepfather was impotent, how he wasn't really a man, how she had only married him so I could have a father.

"I think I realized that she was wrong, that it wasn't fair for her to tell me that it was my fault if things weren't working out for her. But she was my mother! And he was making her miserable, so someone had to make her happy. And that's how I tried to make her happy: I'd sit and listen to her telling me about how wonderful my real father was and how my stepfather was just *nothing* compared to him.

"I couldn't really get myself to dislike him, but I didn't let myself get close to him either. I mean, my mother kept telling me how terrible he was, so I had to take her side. I mean, someone had to make her happy, because, my God, she needed help!

"When I was about ten, she had another nervous breakdown. She never had any big crack where they had to drag her off to a mental institution, but she would go into a decline and just take to her bed for weeks on end.

"I remember that winter; it was very dreary. I spent hours standing in the hallway watching her rock back and forth, back and forth, crying, 'My life is at an end. Why has this happened to me?' I mean, she was a fruitcake. And I remember thinking that, somehow, it was all my fault. She was in an unhappy marriage because I had to have a father. I had been all set to take this guy in, but how could I?"

Both in her reluctance to cross her mother, and in her realization that her needs were quite different from her mother's, Terry reflected the conflict of most girls whose mothers remarry. It's just that, in her case, the tables were turned: she had to forfeit her stepfather's love, rather than wish for it, pretend for her mother's sake that she disliked, rather than that she was drawn to, this man. Into her chaotic childhood, a hero, in the form of a kindly man, had actually appeared. But in deference to her mother, Terry had to deny herself a father.

"Finally, when I was about fourteen, he and I were in the kitchen one day and, for some reason, he put his arms around me and said, 'I really want you to know that I love you just like you were my own little girl.' Well, that was it. I just broke down and cried. It was so important for me to have a relationship with him. He was such a good man. And I suddenly realized that I didn't have to put up with all this grief from my mother. So from that point, I sort of went and made peace with him. I stopped taking my mother's side, and just put up with her anger."

After seven years of living with him, Terry accepted her

stepfather's love. In fact, she said that she thinks of him as her "second father," not a "stepfather."

Four years later, he died.

"He always used to wake me up for school when he was leaving for work, and this one morning he didn't wake me up. I knew that something was the matter, so I didn't even want to roll over and look at the clock to see what time it was. I was just going to lie there and wait until he came in and said, 'Oh, I overslept,' or whatever.

"My mother came into my room and she had this really funny look on her face. 'Something is the matter with Daddy,' she said. Then I knew something was wrong, because she had never referred to him as 'Daddy.' I got up and went flying into his bedroom.

"I opened the door and saw that he was in bed. He looked like he was just sleeping. And I said, 'Daddy, Daddy.' No answer, no answer. I put my hand here and there and no breath, and I said, 'Mom, I think he's dead, you better call the doctor.'

"But she couldn't do anything. She had her nightgown on and she went into the bedroom and put on this apron and then came into the kitchen and started taking down plates and dusting them off one by one, and talking to herself: "Oh my God, I can't believe this is happening to me again.' And I kept saying, 'It's happening to me, too.'

"But she wouldn't listen to me, just kept dusting the plates. So I got on the phone and I called the doctor, and the priest. I called my uncle, I called my brothers, I called my sister. I made all the arrangements for the funeral. I called my school to tell them I wasn't coming in. I called my car pool to tell them not to pick me up. I just sat there making phone calls. Just picking up the phone and making calls.

"After the initial shock, I think my mother was actually joyous. And my brothers and sister didn't care, because they had never lived with him. I think they even might have been happy that, thank God, that was over, because Mom's been so miserable for so many years and maybe now she can have a chance to be happy.

"Nobody seemed to realize that I had been living with Louis all these years too, and that maybe it wasn't like that for me. I felt so alone in my grief, and that was the worst part of it. I was the only one who had really lost someone.

"On the outside, I took it as a very matter-of-fact thing, just like everyone else was. I just held it all inside until my stomach started burning up, and at eighteen, I had an ulcer.

"Mind you, I'm not one to feel sorry for myself. But I remember always sort of feeling, 'When is this thing going to get right? When is my life going to get right or normal?' "

Terry pauses, apparently pondering the question. "Well, anyhow," she resumes, her tone a tad deflated, "that was Louis. No warning, in his sleep, gone."

Just as the four-and-a-half-year-old was suddenly abandoned following the death of her father, her love and grief for her "second father" must also be borne in isolation. The two men had been very different but for one poignant detail: they had both loved her, and they had both "left her." What was she to make of men?

"Well, it's tough for me to believe in permanence," she declares matter-of-factly. "And then, wouldn't you know it? It happened again!"

Despite hysterical pleading that she stay close to home, Terry went away to college. A year and a half later, her mother remarried. "He was a super guy, a lot of fun and very affectionate. It was as though I had this great weight taken off my shoulders, because I didn't have to worry about her any more.

"Of course I went to the wedding. I have to go to all my mother's weddings. And it was great, because the house seemed alive again. Everything had kind of died when she married Louis, and now, with Charles, everything came alive."

Ten years later, in the throes of an unhappy marriage herself, but feisty and talented enough to be making tremendous strides up the corporate ladder, Terry attended Charles's funeral. His death hadn't been sudden, but, rather, preceded by a long illness.

Emotionally wrenching as it was to bury yet another "father," the aspect of his funeral that affected her most was that her husband wasn't there with her. Once again, she had to say goodbye alone. "I was angry like you can't believe. I didn't know I had that much anger inside of me."

Terry, divorced now, theorizes, "I never expected to have a marriage that would work. I knew my marriage to Bill wouldn't last. Maybe I chose him on purpose, just to test myself. Like, how would I behave if my marriage failed? At a very young age, I knew I didn't want to be like my mother, crumbling without a husband. So maybe by setting up a marriage that I knew wouldn't work, I'd get to prove how strong I could be once it was over."

Whether her father was a good man, an exceptional man, a domineering or indifferent man, the little girl who lost him knows at least this much: fathers can't really be counted on. Negative experiences with a stepfather only reinforce that early impression, making her feel, if anything, more acutely abandoned.

But soon the little girl is an adolescent, a teenager. She is beginning to notice, and be noticed by, boys. How does the disappointment of her childhood affect her encounters? Who are these alien creatures, boys, and what can she expect of them?

NINE

FATHER WHO ART IN HEAVEN . . . OR ELSEWHERE

Adolescence and Boys

Bobby Budhias changed my life. Or, if that is overstating it, he may at least be credited with altering the way in which, until that fateful afternoon in 1959, I had perceived myself. He, the golden curly-haired dreamboat of the sixth grade, noticed me.

Serious, shy, hopeful yet highly dubious about my physical attributes, I deemed myself a singularly unnoticeable type. So it was on that spring day that I slowly walked, with my usual slightly hunched demeanor, along the gate that led to the schoolyard entrance. It is fair to surmise that all my energy was directed toward trying to look casual as my darting eyes shifted among the assorted clusters of students within, searching for the small female band that would constitute safety. Bent on a quick and nonchalant approach to my modest group of mutual protectors, I was no doubt eager to lose myself in the familiar huddle that could be relied upon to temporarily camouflage my twelve-year-old's self-consciousness.

Thus subversively engaged—or so I can with some accuracy speculate—and not yet having reached the steps that led inside, my eyes swept past his, then stopped. They were blue, very blue, and they were smiling, it seemed, at me. Reflexively, I turned around to see whom he was really addressing with that piercing, welcoming smile, but there was no one. Incredulous, I glanced back toward him to see that, indeed, he, from within the schoolyard, was smiling up at me. More impossible to fathom, he had actually been waiting for me.

I don't remember the ensuing encounter, nor do I have the slightest intelligence on whatever became of Bobby Budhias, though I hope his every wish has come true. Yet that blue-eyed welcoming smile will be forever with me, a symbol of my debut into the society of people of the male gender, and the possibilities of reassurance that may reside there.

Men, boys, were strange to me. Exotic and alien, they existed only outside the household. Like most of my peers, I fretted or giggled by turns when anywhere near, or even discussing, an especially "cute" one, but to be sought after by a boy, coming as I did from a family united by the hope of male recognition, was for me a matter of particular urgency. Winning male approval was tantamount to validation, not only as a girl, but as a normal person.

Yet men and normalcy were unknown to me, and therefore frightening. I believed myself eager to partake of the co-ed expanse that would finally admit me, but, unconsciously, I was continuing to protect the emotional expanse within. When Eddie, that great and glorious teenage love of whom I spoke in Chapter One, asked for my hand, I looked down to realize that it was closed against him.

As illustrated by the table below, women in our study who had grown up without fathers or stepfathers—girls to whom men were truly unfamiliar—fell in love later than any other group.

MEAN AGE:	STEPFATHER	BIOLOGICAL FATHER	NO MAN AT HOME
Began dating	14.0	14.9	15.2
Fell in love	16.8	17.5	18.5
First sexual experience	18	19.9	19.2

If girls with stepfathers were most eager to establish distance from the home, girls without a man in the house felt most compelled to keep their distance. This is not to say that they repelled male company, for they began dating at nearly the same age as girls with fathers, even had their first sexual experiences a little earlier; but succumbing to emotional attachment? For that they would, in the ongoing interest of protecting themselves, wait a little longer.

Jan, an educational therapist in her mid-thirties, put up her protective armor at an early age. She was four years old when her father became ill. Like Terry, she had been an unexpected baby, born thirteen years after the other children. "I guess my mother would say I was a 'mistake.' To my father, I was a 'love child.' He and I had a wonderful, loving, special relationship.

"When he got sick, my mother, in her wisdom, decided that I should be sent to boarding school, so that I wouldn't be exposed to all the suffering and grief. He had cancer.

"But being sent away was horrible. It was like I was being punished for some terrible thing I had done. I vividly remember my brother taking me, and I was screaming and carrying on. I had no idea why I was being sent away.

"Sometime later, I was summoned back home. My sister was sitting in a chair, wiped out, and my mother took me upstairs and told me my father had died. I had no idea what that meant —I was four years old—except that he wasn't going to be there any more.

"My immediate reaction was 'I'm gonna be brave.' And I operated off that from the time I was four until about a year ago. I became this overadapted kid who was terrified of losing people and terrified of letting go. I held on to my self-control real tight—and proceeded to live out a life where I lost people a lot."

As Jan talks about the years following the loss—describing a "deprived" childhood in Trenton with a demanding and volatile mother (her brother and sister, like Terry's, left home soon after their father's death), there is an overt conflict between anger toward and glorification of the man that got away.

"Because I didn't have a father, I grew up feeling a lot different from the other kids. I got left with this woman who was totally miserable with her life, and who became progressively more terrified over the years. So I became the mom, the kid who grew herself up. I was responsible for keeping the house together, making dinners, a lot of things. And the freedom to just be a child was not there for me. I handled it by pretending it wasn't true, that my life was the same as everyone else's.

"Now, for the first time, I'm allowing myself to acknowledge the pain I felt. And what I'm finding is a lot of anger, like: Where the fuck was he? Why wasn't he around? I appreciate that I had four years, but that wasn't enough.

"All my relatives painted him as a romantic hero, and that's how I thought of him—as a wonderful, loving man who had mysteriously disappeared from my life. The anger was there, but I totally repressed it. In fact, I pushed him out of my consciousness altogether."

The conflict between anger and idealization created a skewed vision of men and informed Jan's attitude toward them through most of her young adulthood.

"There were all these relationships that just wouldn't work out. Things would start to get good with a guy, and I'd get scared. Because if anything gets too good, you lose it, right? So I'd start testing, making demands to make sure that the person was really there; but what I was actually doing was pushing, pushing him away. Then he'd leave, and I could get angry. I could let some of the defenses down, because you don't have to be defensive when you're alone.

"The few guys who stuck it out, who persisted in caring for me despite my carrying on, I left. That's how I took care of myself—by not letting anyone in. I mean, I knew that nothing could last, so I made sure it wouldn't.

"Then, about ten years ago, I was twenty-five already, and in a lot of pain over yet another failed relationship, I said, 'OK. This is it. I'm not going through this again. I'm tired of defending myself, I'm tired of testing, I'm tired of always having to be in control. I want to live.' So I went into therapy."

Jan came to recognize a consuming distrust of men and, after ten years of therapy, the anger toward her father that had fostered that distrust. Yet the price of conscious rage was high: admitting the anger meant admitting the loss. The brave little girl had to say good-bye to her father.

Only by relinquishing the "romantic heroes" that absent fathers frequently become can we begin to value real, human men—the kind that exist on earth. Until then, we pursue and repel them, challenge them to improve on a fantasy that keeps us at a safe distance from further disappointment, abandonment, pain.

*

The fatherless daughter approaches adolescence with more than the usual awkwardness of that age. "Rejected" by the first man on whom she tested her feminine charms, she is a wallflower before she even gets to the dance. Yet male attention, finally available within her peer group, means more than being noticed at a boy-girl party. It is the key to self-esteem that has eluded her through childhood.

But how does one behave around boys? How does one attract them? If, as suggested in Chapter Two and throughout the psychoanalytic literature, father is a key element in shaping sex-appropriate behavior (in boys and girls), the fatherless girl is at an obvious disadvantage. She can rely on books and movies and hearsay, but she lacks the personal experience of direct reinforcement. And beyond the absence of the all-important reciprocal relationship with father, she has been deprived of a role model in mother. She has had the opportunity neither to act in nor observe firsthand a mutually fulfilling male-female bond.

The behavioral results of this void in the fatherless daughter's experience have been documented in an invaluable study by E. Mavis Hetherington. Observing three groups of adolescent girls in a community recreation center—the girls were divided according to intact family, father died, father absent owing to divorce—Hetherington discovered distinct differences in the ways that the girls interacted with males.

Describing her findings, she writes: "Adolescent girls who had grown up without fathers repeatedly displayed inappropriate patterns of behavior in relating to males. Girls whose fathers had died exhibited severe sexual anxiety, shyness and discomfort around males. Girls whose fathers were absent because of divorce exhibited tension and inappropriately assertive, seductive, or sometimes promiscuous behavior with male peers and adults . . . Girls whose fathers had died spoke significantly less with a male interviewer and were generally more silent than any other group of subjects. Girls whose parents were divorced tended to talk more with a male interviewer than with a female interviewer . . . Our study suggests that the effects of father absence on daughters appear during adolescence and manifest themselves mainly as an inability to interact appropriately with males . . ."

Respectively shy and aggressive, daughters of deceased fathers and daughters of divorce bring to their adolescent behavior the circumstances of their loss. While both groups in the Hetherington study reported insecurity around men, their differences in coping with the insecurity reflected their attitudes toward their fathers.

"Daughters of widows often had aggrandized images of their fathers. They may feel that no other male can compare favorably with him, or alternately, they may regard all males as superior and as objects of deference and apprehension." Hence the overall shyness.

Daughters of divorce, more challenging in their approach to men, may be acting out their lingering hostility toward father— a man with whom they might still have a relationship.

Supporting the theories of other professional investigators, Hetherington further concluded that the earlier the separation from father, the greater the anxiety around men. Jan, for example, losing her father when she was four—and theoretically right in the middle of the Oedipal crisis—remained stuck in an unresolved attachment to him. She could neither give up the ghost of idealized expectations nor acknowledge the starkness of her disappointment. Her subsequent attempts at relating to boys/men reflected her fixation on the unresolved conflict. With the awkwardness of the adolescent, she was groping toward resolution with her father: after each man left her, she was able to feel anger, the emotion that would lead to acceptance of her father's death.

"We may see what appears to be a compulsion to repeat relations in which the object is again lost. The motive, however, is not to repeat the loss, but to approximate the earlier tragedy and to undo it by giving it a happy ending."

One happy ending, suggests the author of the above, would

be for father, upon seeing how lost his daughter is without him, to return. An even happier ending, however, would be the daughter's recognition of the true object of her disappointment, and the ultimate relinquishing of her father as a romantic ideal. Yet, psychically demanding as is the abdication of father's lap for the girl with a living, present father, the fatherless girl— particularly if she was younger than five when he left—struggles with singular determination against disengagement. Giving him up romantically would mean giving him up altogether.

It is little wonder that fatherless girls are visibly anxious around men. In fact, both fatherless groups in the Hetherington study scored a higher overall anxiety level on the Manifest Anxiety Scale than did girls with fathers at home. Craving male attention, they are equally resolved to remain invulnerable. They would like to be loved without the threat posed by loving. That way, the need for approval may be safely gratified and the attachment to father unrelinquished.

Stepdaughters who reportedly "fell in love" at a particularly early age would seem to be the exceptions. But, as we have seen, they are *determined* to achieve disengagement—from their stepfathers. Disillusioned by their premature relationships, however, they soon come to resemble, in awkwardness and attitudes toward men, fatherless daughters whose mothers did not remarry. Their hearts, like ours, still belong to Daddy.

The bittersweet irony of the fatherless daughter's adolescence is that she has set as her standard a man who gravely disappointed her. Yet, by keeping his image before all others, she protects herself against further disappointment—and the agonizing acceptance of her father's irreversible absence.

The image of the deceased father is usually an idealized one with which no earthly creature can compare. As long as the fantasy father is perfect, daughter need not deeply feel the imperfection of reality, past or present.

The daughter of divorce uses her father as a protective shield, also. He, of course, is not perfect but, rather, stands as a living symbol justifying daughter's distrust. Since he committed the unforgivable crime of walking out on her, she seeks male approval with a vengeance, so that, perhaps, paternal rejection may be obscured. Yet the possibility of reconciliation is a strong subconscious force, acting in concert with her resolution against emotional commitment to other men.

The following data from our study reveal the dramatic correlation between father's status and daughter's perception of him:

| | | FATHER: | |
I WOULD DESCRIBE MY FATHER AS:	DIVORCED	DECEASED	AT HOME
warm and loving	20%	64%	43%
good to mother	3%	60%	43%
special	17%	52%	41%
tender	8%	47%	24%
indifferent	32%	3%	18%
weak	35%	10%	18%
irresponsible	52%	6%	8%

When considering these categories, it becomes clear that women whose fathers died idealized their fathers; those who lost their fathers to divorce felt most negative toward the male parent.

As documented throughout the professional literature, and coming as no surprise to anyone observant of human behavior, there is a marked connection between a girl's perception of her father and her attitude toward men:

If father is perfect, all other men must pale in comparison— even as the self-doubting girl suspects that all men are too good for her.

If father is lacking in admirable traits, so then must all men be, even as the self-doubting girl suspects that she elicits these shortcomings.

As we have seen, the mechanisms for relating to men are quite different, as are the attitudes the daughter brings to them. But whether father died or left home, whether he is the object of devotion or of scorn, it is the shadow of his presence that keeps his daughter safe and emotionally separate from that gender that might duplicate her failure.

M. Esther Harding, a disciple of C. G. Jung and so an advocate of the presence of the masculine and the feminine within us all ("animus" and "anima," in Jungian terms), could be referring to this shadow when she speaks of the "Ghostly Lover . . . a living reality to every woman." Particularly during adolescence,

Harding feels, this fantasy lover assists the young girl in feeling comfortable with her dawning awareness of the opposite sex, playing ". . . a necessary part in the psychological changes of puberty."

Within the fatherless girl, however, this masculine consciousness—or fantasy father—overstays his usefulness. Rather than becoming an integral facet of the well-rounded female personality, he asserts dominion over her. He becomes the leading player in the emerging romantic drama, isolating her from the real world of boys and men. At the point where he withdraws attention from, and diminishes, reality, the "Ghostly Lover" becomes a menace.

Though Harding is not writing specifically of girls without fathers, she makes note that ". . . the Ghostly Lover is occasionally personified in the memory of a dead or absent lover." From our discussion thus far, it is easy to see the applicability of this concept.

> It is as though [the girl's] acquaintances have an unseen rival whom they must surpass before they can hope to win her attention. As time goes on the developing woman may forget her fantasy . . . But that does not mean that her problem is solved. The Ghostly Lover has fallen into the unconscious. He is not conquered or dispossessed. He is still the Beau Ideal, the Prince Charming, before whose attractions all other men seem insignificant. He is invisible, but his presence can be inferred from the reactions of the woman who possesses him or, rather, who is possessed by him . . . This unseen hero may show himself only through the woman's depreciation of real men. But this depreciation is proof of his presence in her unconscious as a criterion.

Thus the absent father may be seen to function as the "Ghostly Lover," fetching some of us on Friday nights in the guise of a heavenly star; pushing us to pursue, then dismiss, male attention.

Haunted by our inability to hold him, we yet hold on to his ghost. He is the first man we ever loved. Relinquishing him as a romantic object would be a major step in our development—as it is for all girls. But when he is not there to help us through the adjustment, we can remain stuck in our unrealistic attachment to him.

Since a shaky self-image and a growing awareness of boys are generally acknowledged as hallmarks of female adolescence, it is not surprising that these closely connected phenomena become the primary areas of anxiety for the fatherless girl. While her observedly awkward approach to the opposite sex may be the most common manifestation of her anxiety, there are other ways in which her lack of self-confidence is acted out.

Delinquent behavior in teenagers is often attributed to father absence. As noted in Chapter Four, Anna Freud was the first to recognize the correlation in both sexes, and according to our study, fatherless women did indeed report a higher incidence of having given their mothers "trouble as an adolescent" than did women who grew up with both mother and father.

An additional characteristic of discontent among adolescent fatherless subjects was described as follows: "Among young adults . . . those from divorced backgrounds are significantly more likely to report symptoms of poor physical health, often assumed to reflect higher levels of individual stress."

Stress is a natural part of adolescence, which itself may be perceived as a time of loss. Mirroring in many ways the earlier period of separation from mother, it requires that the child gather all her confidence so that she may step boldly into adulthood. This is rarely done gracefully or with ease.

Fear and guilt taunt the instincts away from home and mother, even as the adolescent insists on her desire for independence. Hence the battles and tension we associate with that stage. Certainly, a participating father's presence—as during the separation-individuation phase—can go a long way toward facilitating the child's passage toward adulthood. A single mother, by comparison, often presents a confounding obstacle.

How can we leave her? How can we leave her *alone?* If only father were here, we hypothesize . . . reinforcing his position as "Ghostly Lover" and enabling us to further delay the final farewell to our dependence on him. At a time when we are mourning parental ties, our yearning for him becomes that much more intense.

Pseudo-mature, we couldn't enjoy the spontaneity of childhood. Now confronting the future, it is the child and all her insecurities that we must face.

*

Though early loss is consistently regarded as more traumatic than later family disruption, many theorists are investigating what may be an equally significant time of loss: adolescence itself.

Just as daughter requires father's presence to dispel romantic fantasies in early childhood, she needs his reassurance when her fantasies are beginning to be directed elsewhere. She is stepping out, as it were, from the protection of home and into a world largely dominated by fathers. A paternal pat on the back can convey that she is ready for the transition, that she will succeed in that outside world, that she is appealing, capable, viable.

The separation of which we speak, however, must be perceived as the adolescent's own choice. It is a gradual, painstaking process occurring in a highly sensitized person. If father, the champion of her endeavor, suddenly withdraws, the effect can be devastating. Not only is her worth as a female called into question; her developing ability to control her environment is thwarted. She was aspiring toward an independent identity—but not this quickly. Just as she was beginning to feel comfortable with her new power, comes this stark reminder of her powerlessness. What did she do wrong?

Anger, frustration, loss—natural components of her age—may overtake the newly father-bereft adolescent. Yet her determination to act grownup usually reigns. She'll "be there" for mother, repress her own neediness, and probably forestall her true development toward maturity in the process.

For Ann, the turmoil of adolescence became a way of life. She was thirteen when her father died suddenly of a heart attack, and the "shock" of his death continues to reverberate through her outgoing, gregarious personality.

She was born and raised in British Guiana, a third-world country where family, not television, was the center of existence in the 1950s. Her father was a "quiet, peaceful, family man," who set the tone of the household. Clearly, he was Ann's hero and champion.

"He was a proud man, a great man," she rhapsodizes. "He was tall and slim and he had a lot of style. He always looked so good when he dressed up, and he always smelled good.

"My mother always had something to complain about. She was much more aggressive than he was, but he kept everything peaceful. And, of course, he would spoil me. When I'd want something and my mother wouldn't give it to me, I'd go to him and he'd say, 'Oh, let her have it.'

"I remember when I was about twelve, my mother took me shopping because I had this wedding to go to. I was dying for a pair of those Queen Anne heels that were in at the time, but she insisted on buying me these socks with lace around them, and shoes with a strap across the instep. She insisted on dressing me in frills, and I was so upset I cried all the way home.

"As soon as I got home, I went running to my father and he said to my mother, 'What's wrong with you? Let the girl have the shoes she wants.' So an aunt of mine came over and got me the shoes I wanted. See, he could always get her to do what I wanted, and it was wonderful."

In this classic example of a mother / female-adolescent battle, it was the father's support of his daughter's need for independence that prevailed.

"When he died, the bottom just fell out. We buried him, packed everything up, and moved into my grandmother's house. We had a large family, and they were very helpful. Everybody made sure that my brother and I had what we needed.

"But my mother went to pieces, literally went to pieces. She didn't know what to do. She just sat around feeling sorry for herself and grieving instead of going on with life. It was like she just wanted to drown in her sorrow, and she has still not recovered, not even now.

"I was just in a state of shock. It was like God had hurt me and I couldn't understand why. I needed my dad; why did He come and take him away? And what was going to happen to us?"

Thirteen and busy with growing up, Ann responded to her loss with a fervent desire for independence, and fashioned a life that she feels is quite different from what it would have been had her father lived.

"I felt this hunger for life, for experience, for growth. I had to stand up and be my own person, fighting my mother every step of the way.

"She started coming on real strong, crowding me, doing things that she said my father would have done, but it was her. I'd feel this emptiness inside me because I really had nobody to go to. Everybody was on my mother's side, and if she said no, it was definitely no. And I'd figure this wouldn't be happening, I wouldn't be punished or disciplined, if Daddy was alive. He knew how to get her to relax, he could convince her to take it easy. I probably would have never left home if my father was alive. I would have gotten married there and I would have wanted to give him grandchildren. But the more fussy and demanding my mother got, the more rebellious I became. I couldn't get caught up in her needs, so I had to act very, very independent.

"She used to make us go to his grave and she'd stand there crying and carrying on and saying, 'You wouldn't believe what these children are doing to me.'

"So, yeah, I had to be independent and grow up fast. Of course, I see thirteen-year-olds in America today and I realize what fast really is. But, by Georgetown standards, I was growing up fast. I knew that I was capable of making things happen, of a certain strength that was unbelievable compared to my girl-friends. And I made one vow to myself: I was going to get out of there. I was going to leave Guiana and go to England, Canada, or America. That was my dream, and I spent a lot of time by myself, just fantasizing about it. I was going to live in a big city and be single. Living a life like in the movies. Above all, I didn't want to get married. But don't fool yourself, I had a lot of boyfriends.

"When I got to sixteen, I started having an attraction for older men. They were smarter and wiser and they could help me with my growth. Younger men expect you to meet them halfway, whereas with older men, they just take over and do. I felt an urgent need for that kind of male authority—and I still do. I just find myself more comfortable with somebody older. They're so much easier to relate to, because they've already grown up."

When acquaintances learn about the subject of this book, they frequently, and with undisguised confidence in their psychological acumen, ask if fatherless daughters are attracted to older men. The readiness with which they allude to "father figures" is testament to the recent proliferation of "pop psychology"—which may be appreciated here in *both* its literal senses. Yet the assumption that fatherless daughters seek father figures turns out not to be substantiated by our study.

Very few of the women I interviewed were currently involved with older men, and the fatherless daughters in our study were less likely to be attracted to older men than were women who grew up with fathers. Similarly, the latter group showed a preference for men who are "brighter," "assertive," "dynamic." Fatherless women want their men to be "tender," "protective," and "kind." They are not nearly as interested in typically masculine characteristics, such as athletic prowess or financial success, as they are in the more subtle validation that a caring and thoughtful man can provide. Yet, among fatherless daughters, there did emerge one group to whom "stronger" and "older" men *are* appealing: those who lost their fathers during adolescence.

Perhaps these women, like Ann, remain interested in "growing" and "changing," and doing so under the approving eye of an older man. Meeting a contemporary "halfway" might demand a maturity and commitment they're not willing to take on. Indeed, women who lost their fathers during adolescence, more frequently attracted to older men than any other group, were also least likely to say that their relationships are "strong and long-lasting."

Explained Ann, "I was hurt when my father died, and after that it would take a lot to hurt me, because that was a pit hurt—a hurt that went to my deepest core. I've never had a man treat me bad and I've never really been hurt by any guy. I just don't let it happen.

"There was one guy in San Diego—I loved him so dearly, I don't think I could ever love anybody as much as I loved him.

But I had to get a lot of things out of my system. I was going through a phase where I was a player, I liked to play and I wanted the excitement of a new date, a new boyfriend, so I ended it. I ended it. I didn't want to make that commitment, and I didn't want to hurt him the way I had hurt Don."

Don had been Ann's passport out of Guiana. Eleven years her senior and an undercover agent for the United States whose overseas assignment was coming to an end, he proposed, and she saw her dream of "getting out from next to my mother" coming true. They became engaged, he returned to his home in Seattle to set things up, and Ann started packing.

"My mother went crazy. She didn't want me to leave home without being married, but for me the marriage wasn't the urgent thing. I just wanted to get out of the country. By then, Guiana was an independent republic, and severe economic problems were setting in. A lot of people started leaving.

"Don paid my ticket and everything. I stopped in Toronto to stay with a girlfriend for two months, and it was like a butterfly was let out of a cocoon. All of a sudden, I'm out of my mother's house, I could sleep out, I could sleep late, I could drink, I could smoke, I could go to clubs. I could do as I goddamn well pleased. It was like a freedom that I never even imagined and I OD'd on it. When I finally got to Seattle, I was a totally different person from the girl Don had left in Guiana. The last thing I wanted to do was set up house. I wanted to go out and hang out, just hang out."

Ann wanted Don to wait while she got all of this "growing" out of her system, but he wasn't interested. " 'I don't need that. I'm not looking for a daughter,' he told me. 'I'm looking for a wife, and I don't think you're ready. I can't sit around and wait while you grow up.' So he went on his way," Ann concludes the episode, "and I went on mine."

"Her way" was a series of business ventures, relationships, and exercises in "freedom." At times she was homesick and would call her mother for comfort. Yet just when she was beginning to feel at home in her adopted country, and her financial status was uplifted by a successful restaurant which she and her brother were operating, she sold everything and moved to be with the man from San Diego whom she loved so well but would ultimately leave. By her own admission, she was almost thirty before this impulse to "move," to "grow," to "change," began to ebb.

In her mid-thirties, the robust Ann exudes energy. Like an earth mother in overdrive, she welcomes her interviewer with warmth and ready responses, the lilting accents of her native country flowing quickly and exuberantly even as she describes her more reflective aspect.

"I think about my father a lot," she tells me. "I do a lot of deep thinking, retracing my life, what it would have been like. I know I would have been able to go to him and sit down and talk to him and he'd know what I'm talking about and he'd really relate to me and he'd appreciate me and he'd be proud.

"There are so many things I want to say to my father and I didn't get the chance, because at the time I didn't know I wanted to say them. At that young age, I didn't have anything to say to him. I was always begging for something, asking for something. I never went to him to say, you know, 'Tell me about life, tell me about your life, Dad.' We never got to really talk, and that's what I've missed the most.

"Everybody's got a little corner of them that nobody else knows, and I feel that that little secret soul inside me—my little diamond, as I call it—my father would have understood."

For the past several years, Ann has been living with a man who is eighteen years older than she. The attachment suits her because Tom "doesn't interfere" with her need for independence. "He lets me be me. And I have good soul talks with him, the types of talks I could have with anybody who could be my father. He is wise, but my father is really, really wise."

Perhaps Tom's "wisdom" is best illustrated by the indifference to marriage that he shares with Ann. "I don't want to get married at all," she matter-of-factly asserts. "I don't ever want to be that dependent on anyone. You can move fastest when you're alone. If you want to change or if you outgrow the person you are with, you can do it easier without the marriage commitment."

Adamant at thirteen about her desire to leave home and grow up, Ann continues to resist a permanent home, because it would imply that she is grown up. That final acceptance of her age would demand a separation for which she is not yet ready, while her persistent high regard for the value of nonconformity allows her to maintain her profound attachment to her father.

Free and independent as she presents herself, she wanted to make a point of noting that "All the good things that have happened to me have happened because of the force of my father. He's around, watching over me, and making things go right."

Seeing our mothers crumble, or losing them to stepfathers or the workplace after death or divorce, fatherless daughters adopt a grown-up stance whose precariousness begins to be felt in adolescence. At the precise moment that attaining true maturity is the age-appropriate impulse, we find ourselves face to face with the neglected child within; she has been revitalized by the very events—our new relationships with men—that were meant finally to silence her. For, in seeking male approval, we are reminded of the pain of father's rejection, and of our unresolved attachment to him. We are not yet ready to grow up, because we have not as yet finished with childhood.

Saying good-bye to our parents, a task of adolescence, calls forth the pain of loss that fatherless daughters have for so long tried to repress. The degree to which we acknowledge and exorcise that grief will have a direct bearing on our ability to succeed as adults.

> Ever since this world began,
> There is nothing sadder than
> A one-man woman looking for the man
>   that got away.

Not unlike the thwarted lover of the Judy Garland classic, we must recognize that the man that got away—in our case, father —is gone for good. However much his absence has affected us, we must focus our sights not on a quest for his love, but on the reality of its loss. And then we can move on.

PART FOUR

THE WOMEN WE'VE
BECOME

TEN

IT'S THE CHILD
THAT MAKES THE
WOMAN

Self-Image and Others

The profound effect of childhood events on personality development was appreciated long before Freudian theory burst upon a dubious world. "The childhood shews the man," wrote John Milton in 1671, "As morning shews the day." An event as shattering as father loss shows the woman. Regardless of all other variables, the inescapable reality is that she has attained adulthood having been deprived of a key relationship in childhood. A healthy expression of mourning, a strong, sensitive mother, a surrogate father—these may have been crucial elements in helping the girl adjust to her loss, yet growing up female and fatherless necessarily conveyed a unique perspective on herself and the patriarchal society of which she was to become part.

The world of childhood is largely a female realm. From the kitchen to the playground, and then in the schoolroom, we are guided by the figures and voices, the scents and sensibilities, of women. Father is a gift, a remote authority whose evening arrivals deliver us from the maternal bond, his encouragement suggesting our own possibilities in that other world: the world away from home and mother.

Gradually, as we go through adolescence, men become a

more visible part of our daily lives. Some of our teachers are men, and boys increasingly emerge as the objects of our most fervent wishes. We are stepping out of a female into a male society, where fulfillment will depend to a large extent on male acceptance.

The transition, reminiscent of the female Oedipal crisis itself, is a harrowing one for all women. For fatherless girls to become women demands singular courage. Men are strangers to us, yet their approval is more prized for its past elusion. Now in a world where we must admit and ingratiate men, we are simultaneously tentative and eager, up against the myriad ways in which we have been shaped by father's absence.

Nearly half the women in our study agreed that losing father was the most significant event in their lives. Only 14 percent felt their lives would have been the same had father been there. Though the older women seemed happier than the younger ones (suggesting the proverbial healing effect of time), the notable number of responses from women in their fifties, sixties, and seventies attests to the long-range importance of father loss in a daughter's life.* As illustrated in our findings, every aspect of her existence has been colored by that early dark rejection.

". . . The effects of father absence on females may find its most important evidence in the lives of mature women," wrote E. Mavis Hetherington at the conclusion of her article on fatherless adolescent girls. This, then, is the woman that emerged in our study, and whom you may recognize as wife, friend, lover, daughter, colleague, mother—or yourself.

Compared with women who grew up with both parents, fatherless daughters were much less likely to describe themselves as "extroverted," "aggressive," "impulsive," "dynamic," "flirtatious," "self-confident." We are a cautious lot—controlled, serious, and guarded.

We are less secure than other women about our body image, seeing ourselves as less "attractive" and "feminine." Given this comparatively inferior image of ourselves, it is not surprising that we are *much less* demanding of others. Moreover, the way we feel about ourselves translates into diminished expectations

---

* The mean age of the women in our study was forty-two.

of all women. As we saw in Chapter Seven (table on p. 133), this overall disenchantment with the female gender may be a result of our anger toward our mothers. Our fathers weren't there to help us to feel good about ourselves, and our mothers' perceived inadequacies highlighted our low opinion of ourselves/them/other women.

We enjoy sex nearly as much as women from two-parent households, but are more likely than they are to "prefer cuddling." We are much more attracted to "tender" than "assertive" men. And unlike women with fathers, we value kindness over excitement in our mates. We are fearful of the unexpected; perhaps that is why we are much more likely than other women to doubt whether we'll ever be able to love a man totally.

Inexperienced, yet eager for a place in this world of fathers, we are careful not to ask too much of it. We are determined to succeed, but dare not characterize ourselves as "ambitious." A subdued profile is more suitable to our needs; as long as we are inconspicuous, we may be safe from further rejection.

The above conclusions were drawn from an overwhelmingly white, heterosexual sample. Based on the study conducted for this book, there is little evidence of a connection between father absence and homosexuality in women. In fact, as mentioned earlier, women who grew up without fathers are particularly eager for male approval.

There is a strong connection, however, between father absence and the black female experience. Indeed, father absence is almost the norm for these children. Compared to 14.2 percent of white girls under the age of eighteen, 42.4 percent of black girls were "living with mother only" in 1981. The impact of this stunning statistic on black culture—past, present, and future—has been, and (let's hope) will continue to be, a specific subject of scholarly investigation. Its far-reaching implications vis-à-vis black female attitudes are outside the scope of this study. Yet because nearly two million of the five and a half million girls currently growing up fatherless in the United States are black, some attention here is necessary.

Does the comparative "normalcy" of the experience within the subculture alter its impact on these women? How does it

affect the way in which they approach the larger culture? Only
2 percent of the fatherless women in our study were black. Yet
even their scant participation offers some insights.

May's questionnaire was conspicuous for its tenacity. Its message—that her life, had her father stayed, "would not have been
very different at all"—was emphasized again and again. Black,
bisexual, and indubitably strong-willed, she had a powerful personality that leapt from the page, a contrast to the milder
profiles suggested by most of the questionnaires.

By her own account, this bold persona has only recently
evolved. "I've always been very sure of what I thought about
everything," she said during our subsequent interview, "but I
never really put myself out front. I had to be drawn out. Now I
speak up, say what's on my mind." The open-faced, heavyset
woman, in whom it is hard to imagine timidity, decided to
become more outspoken after a humiliating love affair (a year
prior to our meeting) threatened to topple her carefully constructed self-confidence.

"The one person that I always had been sure of in my life, that
I could always depend on, was me. But with Nell, I found myself
losing control; I became totally unsure of myself and the rightness of my responses. After getting jerked around so much, and
feeling like a buffoon, I realized that the only way to keep it
from happening again was to let everybody know up front that
I'm not a fool. If you're going to maintain control over your life,
you've got to let people see who you are.

"I used to be more low-key," she continues in her slow, deliberate manner of speaking, "until it stopped working. It's like,
just when I thought my life had settled down and I was safely
away from aggravation, this sore spot acts up that won't quite
heal. It's like having an old broken bone: you are walking on it,
it's doing good, but it aches when the rain comes; it's always
there."

The heady romance was proving dangerous to her foundation, and May needed to refortify. Rather than heal the "sore
spot," she chose to fight it by making her theretofore under-
stated strength more prominent on the surface. Like most fatherless women, she thrived and functioned on control; like

most girls growing up in black America, she was not unfamiliar with the ways in which females exercise that control.

The black women in our study were markedly more aggressive than other fatherless women. Their relationships with their mothers were far less conflicted, and their self-images much more positive. Their fathers' absence, a familiar condition in their immediate surroundings, was less a strain on their self-esteem, primarily because their mothers knew how to handle it.

May's parents were divorced before she was two years old. She has not even a visceral memory of their marriage, though she knew her father from the neighborhood in her small Alabama town and was accustomed to his occasional visits to her three older siblings.

"Yeah, he was around, but I definitely grew up without a father. He sure didn't do any of the things that Beaver Cleaver's father did. He was just a nice, innocuous man. He liked baseball, he liked beer, and he used to like to get dressed up. I really don't think I ever took him very seriously, or thought that he could make a difference in my life. He made no contribution whatsoever to my growing up.

"The term 'father,' to me personally, it has no responsibility with it. You have to remember that we came from a social level where fathers didn't have much to do with their kids. Fathers worked and slept and hung out with the men. It was the mothers who did everything with their kids. It's funny, when I think about my family, I can see everyone in a state of high emotion, except my dad. The most emotional thing I can remember my dad doing is chuckling to himself when something tickled him."

No amount of probing could provoke in May any anger toward her indifferent father; her attitude toward him was one of patronizing fondness. There is no sarcasm in her voice, or bitterness in her tone, just a knowing acceptance that this is the way things are. "What can you expect of a man?" she actually says. "I know that sounds offhanded, but I really do expect more of women. I'm always more disappointed when women do stupid things than I am with men. Like, a woman should know better; but when guys do something stupid, well, they just did another stupid thing. The one time I did give a man the opportunity to make a difference in my life, he showed no desire at all to work at it."

When she was twenty-three, May married a friend she had known since high school. She wasn't in love, but the relationship was comfortable, and the circumstances suggested that marriage might be a reasonable step. "We were spending more and more time together, and somewhere along the line, we got physically involved, and so we just agreed to get married. I guess I should have known better than to let it be that serious, because even then I was the one who took care of business.

"To him, life was just one big party. He could consume beer by the barrel, he would have accidents on his motorcycle, he would get in fights. And of course, he'd always come home with these wild moneymaking schemes.

"One day, he said to me that he never intended to grow up, because then you get old. And I told him that what he didn't realize was that he was going to get old whether he grew up or not.

"Well, I ended up being mom, manager, banker. I never had anybody to help with anything. And I just got partied out."

Though not officially divorced, May and her husband separated after six years and, again, she bears no malice. "I'm still very fond of him, we see each other occasionally. He's a nice, immature man. Everybody likes him, he's a lot of fun. He just has no business in any kind of serious relationship."

If May's seriousness is an attribute of fatherlessness, and her acceptance of female authority characteristic of her background, her particular wealth of self-reliance is a result of more than the sum of these two factors. For when she was eight years old, the circumstances of being black and poor and the daughter of a single mother conspired to impose a change in her life that would require an unusual reserve of inner strength.

"My mom recognized the trend of events in the South, and the fact that there was going to be a lot of civil unrest, so she decided to get us out. We moved to Sacramento, because my oldest sister lived there with her family. The neighborhood was very mixed, and it was amazing to me to have white neighbors and to go to a school with white kids.

"Being the new kid in school was very hard. As a matter of

fact, we moved so many times that year—I went to four schools in fourth grade—that I was always the new kid, the fat kid. You feel every possible negative in that situation. You don't have any friends because you haven't been there long enough, and everything you do is closely scrutinized. They're always waiting for you to screw up. I guess that's why I've never tried to be part of the in crowd. I'm my own crowd.

"The one and only time that I can clearly remember feeling the lack of a father was that year in fourth grade when Father's Day came around. Of course, like everybody else, I made a Father's Day card, but I remember feeling embarrassed because I didn't have anyone to give it to, and I didn't want to tell anybody, not even the teacher. I don't even remember what I did with it. You know, you're not good at sports, you can't do this, you can't do that, you don't have any friends, and then, bingo, here comes Father's Day. And you haven't even got one of those. One more thing that I couldn't do, didn't have, or was left out of.

"But see, even when things got real rough for me, it was never my father that I thought about or wished for. When I needed somebody, it was always my mother. 'If Mom were here, this wouldn't be happening, everything would be fine.' Believe me, I worked very, very hard on Mother's Day projects."

Mrs. Hanes wasn't around because the only work she could find in Sacramento was live-in housekeeping. From Sunday night to Friday night, "I didn't have my mom. It was thought that I would stay with my sister, but after a few months, it was clear that she didn't want me there. So here I am, in a new city, a new school, and my mom has to find a new place for me to live.

"So she meets this woman in the neighborhood, says she'll give her room and board, and off I go living with somebody I never saw before. And my mom is away all week, comes home weekends, away all week, comes home weekends. Then things calmed down at my sister's, so back I go, changing schools again, of course. Then I'm kicked out of my sister's, and have to live with more strangers, go to another school. And through all this, my mom is working five days a week at someone else's house, taking care of someone else's kids, seeing me only on weekends.

"So, that's how I learned that the only person I can depend on in this life is me. And it's possible that I overcompensated. But when you get kicked around from spot to spot, and you're at strangers' houses, the one thing you always know how to do, well, you learn to keep a low profile. You aren't allowed to watch TV much, because it's their TV set and their kids have first shot at it. Besides, if you're watching TV and you're at my sister's house, and she gets upset about something, you're close at hand and you might get punished. So the only thing that I ever had to count on, and it was the one stipulation that my mom always had in any of the places, is that I had my own room. And that was our room when she was home on weekends. So I spent a lot of time in whatever that room was, because that was the one place that was mine. And that's what I mean when I say that I may have overcompensated, because what do you do with all that time alone in your room? You read. I read *a lot.*"

Beyond being a salve for isolation, the reward for all this reading was not immediately apparent. In fact, a few months into fifth grade, terror struck when May was quite matter-of-factly called to the principal's office. Finally settled with her "good" sister, who had recently moved to Sacramento, things were just beginning to look up. "But that morning I was scared to death. After going through all that stuff, bouncing all over creation, going from school to school and now finally settled in one, the principal calls me in, and then wants to talk to my teacher, and then talks to my mom, and then they're all in there talking while I wait outside. I was real scared. Then they called me back in . . . Son of a gun, I don't know how I did it!"

She stops talking, obviously transported back to the principal's office, hearing her fate. In the temporary lull, I wonder what further blow might have befallen her, the lonely child, who sits opposite me now, a miraculously proud and powerful woman.

"What had you done?" I finally inquire, all sympathy.

"I had gotten accelerated!" she fairly whoops. "I was put right into the sixth grade. Now, how the hell do you do that when you've been in four different schools in the fourth grade? You see, all that reading paid off." She basks in the delight of her accomplishment, the unexpected joke she played on those whose insouciance pushed her to make companions of books.

By the time she reached high school, her academic and inner strength were well established. Permanent residence in her kinder sister's home made her mother's continued week-long absences more bearable, but May remained a loner.

"I learned to cultivate personal time so that it blossomed into something I could really look at, see, and enjoy. I still relish it.

"I wasn't dating in high school and didn't have a lot of people who even cared that I wasn't dating, because they weren't asking. But I joined clubs—the art club, the thespian club—so anytime you saw a list somewhere, my name was probably on it. Anyway, somewhere in there, I became friendly with this girl, and she thought I was wonderful, and I liked somebody thinking I was wonderful. We didn't have sex, exactly, but we had a lot of fun with maybe some hugging and snuggling up. I was introduced to sex by somebody else, a guy. The physical attraction to him was sort of cursory, but I figured you gotta do it sooner or later. I liked him, he was nice, we had fun, that's it. Then he got married and I met Lorna—with whom I had my first fulfilling sexual experience.

"Since I was seven or eight I was interested in girls. I played doctor with little girls, never little boys. And when we played house, I was always the daddy. Never, as I was growing up, did I ever plan to be married. I was going to be a professional woman, or maybe an artist, but I never even thought about marriage."

Nevertheless, following her two-year affair with Lorna, May did marry, with what she considers the predictable results already described. With the breakup of her marriage, she retreated into the safety of her cherished solitude. Working as an executive secretary by day, she would on an evening venture out, "cruising everything: that's a nice-looking guy, that's a nice-looking girl. I'd appreciate it, I'd recognize it, but that was all. I was not, definitely not, looking for an emotional involvement.

"Well, after a few years of this, I agreed to be introduced to someone that a friend of mine had been talking about, someone he thought I'd like a lot. We met, and I liked her. And she, well

she came out of the chute like a bull at a rodeo. She was everywhere at once. I was wooed, I was pursued, I was courted and
flirted with. I got roses sent to my office, I got balloons delivered
to my door at seven-thirty in the morning.

"It was like being awakened from a deep sleep. You want to
wake up, but it's hard to wake up. I wanted it, I didn't want it. In
the course of a few months, she had avowed deep and undying
love and while I wasn't consciously buying this package, it was
sure nice to have all this thrown at me.

"So, I thought to myself, 'You don't believe this . . . do you?
You know this is nuts and it can't possibly be true . . . can it?
But it sure feels good and why not go ahead; you've got control
over things . . . haven't you?' So I stepped in, and that was all
she needed. She had me by the hand and it was like watching
kids play pop the whip at the park and I was the last kid on line.
I was all over the place. I was up, I was down, I was ecstatic, I
was hurting. The caress and the jab, the caress and the jab.
Accusations, apologies; fury, flowers. I never knew what the hell
was happening, what I had done wrong. She was always getting
angry, out of the blue, and I never knew why. The one thing I
did have sense enough to recognize, finally, was that I was
bleeding, and when you're bleeding and the Band-Aids don't
work, it's time to call in the paramedics."

The self-sufficient, self-reliant pillar of strength, crumbling,
went into therapy. It was brief, but long enough to reveal to
May that the wound was an old one, sustained at the hands of a
volatile sister and schoolmates who made fun of her—while her
mother, by necessity, tended to others. Like so many girls who
"grew themselves up," May had succeeded for a time in denying the pain, but now, in the grip of a volatile relationship, the
wound was once again beginning to throb. Rather than confront her reopened vulnerability, however, May elected to ap-
ply a fresh, less penetrable bandage. She terminated therapy
and became more resolved than ever to be, first and foremost, a
woman in charge.

Yet there lingers a disturbing rub. "I have always intensely
disliked having to commit myself to stating sexual preference.
In fact, that was the one question I had trouble with on your
questionnaire. After giving it a lot of thought, I finally checked

'bisexual,' because I have had relationships with both. But at this time, I am gravitating towards women, and I have no problem with being called a lesbian.

"Certainly, on an emotional level, my strongest feelings have been for women. But, more important, if I ever get involved to the point of living with someone again, I'm resigned that I'm going to be head of household. And if I'm going to take the responsibility, I want the title, and that's simpler with a woman.

"Ideally, I would like to find someone who's going to give me equal time and equal support. But I'm going to be a little bit equaler." She smiles mischievously at the prospect, yet reveals visible uncertainty at the immediacy of her prospects.

At thirty-four, and just getting over a self-image crisis, she has reestablished her boundaries by defining them in the way she presents herself. Strong, steady, articulate, she is highly regarded at work, progressing through night-school classes, being sought after as an inspiring speaker by gay rights organizations. She is content, for now, to live alone, and takes pride in the nicely decorated, muted colors of her suburban apartment, just down the street from where her mother worked as a domestic.

"It was one of her last jobs before she died." The voice continues calm, composed, even as her eyes accommodate an instant pool of tears.

"The house was right here on the boulevard. I pass it every day when I go to work. It was a real big deal working in a house like that, and I sometimes think, gee, if my mom only knew when she used to work there that I'd be living right down the street one day . . ."

The deprivations of May's childhood—father, mother; constancy of home, school, friends—perhaps atypical in circumstance, explain the resilience adopted by generations of black women. Neither mothers nor daughters are unfamiliar with female-headed families, the older women providing progressively more effective means for survival: Mrs. Hanes, forced to place her daughter with strangers, insisted on a private room.

Now comfortably ensconced in home and job, May has reaped the benefits of resourcefulness—her mother's and her own. Yet even her house on the boulevard strained under the turbulence of a romantic love affair.

It would seem to be romance, more than any other experience, that threatens the fatherless woman, her highly prized control ceasing to be a matter of black and white. Here her guard is grayed, overcast by the shadow of her first lost love. In other areas of her life, she can hold down the fort to protect the child within. But, once enticed by someone who may love her, she swings open the gate, allowing admittance, she knows, not to a stranger, but to the familiar form of vulnerability.

Perhaps she actively seeks those who will not stay, intuiting that, like a lesser earthquake, their disruptiveness and the painful feelings they evoke will relieve pressure on the larger fault.

*

Upon first considering the questionnaires, I had been surprised to find that the composite fatherless woman in our study steered away from hurtful relationships. Instead of the romantic disappointments to which I would have assumed her prone, she revealed marked good sense in the characteristics to which she was attracted.

Yet, didn't we need to relive pain and rejection as a way of coming to terms with childhood abandonment? Weren't hurtful attachments a preoccupational hazard of father absence? Certainly research, and my own experience, would have so indicated.

Further examination of the questionnaires dispelled my earlier surprise. The fact that the composite fatherless woman in our study is forty-two years old is significant, because an older woman would seek safe, rather than risky, relationships. Experience and more years of mourning have helped her integrate childhood loss. Younger women have not yet come that far.

As reflected in the study, fatherless women under the age of twenty-five do have a penchant for disappointing romances—not only because of the relative lack of experience common to all young women, but because of the specific experiences attendant on father loss, major among these being disappointment, abandonment, pain. Until we recognize the rightful object of our disappointment—father—what more appropriate arena for venting unspent anguish than that created by love for a man?

As young women interacting with men, we may reenact the climactic scene of childhood: over and over again, the heroine's life is altered by the rejecting protagonist, and at long last, she allows herself to grieve.

Like May, I had been driven into therapy by a tortuous love affair. It was a twisted, twisting relationship, an obsession, during my early twenties, from which I could not disengage. I knew that his feelings were far from reciprocal—he told me so quite plainly—but didn't that make him much more attractive? And weren't the despair and the agony of rejection somehow sweet in their familiarity? A year before, I had been immersed in a similar situation, and also, farther back, as a teenager. Introspection soon illuminated the pivotal experience in my childhood as the source of my fixation, but still my days were haunted by it, and my nights uninterrupted by sleep.

"Knowledge has no power to lessen pain," Charlotte Brontë writes. In fact, I needed to feel the pain; intellectual understanding was not sufficient to the task at hand. The sadness that my husband was to perceive several years later lingered, but through those earlier unrequited loves, the hurting, abandoned three-year-old was finally able to suffer loss. Without my even realizing it, much of my adolescence and early adulthood were taken up with mourning. Had I been deprived of those seemingly depraved attachments, I probably would not have been able to accept the love of the man who is my husband.

I do not mean to prescribe masochistic relationships as an antidote to father absence. Mourning at the time of loss is far healthier, and prevention is the most effective cure for repressed mourning. Only 18 percent of the women in our study, however, were encouraged to express their feelings about their fathers' absence at the time it occurred, so that the vast majority of us had to ignore, or control, or delay grief until such time as another abandoning man forced it to erupt.

As fatherless daughters, we have little trouble recognizing such a man, for if men are alien to us, the rejecting type is less so. He is familiar in the feelings of self-doubt that he evokes, and in his ability to seduce and disappoint us by turns.

Various studies have concluded that people with a low self-concept gravitate to negative experiences, and the young fa-

therless woman is no exception. According to our findings, the
adolescent anxiety reported by Hetherington would seem to
persist into early adulthood, for the fatherless women in our
study who were under twenty-five were less self-confident than
their older counterparts. They were much more likely to be
"anxious" and "insecure," and felt much less "feminine." The
correlation between low self-confidence and a penchant for
relationships that reinforce it is illustrated by the fact that our
younger subjects were more likely than older women to become bored with men who appreciate them, and showed a
greater propensity for those who were "unavailable," "older,"
and "bad for me."

Fortunately, these hurtful relationships are not usually self-
perpetuating. In fact, they serve a very useful purpose. It is as
though some unconscious internal mechanism were at work,
prompting the insecure woman to seek reinforcement for her
low self-regard, so that she may experience grief, and finally,
achieve separation. For until she has separated from her father,
it is not a long-term relationship that she is looking for. Such a
union would threaten her standing with the man that got away.

It is the goal of mourning, we will remember, to bring about
separation from the loved one. This cannot occur before we feel
the pain and accept the fact of loss. Now an adult, functioning in
all probability for the first time in a male milieu, the fatherless
daughter may at last, through the ever available services of the
unwitting Don Juan, bring mourning to the light of day. And
having grieved, she need no longer seek those who would make
her miserable. She has achieved a greater degree of separation
from her father, and thus, as reflected in the more sensible
choices of our older women, she is available to men who will be
good to her.

The fatherless daughter will still think less of herself than
women who grew up with fathers—one doesn't ever outgrow
the trauma of childhood abandonment—yet, in her case, it is
better to have loved and lost than never to have admitted loss at
all.

Just as men reinforce our low self-esteem during early adulthood, they continue to be a major source of validation for the

self-confidence we have acquired. To be known by a man, and
approved of by him, is our dearest wish. That is the legacy of
having been left—disapproved of—by father.

A common misconception about fatherless women is that we
dislike men: that we resent their inability to live up to father, or
that we assume that all men, like our fathers, will be ultimately
disappointing. In fact, because of our ongoing need for their
approval, we tend to glorify them. If anything, mothers/women
are the more likely objects of our ambivalence, as fathers/men
remain idealized.

The one exception to this overall positive attitude toward
men reportedly exists within the black community. Just as these
women were found in our study to be more aggressive than
their white counterparts, and just as their relationships with
their mothers were found to be much less conflicted, the preponderance of father absence in their backgrounds has evolved
into a generalized distrust of men. Researchers Henry B. Biller
and Stephan D. Weiss conclude:

> . . . Negro girls, in families where the father is absent or
> ineffectual, develop derogatory attitudes toward males.
> There is a tendency in lower-class Negro families with
> somewhat different sociocultural backgrounds, to down-
> grade males in terms of their seemingly social and eco-
> nomic irresponsibility. These negative attitudes are trans-
> mitted by mothers, grandmothers, and other significant
> females, and unfortunately are often reinforced by obser-
> vation of, or involvement in, destructive male-female rela-
> tionships.

May's comment about not associating the word "father" with
responsibility comes to mind, as does the earlier query about
the effect of so much father absence on black women's approach to the larger society. Surely, as fatherless women reared
in deprived economic circumstances, they have every reason to
feel cheated by, and hence defiant of, both men and society—
and they do. "There is only one person I can depend on in this
life," May said repeatedly, "and that's me."

In their attitudes toward themselves and others, daughters of widows and daughters of divorce share the characteristics already mentioned, and thus emerge as a group distinctly different from women who grew up with fathers. The following table will illustrate, however, that the childhood experience of household dissension, and the subsequent rejection by a *living* father influences a girl differently from the sudden disappearance caused by death.

| | FATHER: | | |
I WOULD DESCRIBE MYSELF AS:	DIVORCED	DECEASED	AT HOME
extroverted	42%	38%	53%
aggressive	35%	25%	41%
impulsive	44%	39%	51%
dynamic	34%	26%	49%
flirtatious	32%	26%	47%
self-confident	59%	53%	67%
feminine	65%	58%	73%
ambitious	51%	41%	69%
demanding of others	42%	34%	53%

As these numbers show, parental divorce promotes a feistier, more assertive attitude than the irreversibility of death. Though still much more closely aligned to the overall low profile adopted by fatherless daughters—and even more inclined to describe herself as "anxious" and "insecure" than women whose fathers died—the woman with the hope, however dim, of reconciliation, was less given to quiet, passive acceptance of her fate. Consequently, she participates in the world with just a little more daring.

Our expectations of others are shaped by the image we have of ourselves. And this image is molded by experience. The girl who lost her father at an early age, owing to death or divorce, was gravely disappointed by the first man she ever loved. As a child, she interpreted his absence as a personal rejection; as a young adult, she is likely to struggle with the rejection through her relationships with men.

Regardless of the success she has found as an adult, she will always be apprehensive of abandonment, for that is the key event of her childhood. She will participate in the world with just enough caution to keep herself safe, alert to the potential disaster of total commitment. Central to the fulfillment she will find as an adult is the willingness with which she has allowed the child to venture from her guarded boundaries. To be strong is not the same as to not feel.

*

"It was a discomfort that was not to be relieved, like an itch in an amputated limb." The woman who has never allowed herself to feel, participates in life through an ever present numbness that is characteristic of a dull chronic ache. She recognizes the pain but has chosen anesthesia over treatment, a preference that will influence all her choices, as well as her demeanor. One third of the women in our study revealed that they had not yet accepted the loss of their fathers, and the result is perpetual grief, mourning casting its shadows over all their days and nights.

Immediately upon opening the hotel room door, Jayne encircled me in an embrace. We had never met, but her gratitude assumed familiarity. Except for her therapist, none of her acquaintances had ever addressed the significance of father loss, and until hearing of this project, she had endured her sorrow very much alone.

The initial effusiveness belied the monotone that was to characterize her delivery, however; within moments after settling into conversation, her eyes and speech modulated to a decidedly low key.

She began by talking of depressions that have visited her over a lifetime, of going through the motions of activity without the emotions. As a wife and mother, she had fashioned an apparently fulfilling existence, but all the while, the purpose of her busyness was to squelch feeling. "I kept trying not to feel any more pain, but of course that meant not feeling any of the good stuff either.

"I guess I've always been serious, even as a kid, but I was also very successful. My image of myself in sixth grade is that I was super: I had the lead in the class play, all 'excellents' on my report card; I had a lot of friends and everything was just great. I don't think I've ever felt as good about myself as I did that year."

It was during her exemplary sixth-grade year that her father's lung cancer was diagnosed, and the juxtaposition surely taught the eleven-year-old the inherent dangers of feeling good about herself—a lesson she has carried into her mid-forties.

"Of course, I didn't even think about the possibility that he might die; I didn't understand what death was. But I knew it was serious, because I was allowed to visit him in the hospital, and I had been told that that was something that was not ordinarily done. You know, that usually you had to be sixteen to visit someone in the hospital.

"I remember thinking that if only he weren't in his pajamas, he wouldn't be sick. I wanted to tell him to get dressed and come home. He didn't look sick.

"Right after graduation, I was sent to stay with my aunt, and on July 3, I was abruptly shipped off to the camp that my younger brother was at for the summer. My mother was crying on the telephone as she said good-bye to me, but I figured that was because she was worried about my father, and that she would miss me."

Jayne learned the true reason for her mother's tears about a month later. If not for the daily letters she was writing home, it might have taken longer.

Her father had died on July 3, and the doctor had advised against telling the children until after the summer. But the unanswered letters were piling up, leading her distraught mother to finally succumb to her wiser instincts. She appeared at camp unexpectedly and told her daughter the truth.

"She told me that he went away, and for an instant, I thought she meant that he had gone to Canada—he had been promising that we would take a trip there—so I thought he had gone without us. But then, of course, I grasped what she was telling me, and I remember silently counting the days, all the days that he had been dead and I had been writing to him. I tried not to be angry at her, I knew she had kept it from me for my own good, but the reality of the deception was overwhelming.

"I remember I did cry, but then the weirdest thing happened: the bell sounded to signal flag-lowering, and I actually went. I mean, there I was, standing among my bunkmates, the bugle playing taps, putting all my energy into trying to stifle the sounds emanating from my chest. And I think that pretty much characterizes what I've been doing ever since.

"I've always felt some kind of shame about my father's death: about his dying, and about my feelings about it. I never could talk to anyone about it, because my mother and I were always at odds; she and my brother got along and I was more my father's child. I remember even saying to her that I should see a psychiatrist because of the depressions I was experiencing, but she wouldn't hear of it. She thought that would mean I was crazy. She even hinted that I was so much like my father's family that I would end up having a nervous breakdown, as his sister supposedly had. So naturally, I came to believe that if I expressed the feelings that were rumbling inside me, I'd end up crazy in a hospital.

"I think one of the ways my mother dealt with my father's death was by convincing herself that he hadn't been a good husband. She became a perpetual complainer, blaming practically everything on him. She even told me that she had found a note in his drawer from another woman, and that that had helped her to get over him. Of course, I didn't want to know that, and to this day, I hope it wasn't true. You see, my mother had some serious mental disturbances as a result of childhood illnesses, and I really don't think that she was ever totally well. We never got along, and I think that's another reason I had trouble mourning my father.

"I had a tremendous amount of guilt, and really thought it was my fault that he had died. You know how children are, the fantasies they sometimes have. Well, I remember wishing once that my parents were dead, and that if I were an orphan, everyone would feel sorry for me and give me everything I wanted. Well . . . so . . . well, I guess I once wished that. Only it was probably directed at my mother."

Her eyes fairly glaze over. Though she says that therapy finally succeeded in alleviating her guilt, it is apparent from her halting presentation that she is still not totally convinced. Her mother's death, during Jayne's twentieth year, only strengthened her suspicions.

"Even before she died, I was in a very depressed state. I
carried my father's death around throughout my adolescence.
It's like I reached a peak in sixth grade, and then, after that
summer, everything changed. I was a loner in junior high
school, and my relationships with boys were terrible. I never
felt comfortable with them; I was shy and felt very unattractive.
I always liked people who didn't like me, or who liked me only
for a while and then I would hang on. I think, more than anything else, my relationships with men have been dramatically
affected by my father's death. I am absolutely terrified of rejection."

Jayne's lack of self-regard, fostered by guilt and the denigra-
tion of feeling, led her to pursue hurtful relationships. By
"hanging on" to a rejecting man, she was enforcing her own
punishment and allowing herself to approximate the grief she
dared not manifest, lest she be deemed insane.

Though the edict against mourning was exaggerated in her
particular case, her continuing dread of rejection is not unusual
in those whose grief remains unspent. "Childhood parental loss
to which emotional response has been curtailed leaves the individual liable to massive reactions of panic in circumstances of
loss or threatened loss of a love object in later life," a panel of
mental health professionals concluded. As the events leading up
to the termination of Jayne's marriage will illustrate, panic in
the face of loss led her to believe that a painful relationship was
preferable to none at all.

"I think when I married my husband, I also married his family. It didn't matter that he was cold and unaffectionate, because, first of all, I didn't know that I deserved anything else,
and I needed a large family to compensate for the fact that I
didn't have one.

"Even as I was fulfilling the duties of wife and mother, my
lifelong bouts with depression would reappear. But then I
would just throw myself into activity. I think I always felt that I
had to be an achiever, to prove that I was worthwhile. I was
afraid that if I ever gave in to my feelings, I'd stop functioning
altogether.

"I was pretty much able to repress everything until my husband's job necessitated relocating. Without the company of his

family, I began to feel very isolated, and the depression became impossible to ignore. My husband's attitude was that I should take care of my problems and not demand any help from him. So, finally, at thirty-five, I went into therapy.

"I found an excellent analyst and commuted an hour each way to see him, but if I attempted to share any of my insights or feelings with my husband, he'd back away. Whenever I'd reveal anything, he'd say, 'Oh, I thought you solved that already.' He just couldn't relate to the idea of a deprived childhood, or to emotional pain. He wanted me to take care of things with the therapist, not bring anything home. The more I reached out for emotional contact, the angrier and more remote he became. When he finally told me he wanted out of the marriage, I was devastated.

"Of course, his distant attitude had always upset me, but I assumed that if I was unhappy, it was because there was something wrong with me. I had no idea that I could expect warmth from my husband, and of course, my mother had convinced me that my emotional needs were not reasonable.

"I guess the thing that made it toughest was that my kids knew he wanted out before I did. For months, I had this gnawing feeling that something was going on that I didn't know about. When he finally did tell me, I became hysterical. We had been married for twenty years, and I'd much rather have stayed in a terrible marriage than be left alone. I only came to accept it after a great deal of suffering. Also, I began to write, and that has been very helpful.

"We've been separated for three years, but it's still hard to be alone. The kids are off to college, and I'm frequently afraid. Therapy has been invaluable, and I've come to realize that there are people out there who can be affectionate, and that what I want isn't so unreasonable. I guess I still have trouble thinking I deserve it.

"I would like to think that I've worked through my father's death, but on certain levels, I think I haven't. At least, after eight years of therapy, I know he isn't coming back. But still, I'm always afraid that the men I love will die."

We end the interview with my repeated assurances that we'll remain in touch. It is evident even in the way that she "hangs

on" to me that Jayne has a long way to go in accepting separation. Plagued by the fear that "things are going on that [she]
doesn't know about," she has accepted the fact that her father
isn't coming back, but she still expects that no one else is either.
Perhaps it is that haunting childhood fantasy for which she must
perpetually repay; or maybe it is her emotional need itself, she
suspects, that causes people to disappear.

Unless thwarted by extreme circumstances—such as those
brought about by Jayne's mother—most fatherless women, with
age, come to terms with their loss. This is illustrated by the
improved self-image articulated in our study, as well as the
prudent romantic choices that evolve from it. We no longer
seek men who will hurt us, or cling to men who are hurting us,
because through their earlier services, we have grieved and
separated from father—we are free to love and be loved. Mis-
treatment ceases to be the better part of rejection.

Yet our expectations are shaped by experience. If we no
longer gravitate toward disappointment, or prefer emotional
indifference to the cessation of a relationship, this is not to
suggest the reparation of childhood abandonment. It is a chasm
whose echoes resound not only in sickness, but in health, frequently reopened by the occasion of marriage: according to our
study, the worst fear of married women who grew up with
fathers is that their mates will take them for granted; the worst
fear of the married fatherless woman is that her mate will die.

In many instances, this expectation of doom becomes a palpable aspect of the fatherless daughter's marriage, a chink in her
armor that will continually threaten to sever the bond. She lives
under the shadow of loss, and this she and her husband learn
almost immediately. For even as she walks down the aisle toward her betrothed, she may very well be thinking of the man
who is not there to give her away.

ELEVEN

A MATCH
MADE IN HEAVEN . . .
OR ELSEWHERE

Attitudes
Toward Marriage and the Family

The emotional turmoil of our young adult years frequently yields to a period of more external concerns. Having struggled awkwardly through our initiation into male company, we emerge better equipped to function in male society, more confident for having allowed ourselves to be vulnerable. Our hurtful relationships with men have served their purpose, acquainting us with the pain which, had it remained smothered, might have blighted us as well.

Now the independence and determination learned in childhood—temporarily shaken by long-silenced feelings—reassert dominion over our choices, encouraging us to participate actively in the world. We still desire the kind of male validation accessible only through love, yet we are creatures of habitual self-sufficiency and may operate from a position of greater strength now that we don't have to expend so much energy pretending to be strong.

Thus, in the midst of calamitous, if psychologically liberating, romances, we continue to pursue practical objectives, and gradually the rewards and excitement of participation in the adult world override as yet unresolved psychic dilemmas. We become absorbed in forming friendships and fashioning a viable identity for ourselves, buoyed by the receipt of hard cash in exchange for our capabilities. The childhood grief so recently reawakened by romantic entanglements, though hardly eradicated, is for a time superseded by the challenge of entering society. As girls growing up without fathers, we were bred to accept responsibility; now we may exercise that training as real—not pseudoadults.

According to our sample, fatherless daughters enter the work force earlier than those with two parents. We are not, in retrospect, happy about this. In fact, one of the most prevalent remarks I encountered during interviews was the regret of not having gone further in school. Had father been there, we imagine, his intellectual and financial backing would have promoted greater opportunities and higher education. Whether this speculation would have been supported by fact is impossible to say, yet the evidence of our numbers is clear:

	FATHER:	
HIGHEST LEVEL OF EDUCATION:	ABSENT	AT HOME
High school	17%	4%
Some college	32%	15%
College graduate	24%	37%
Postgraduate work	25%	43%

Women with two parents did have more education than we did—yet 80 percent of both groups are now working. And it is only in hindsight that we wish we had gone further with our formal education.

Immersed in the universally appreciated delights of establishing herself in the adult world, the fatherless daughter, like all young women, is focused on the present and planning her future. The deprivations and disappointments of her past belong to a younger, less resourceful person than herself; there is no place for them in her busy, bountiful agenda. Everything is going quite well for her. She is out on her own and feeling good about it.

In the majority of cases, work, friendships, and the exuberance of young adulthood are soon crowned by the greatest prize of all: she is going to be married. She is going to live with a man, be part of a couple. She is going, after all these years, to be normal.

The state of wedlock has loomed like a promised land, and now, thanks to the forces that bring people, however troubled, together, the fatherless daughter has been granted entry.

Yet, as she walks toward the altar, she treads on unsettled ground. Absences thought forgotten accompany her down the aisle, and doubts about her worthiness are tucked in with her trousseau. Is she prepared to live in harmony with a man? Does this commitment forever separate her from her father? Is she willing to accept that separation? Above all, what does she know of the male-female love relationship? Only that it ends.

"To me, being a daughter had been an apprenticeship," wrote Irene Mayer Selznick on her thoughts before marriage. Most professionals agree that our behavior during marriage is informed by what we observed in our parents' behavior; that the intimacy of married life recalls the nature and quality of our earliest intimacy (that which we shared with our parents); that conflicts unresolved with our parents are played out with our mates; and that mourning is revived when a new relationship begins.

Margaret, whom we met in Chapter Three, first saw her future husband on the afternoon of her graduation from junior high school. He was standing in the line next to hers.

Theirs was the time-honored courtship of high school sweethearts: periods of bliss punctuated by hurtful jealousies, all to the accompaniment of jukebox favorites.

"He was a very romantic character, and I really liked that," she tells me at the kitchen table in their house near the beach. I can see that she enjoys this line of questioning, her brown eyes twinkling on those early days. "I felt very proud that he was interested in me, because he was very popular at school. A lot of people liked him, and it made me feel special to be the object of his attention. He was generally very gregarious—you know, the class cutup—but with me, he was very warm and tender. As I think about it now, it was just the kind of nurturing I needed from a man, even such a young one.

"My father had been dead for five years and I was still going through life feeling numb. His approval had been very important to me. It's like he was someone to come home and bring achievements to, the audience that everybody in the family performed for. As a teenager, I longed for a man to look upon me with approval, to tell me I looked nice, things like that.

"Of course, I kept my needs bottled up inside. My mother didn't want to hear any of it. In fact, for some reason, Larry was the only person I could open up to. With him, I talked about my father a lot. And he understood. On the morning of our wedding, he sent me a telegram and it said, 'Love me as much as you loved your father, and I'll be the happiest man in the world.'

"As I think of those high school days, I can see that I expected much too much from him. We would hit a point in which he wasn't meeting my needs and I would go through terrible times. I was very dependent on him and at the same time terrified of the attachment. We broke up and got back together a lot over the years.

"In fact, now that I'm a mother, a lot of those same conflicts are coming up. I've had to acknowledge how much risk there is for me in putting Larry in the category of father. Fathers can die or disappear.

"I went through the same thing before we got married. I had such a strong inner feeling that we ought not to marry. It was almost like a taboo. Again there was that powerful sense of risk."

As verified by the theoretical literature, and illustrated by countless other women's experiences—including my own— marriage is a risky proposition for the fatherless daughter. At stake is a lifetime of carefully constructed defenses. Toppled though they may have been by previous romances, we were able to regroup in privacy. We could thrash and rail and ruminate alone, going out to face the world with our ever present aura of control, until soon even we believed in our mended fences. Now capable of accepting love, we are reminded of its ramifications: for the woman whose father died or abandoned her, love and loss are inextricably bound. And in the state of wedlock, private fears risk exposure.

Yet, if marriage is vital to female legitimacy, it is for the fatherless daughter the symbol of validation. She embraces her marital status with the relief of having arrived, even as she unconsciously awaits the impending arrival of childhood trauma. It is worth the risk, she ultimately decides, even the risk of exposure.

"We were married right after college, and that first year was really tough for me," Margaret continues. "I tried instantly to be this wonderful wife who cooks and cleans, but it didn't feel right. I was also working a full-time clerical job which I hated. I didn't like the way I was treated when I was working in secretarial jobs. I felt very prestigious as a student, and now everything was different.

"Larry treated me differently too. I think he had some notions about what husbands were supposed to be like, but for whatever reasons, he was much less romantic, less attentive.

"I was not happy at all. I remember, I cried a lot that first year. Overall, I just felt very lost and very angry."

After a year and a half, Margaret's dissatisfaction reached a crisis point and the young couple mustered enough of the romantic spirit to try to save the marriage. It was an adventure that they needed, it was decided, so they packed up and moved to England.

Listening to her account of the excitement and energy they found on foreign soil, I remark that it must have been a happy time for her. She smiles wistfully.

"You know, I can never look at any period of my life and call it 'happy.' Honest to God, there's really always that inner suffering. But it was a good experience. It was fun to discover a new city, strike out on my own and make new contacts. There was a renewed feeling of independence and growth.

"There were still hard times in the relationship, where I felt I wasn't getting enough attention. That's what it always comes down to, I guess, that lack of attention. But whenever I felt I wasn't being appreciated, I would look for another man. It would always be another man who would give that to me, make me feel special. Nothing sexual or romantic, but a man to talk to. And that would help sustain me."

Three and a half years later, and back in the States, an attentive male came in the form of a therapist. "I was so needy and so jealous of Larry's friendships, male or female, and, of course,

therapy was *the* thing. Everybody was talking about it. I didn't
know yet that I had all this repressed mourning to deal with, but
the recurring depressions were becoming intolerable. I'd go off
for weeks in this woeful state, feeling sorry for myself. At first,
my therapist served the purpose of being a man who would
listen to me, and it was wonderful. I felt like I had a father again.
It took a lot of work and a lot of years to get to the true source of
my pain.''

As has already been recorded, Margaret's years of therapy did
indeed go beyond transference to the gut-wrenching experience of grief. The day-to-day dependence on a man that she
loved had been the catalyst of her recognition that there was a
severe underlying problem; and her choice of an ultimately
trustworthy mate had provided the security to confront that
problem squarely.

Like so many other fatherless women, Margaret had been
distracted from psychic pain by the uplifting successes of young
adulthood, which in her case comprised college and courtship.
Her early marriage had delayed for a time the youthful exuberance of newfound independence that she was to discover in
England. Yet it did fulfill its recognized capacity for bringing
childhood trauma to the surface.

Fifteen years and a lot of therapy later, she has managed to
maintain a solid and loving relationship with her husband, but
only by loosening her grip on the man that got away. She is not
entirely liberated from the sense of impending disaster that
haunts most of us—that our husbands will suddenly abandon us
or die—but her anxieties have been put into a workable perspective.

"Whenever I find myself feeling insecure about the permanence of our relationship, I deal with it by fantasizing a plan of
action. I don't see myself as the helpless victim any more. It's
like I'm no longer retreating.''

*

"Because each of us has within himself a 'child of the past,' "
Dr. W. Hugh Missildine writes, "marriage requires that four—
not two—persons adjust to one another . . . In marriage the
child you once were expresses his needs, wants, attitudes, ways

of behaving and desires *more fully than in any other situation.* "* Indeed, the fatherless daughter has a singularly forceful
need to behave like a child, having been denied, or having
denied herself, the opportunity during childhood.

One of the first acts of marriage is setting up house, a presumably comfortable place to come home to. It would seem inevitable, as Dr. Missildine suggests, that the child in us all would be
reawakened in the process, recalling, perhaps trying to
reproduce, the home from whence we came. With two people
—or, as he puts it, four—thus engaged, conflict would also seem
to be inevitable. It is not surprising, therefore, that the first year
of marriage is a notoriously difficult time for most men and
women.

For the daughter of a single mother, home was not characterized by comfort. To be sure, it may very well have been comfortable, but it was both more and less than a port of safety. If
mother was a widow, home may have housed a vague but pervasive suggestion of grief; if father left following marital dissension, there was the anything-but-vague reality of overt hostility.
Whatever the cause of father's absence, daughter's experience
of home was at least in part furnished by disappointment, guilt,
and the pretense of maturity. And prominent among the fur-
nishings was that nagging corner conspicuous in its unfillable
emptiness.

Arranging this table, placing that lamp, outfitting her kitchen
with wedding gifts of china, the inner child of the fatherless
bride struggles to avoid repetition by filling that space. Implicit
in her childhood home was the knowledge of failure, and this
may be her last chance to disprove its overwhelming impact.

With neither home nor relationship to try to live up to, the
fatherless daughter finds herself, once again, very much on her
own. The attentive companionship of her husband may temporarily assuage reawakening doubts, but this is the least reasonable time to rely on their slumber. Her expectations of the
healing effect of marriage will themselves place undue strain on
the relationship, and she persists in testing it for lack of faith.

* Emphasis added.

She had pinned her hopes on the one thing she can't count on: the permanent love of a man.

As the realization of her predicament dawns, so too does her most decisive encounter with mourning. Marriage has eradicated neither her father's rejection nor her chronic feeling of failure as a woman. In the shelter of her husband's arms and in the home that they have fashioned, she hasn't found protection from the past; rather, she is confronted with its reappearance. A man is loving her, and nothing is quite so threatening. Men who love you, and whom you love, leave. Through the medium of marriage, the man that got away, carrying his message that love breeds loss, has returned.

In one of the few professional studies addressed to the influence of father loss on women (conducted by E. Mavis Hetherington), it was found that even in our choice of partner, we are setting up this disquieting confrontation:

> Freud has suggested that girls continue to relive their relationships with their fathers through subsequent interactions with men . . . Freud may be right, *but only for father-absent girls.†* Girls with absent fathers maintain their childhood image of their fathers. Daughters of widows perceived both their husbands and fathers as having many more favorable characteristics than most men. Daughters of divorced parents viewed their fathers, husbands, and most men as having predominantly negative characteristics . . . The appraisals of the husbands on the basis of interviews, tests, and direct observations to some extent confirm the wives' opinions . . . These [father-absent] girls seem to select mates who were similar to their images of their fathers, whereas girls from intact families were less constrained by their relationship with their father in their choice of husband.

As indicated in Chapter Ten, the fatherless women in our sample were comparatively healthy in their ultimate choice of mate (though they continued to fear for their mates' health). It must be noted that, indeed, *within* the fatherless group, daugh-

† Italics mine.

ters of divorce had a greater tendency than daughters of widows to pursue destructive relationships. Yet, as illustrated in the table below, women who grew up with fathers had an even greater tendency in that direction.

I AM MOST OFTEN ATTRACTED TO THOSE WHO ARE:	FATHER:		
	DECEASED	DIVORCED	AT HOME
unsettled	5%	11%	14%
indifferent	2%	10%	8%
unavailable	15%	20%	31%
bad for me	7%	13%	22%

Unlike the subjects in Hetherington's study, and in contrast to the small numbers above, 75 percent of our fatherless sample listed "kindness" and 72 percent listed "tenderness" as the traits to which they are most often attracted. For all their apparent good sense, however, the married fatherless daughters in our study were more likely than the married women from intact homes to report "significant problems" with their husbands, and more likely to be currently divorced or separated.

Hence, though conclusions may vary concerning whether or not we actively seek out men who are like our fathers, that we find ourselves using marriage to work through our loss of father is evident. And regardless of the kind of men we seek, we do seem to seek marriage itself: one third of the women in our study who grew up with both parents have chosen to remain single, as compared to only one fifth of the fatherless daughters.

We gravitate toward marriage as a symbol of normalcy that has for a long time eluded us. But it is also a symbol of security, and perhaps within the relative safety of being part of a couple, we feel that we have permission to acknowledge vulnerability. We may, however unconsciously, seek the security of marriage so that we may plumb our insecurities.

Another explanation for the fatherless daughter's attraction to marriage is offered in Jill Johnston's autobiography. Though very much aware of her homosexual preference, Johnston married to appease convention. But beyond that, she, perhaps like many of us, married to appease the palpable conflict with her mother. Through marriage, Johnston writes, ". . . a total rupture with her was averted. By shifting the arena of conflict just when it threatened to become overt, we preserved the semblance of harmony required to hold things together." A similar function was served by becoming a mother herself: ". . . I was free to be something besides her daughter. The purpose of the marriage has been fulfilled: between us stood two new relatives who were promising receptacles for her attention."

Eager as she is to be married, the fatherless daughter commences marriage with no realistic foundation on which to base her expectations. She is hoping that her husband will rescue her from her past, when in all probability his mere presence will remind her of it. If she is to thrive in her newly acquired status as wife, she must at last give up the ghost of father.

She must learn that commitment does not inevitably lead to disappointment, that interpersonal conflict is resolvable, and that not all men will leave her.

She must gradually become comfortable with the occasional manifestation of anger, as well as the casual exchange of simple affection. Particularly if she lost her father at an early age, she has had no firsthand experience of either of these; in fact, both affection and anger pose a very serious threat.

The psychic demand on the fatherless bride is indeed a profound one, requiring the simultaneous integration of something old and something new. As one paper cogently observed, she must ". . . mourn one close relationship and celebrate another at the same time."

Our penchant for, and unrealistic expectations of, marriage are mirrored in our attitudes toward motherhood. According to our study, fatherless women were more likely than women from intact homes to have children, and less likely than other mothers to feel secure about the success they have achieved with their children.

Nearly half of the fatherless group, as compared to 35 percent of the control group, reported "significant problems" in their relationships with their children. And, considering the comments of these women in light of the voluminous literature on motherhood, it would seem once again to be our fear of loss that creates much of the dissatisfaction.

Part of being a mother is enduring—and facilitating—separation. Knotty though the process may be, we must allow the
umbilical cord to be severed. For women with intense separation anxiety, the task is particularly strenuous.

Unlike the marital bond, which (one hopes) strengthens
union, the mother-child bond is meant to strengthen independence. Our success as mothers may even be measured by the
extent to which we have fostered autonomy in our children. We
love them so that we may lose them to their own secure and
productive lives—a poignant reality to women trying to con-
quer their dread of losing loved ones.

In their attempt to maintain this love relationship, many fatherless women overprotect their children. Yet, in trying to
shelter them from harm, they are nurturing a harmful dependency against which the children quite naturally rebel. The
mother's submissive response to her children's rebellion per-
petuates anger on both sides, so that neither she nor the children are encouraged to grow up.

If, as many mental health professionals believe, our childhood
experiences of attachment and separation are the very bedrock
of our personality development, we can readily understand
why being in control is of such vital importance to the fatherless
daughter: her childhood was shaped by a loss over which she
had no control. Even before she herself becomes a parent, she
has been striving to win back that control:

• Immediately after the loss of her father she controlled
her emotions.

• As the daughter of a single mother, she aspired to control childish behavior.

• As an adult, she greatly values her own self-control, and
is perceived by others as being in control.

Now a mother, she is likely to equate parenthood with being
in control of someone she loves. She enthusiastically embraces
this opportunity to eradicate a lifelong frustration, the result
often reaping more disappointment, more frustration.

"Loss, like the air, surrounds us always," says Dr. Saul L.
Brown, "its consequences enduring through the lives of the

grieving children themselves and later in the lives of their children."

One of the most frequent laments I encountered in questionnaires and interviews concerned fatherless daughters' doubts about their femininity. Had they grown up with father, many women believed, they would be "softer," "more comfortable with men," "more successful in their relationships." Nowhere are these capabilities more acutely tried than in the areas of marriage and motherhood—the latter historically perceived as the ultimate achievement of femaleness.

A conscientious lot, most of us rise to the challenge, getting married and having children—according to several studies— earlier and with more emotional investment than other women. Being part of a couple, and then, part of a "normal family," means a great deal to us. Yet, according to our study, we are more likely, as both wives and mothers, to encounter "significant problems."

*

Though she has been married three times, Roberta states flatly that she has never had a close relationship with a man. "They baffle me; they are the enemy. I can never be honest about myself with a man. Yet I don't feel I can survive without a man in my life. My last marriage, which lasted for twenty years, was terribly stormy. He died. The first two ended in divorce." Recently, the fifty-seven-year-old widow has begun to give some thought to the origins of her alienation from men.

Her father, a farmer, left her mother when Roberta was sixteen days old. "I don't remember when I realized I simply had no father. I was never encouraged to express any feelings about it. It was a subject not to be discussed, except by my grandmother, who had a deep and abiding hatred for him, which she expressed often and forcefully.

"He lived in the same small midwestern town in which I grew up. I saw him frequently on the street, but he never acknowledged or spoke to me. It was known that he lived with another woman, which absolutely was not done in that town in those days, but to me, he, and everything about him, was just like a vague shadow that was part of my background.

"When my older sister was terribly sick with scarlet fever, he never even inquired about her. This made a lasting impression on my five-year-old self."

Roberta's mother remarried when the girl was eight. She describes her relationship with her stepfather as "cordial." He was kind but unconcerned. Her mother, on the other hand, was concerned to the point of suffocating her children.

"She had had a terrible time those years in the twenties and thirties, and I think the multiple disappointments—losing her husband and struggling financially during the Depression— made her terribly fearful and insecure. She would never allow us to do anything for fear of our getting hurt. We couldn't ride a bicycle, or skate, or swim. She was obsessed by the possibility that we'd be injured. I know she was only trying to protect us, but she made our lives so pitifully limited."

As a result of maternal overbearance and paternal indifference, Roberta remains uncomfortable with emotional commitment. Men, though perceived as necessary to her legitimacy as a woman, are not to be trusted; and even her feelings for her children present difficulties: love is, for her, an enigma.

"I love my children, but I try to maintain distance from them. They're grown now and I want us to be friends, but I don't think we should be emotionally responsible for each other. Whenever something sad has happened to any of them, the pain is so great I can't bear it. I try to appear strong and aloof, but really I have wanted to run.

"My therapist, whom I've been seeing for two months, tells me I'm fine the way I am, but I know that I am deeply troubled. I allow myself to be used by men, like the one I'm seeing now, but in reality, I don't even like men very much. Everyone sees me as aloof and strong, but I am so pitifully eager to just feel like a part of the world.

"I grew up with a feeling of shame about my background, and I guess I'll always wonder how much my father's rejection affected my life."

At the age of fifty-seven, Roberta is striving to match external control with internal strength. Accustomed to being perceived by others as independent and confident, she is ready to try to substantiate her persona, and in the process of acknowledging the hurting child inside herself, she uncharacteristically allowed us to hear her cry for help.

Susan, also the product of a disrupted childhood, makes a striking contrast. Even as she describes a lifetime of deceits and disappointments, she maintains her stance of self-determination, not only for the benefit of the listener, but just as surely for her own sense of well-being.

(Unlike the casual presentation of most of the questionnaires, Susan's was typed, neat and tidy. At first perusal, the document looked just so, yet the pages had inadvertently been restapled out of order. Similarly, she mentions repeatedly that she is the one who ends most of her relationships. The facts, like the pages, demand reshuffling.)

Susan is in her early forties, an administrative assistant, twice married, twice divorced. Each of her marriages lasted four years, with, as she puts it, "a twelve-year hiatus between the two.

"I had assumed that the second marriage was made in heaven and would go on until we both died of old age (preferably on the same day)." Her husband, however, who was nine years her junior, told her one day that "he'd never really wanted to get married, that he always wanted to live alone." This was his third attempt at matrimony.

She attributes part of his dissatisfaction to the presence of her daughter, who was fifteen at the time of the marriage. "I'm a very relaxed mother, very easygoing. Although my daughter claims that I was overprotective when she was a child."

Describing both marriage and motherhood, Susan tries to assume a lighthearted, optimistic attitude. Yet the circumstances and the observations of others, which she is forthright enough to include, suggest acknowledgment of her confusion. Certainly her childhood experiences would encourage her to cling to someone she loves, such as a daughter or a husband, even as she tries to minimize the intensity of her emotional commitment.

She was born into the affluence of Hollywood, circa 1940. Her father, a successful cinematographer with a major studio, had died when she was an infant. "I was too young to remember any of the details. But when I was old enough, my mother told me he had died during the war.

"Eventually, when I was around six or seven, a little friend told me that my parents were divorced and my father alive. When I asked my mother why she had said my father was dead, she explained that to her he was dead. And there was no further discussion.

"In grammar school, I was jealous of the other children who had fathers. Even finding out that he was alive didn't ease my jealousy, because my mother told me that he never liked children."

Susan's jealousy extended to the man her mother was planning to marry when the girl was seven. (She later learned that he had been her mother's divorce lawyer.) "I was terribly worried that they were going to send me away to boarding school, because he had a daughter in one. My mother kept assuring me that she wouldn't allow it," but one can readily understand why Susan had reason to doubt her mother's word.

The issue soon became moot, however, as her mother's fiancé died of a heart attack just prior to the wedding date.

At seven years of age, Susan had discovered that her "dead" father was very much alive. Indifference, not cruel fate, had been the cause of his total absence from her life. It is only natural that she expected her new father to be at least as indifferent to her. As if in answer to her fears, the threatening man was, quite beyond question, eliminated.

That she developed into a woman cut off from her emotions is not surprising. In regard to her biological father, she was thrown a curve to set all feeling into imbalance; and her secret feelings toward her prospective father must have seemed unbearably powerful, given the end that he met.

In her attempt to keep her life in order, Susan has made some serious errors of judgment. Like many fatherless women seeking to undo or redo the past, she has mistaken safety for love, and marriage for safety. Both her husbands were poor choices, both precipitated the dissolution of the marriage, and in each case, she resisted. Yet she is the one who does the abandoning, she proclaims; she is in charge; she sets the agenda. "I don't *like* the fact that my husband left me," she says, and then adds in the singsong defensiveness of a scared little girl, "But I know I can exist perfectly well on my own."

In their forties and fifties, respectively, Susan and Roberta are the products of divorce. As such, their long-standing ambivalence toward marriage and children may very well be attributed to the possibility, however remote, of reconciliation with their fathers. In their choices of husbands, they not only echoed the negative choices of the daughters of divorce in the study quoted above, they were also setting up failure, their own divorces, and hence availability for father.

Tess, at thirty-four, has attained earlier psychological understanding. Her father died and, as noted in Chapter Six, the permanence of death usually promotes acceptance of the separation at an earlier age. Yet intellectual insight is merely the beginning of resolution.

"Therapy has helped me understand the choices I've made as an adult," says Tess, "but now I must live with or find the courage to change those choices." Currently on her second marriage, Tess fears that she is not in love with her husband.

"Regardless of how hard I work to establish an emotionally intimate relationship with him, I am afraid the truth is that I married him for safety and security, not intimacy. As desperately as I have always needed to be part of a 'perfect' relationship with a man, I have also been afraid of risking love. Perhaps that is why I have married men who would be nice to me and take care of me but whom I really had no strong emotional feeling for."

Tess's unrealistic expectations of marriage are matched by her unrealistic notion of what love is, the latter having been shaped by an idealistic relationship of which she has little memory. Throughout her life, she has been told by numerous relatives that she had an incredibly close relationship with her father: a man who died before she was three; a man, it was explained to her, who had "gone to live with God"; a man who, to her fantasied recollection, was a god.

The majority of Tess's portrayals of her father are prefaced with "I don't remember, but I've been told . . ." Obviously, the myth of a perfect relationship was very important to her, indeed necessary to sustain her through childhood. For her mother, she says, is a distant and cold person, given to neither affection nor warmth of any kind.

"I've been told that I was very much a Daddy's girl. Whenever possible, I was in his care. He was my primary source of love. My mother has never denied the fact that she is not a loving person, and I've been told that she would often send me off to work with my father when she was losing her temper with me. So he was really mother and father to me. Under the circumstances, his death must have been doubly traumatic. I'm sure I wondered why my only loving parent had chosen to go and live with God. Why had he abandoned me?"

In her relationships with men, Tess has tried to emulate this love of which she has so often been told. No human man, of course, can live up to a god. But Tess suspects that in her two husbands, she purposely selected men who wouldn't even come close, that she shied away from passionate attachments to protect herself from rejection. She was also, it must be added, remaining faithful to her perfect father.

"It is only in the last two years that I have begun to recognize the overwhelming influence of my father's loss and the feelings of rejection it evoked in me. I was always frustrated by my continuous yearning for a perfect love and the fact that I just couldn't get it right. Even with my children, I created a distance, and I'm beginning to think I was just afraid of getting close. With the help of therapy, I've made tremendous progress with them, learning to be more consistently sensitive to their needs, to give of myself emotionally. But I believe that for some time to come, I will be dealing with my fear of risk.

"The relationship with my husband is improving, but I have no way of knowing what will happen. I certainly don't want to hurt him or the children, so perhaps I have to take responsibility for choices I made before I understood my motivations. At least now, my problems are external ones, and I prefer those to the 'hungry' little girl that was inside me, always seeking affirmation in other people's eyes."

Before she was able to acknowledge the impact of her father's death, Tess thought that love had been eluding her, when in reality she had been eluding it. She avoided getting close, "getting it right," for fear of reprisal: If you dared to live with someone whom you loved (like father), he would inevitably abandon you. Only a cold and distant relationship (like the one with mother) remained constant. Understanding the pattern, she is trying to correct it, the first step being an elevation in the regard she has for herself. She is beginning to acknowledge her own worthiness.

If she has succeeded in building her own self-esteem, however, she has yet to cut her father down to size. Like all our fathers, he was merely human; only in recognizing this may we grant our loved ones their mortality.

Compared to 14 percent of women from intact homes, one third of the married fatherless women in our study have been married more than once. Whether father was indifferent or superhuman in his ability to love, he left a void that we feel compelled to fill. Lacking both experience and observation of a successful male-female relationship, we grapple with our misconceptions until, finally, many of us do get it right.

Almost certainly, the early years of marriage will be particularly stressful for the fatherless daughter, and just as certainly, the burden on her husband must not be overlooked.

"I have this recurring dream that I am her father," one man told me. "There's always a different catastrophe, and I'm always trying to save her."

TWELVE

INSTEAD OF FEELING

Women with Wounds That Will Not Heal

It is a widely held belief in therapeutic circles that serious emotional wounds are frequently contained during the crisis that causes them, that the scars only show themselves years later, when relative safety has been achieved. The phenomenon has been observed in concentration camp victims, as well as in the combatants and inhabitants of war-ravaged localities. As long as external danger looms, we maintain an outward focus, reserving the harm inflicted on our psyches for later recognition.

Similarly, during childhood it is our tendency to mask the pain of father loss behind the stiff upper lip of pseudo-maturity. We do indeed fear fear itself, so to keep mother's love, we become brave, stalwart little people. Only later, during the deceptive independence of adolescence, do the consequences of our loss begin to emerge, becoming observable in our reportedly awkward interactions with the opposite sex. From teenage crushes to the crushed hopes of adult romance, the insecurities and doubts of a lifetime ripple through our defensive disguise until, for many of us, they surface completely in the mistakenly safe harbor of marriage.

As a result of our particular determination and the strength of the human spirit (and in many cases the grace of our husbands), the overwhelming majority of us work through our confrontation with father's absence sufficiently able to find pleasure and satisfaction in our lives. We work, get married, have children, fun and friendships, failures and successes, like everybody else.

The anxieties that characterize us are never fully attenuated, but they usually don't prove prohibitive, either.

In this chapter, we will encounter women for whom pleasure and satisfaction have continued to be elusive. Owing to factors that will soon become apparent, it was necessary for them to cope with their fathers' absence by affecting an absence of pain so persuasive as to render them alienated from other feelings as well. Like victims of a catastrophe, they sacrificed emotion in the name of survival and are only now coming to recognize the cost in human life.

Amy, a thirty-year-old social worker, was "somewhere between three and five" when her parents divorced. It was only after her marriage, however, that she felt "permission to get in touch with the loss." She is married to her first and only lover, someone she has known since she was four years old and who is himself a mental health professional. "Without the love and support of my husband, I would not have progressed to where I am today."

The third in a line of daughters, Amy remembers feeling that, because she wasn't a boy, she had let her father down. She tried to make it up to him by going fishing with him, becoming interested in sports, but even these attempts could not supersede the overall tension in the household caused by her parents' unhappy marriage.

"I remember endless nights of their arguing, leaving us in another room. One night, they came in together, woke us up, and told us that Dad would continue to live at home, but Mom was going to take us to live with our grandmother. From that time, there was just this tremendous void in my life. Mom was a very distant, cool parent. I don't recall any physical affection on her part aside from the perfunctory kiss on the cheek. I never really experienced her as being my mother. I think she wanted to be more like a friend. Despite his eventual absence, I remember Dad as the affectionate one.

"I often wonder what I'd be like if I'd had parents who loved each other and us as children. As it is, I'm so grateful to my husband for helping me work through my problems. We have a very strong commitment that only developed after *a lot* of struggle and effort.

"When we were first married, eleven years ago, I was terrified of arguments, as I was certain my husband would ask for a divorce. I used to withdraw and avoid expressing anger for fear of losing him. I feel that I've resolved that, but I'm still very uncomfortable when it comes to intimacy, sexual as well as 'cuddling.'

"I don't really enjoy sex, and I even have trouble with affection. After eleven years of marriage, I think it's getting better, but the truth, I guess, is that I don't really trust men, nor do I feel worthy of them. At least I'm not any longer obsessed by the fear that my marriage will end the way my mother's did. At least I'm capable of being angry."

A professional married woman with a child, Amy is to all appearances a thriving young adult. Eleven years of marriage have assured her that anger does not obliterate love; yet the physical expression of love continues frightening: She never received it from her mother, and her father, the affectionate one, was disappointed in her. Indeed, in the midst of trying to win him over, she lost him.

While Amy is striving to overcome alienation through the help of a relationship, there are many women for whom alienation has extended into the preclusion of a relationship. They, unlike Amy, never felt loved by their fathers, and it is that void which unites them. In some cases, father died or left before daughter had a chance to know him; in others, knowing him was confounded by indifference—and then he was gone.

Faye's father died when she was six months old. He had held an important job in the community and was revered by one and all as a very special, wonderful man. At thirty-six, his daughter is still trying to exempt every man she meets from his "saintly" example. Until she succeeds, she suspects, she will be incapable of enjoying a relationship with a man.

"Growing up without a father continues to pervade my intimate relationships," says the clinical psychologist. "I just don't like the person I become when I'm seriously involved with a man, so I avoid intimacy in favor of friendship.

"I experience myself as becoming more insecure, anxious, more vulnerable, demanding and childlike when I'm romantically involved. As a result of this toll on my confidence, I have come to avoid love relationships altogether. Until recently, I have been content with my life because it is filled with many strong and rich friendships. But something is missing.

"I find myself yearning for intimacy with a man, and I'm coming to realize that it isn't the perfect person that's going to make this happen, because he doesn't exist. I'm going to have to work this through for myself, stop running away the minute an appealing man becomes interested in me."

Betty is also afraid of intimacy. Her father died when she was eleven months old and, although he wasn't a saint, "He and my mother and sister had a good life together before I was born, and after I arrived, everything changed."

Her father contracted polio soon after Betty's birth, and died. "I have absolutely no memory of learning that my father had died. I do remember desperately trying to get around the fact that I had no memory of him. As far back as I can remember, I wanted to find him, either through memories or by dying and going to heaven, where he would be. Eventually, I stopped having these fantasies, but I still haven't totally accepted his death. I may be learning now, through therapy, to come to terms with it."

In filling out her questionnaire, Betty described herself as "lonely," "shy," "deprived," and "suspicious." She states that she is employed, but neglects to indicate what she does. A frequent alcohol user, she regards herself as "independent," yet feels she would be more "emotionally secure" had her father lived.

Like many women who were infants when their fathers died, Betty can't help suspecting that her very existence precipitated the catastrophe. Instead of allowing herself to love another man, therefore, she is loyal to her father, striving with singular obstinacy to "find him" in all her endeavors, and repeatedly finding herself disappointed.

If her suspicions of guilt are strong enough, the girl who never knew her father will have a need to punish herself so that, quite unconsciously, her attitudes and actions conspire to ensure disappointment. This is certainly the case with Betty, who at thirty-five has a most compelling reason for believing that she is culpable in the matter of her father's death.

"When I was around nine years old, my grandmother told me that my father may have caught polio from me. I was hospitalized with some unknown disease at the time that he died. I loved my grandmother very much, so when she begged me not to let my mother know that she had revealed this to me, I complied.

"I don't consciously feel responsible for my father's death, for having infected him with a fatal illness, but in a way I feel that I deprived my sister of the family life she had with my parents before I was born."

Daughter was born and the family was shattered. This is a common conclusion for the girl whose father died soon after her birth. Of course, the circumstance doesn't have to lead to serious emotional disturbances, but if her father was a "saint," or in perfectly good health until she "infected" him, it is likely that her self-image will suffer in, and thus avoid, the company of love.

For fear of confirming the final separation from the male parent, fatherless women are much more likely than other women to fear intimacy. Whether atoning for past sins or hoping for future miracles, they tend to feel some degree of discomfort with the usual manifestations of commitment. Most of us override those fears to the extent of making an outward commitment; many of us, after a good deal of struggle, succeed in honoring that commitment emotionally. Father's death during infancy is, as we have seen, one exacerbating obstacle to success; the eventual withdrawal of an unloving father is another.

Evelyn, an administrator at a large university, flatly declares that she is asexual. Divorced from her husband, who was a virgin when she married him, she is terrified of being abandoned by people she loves. To avoid this eventuality, she makes a point of being the one to end any relationship in which she is involved; moreover, she doesn't get involved very often. In tone and lifestyle, her attitude suggests distrust: her father never loved her, she says, and her overbearing mother did little to instill confidence in her worthiness.

"My father never wanted children," she begins. "My mother did. She managed to get pregnant three times, and each time my father was infuriated. He insisted the third pregnancy be aborted. But she stalled, and I was born. She compounded his anger by having three girls.

"I was almost four when my father came home from overseas. He completed his medical training soon afterwards in a city away from home. By career and inclination, he was never around much, so his moving out when I was thirteen was not a great change.

"He wasn't a cruel man. He never abused us—in fact, he rarely touched us. He fed, clothed, and educated us and left our rearing to my mother and the servants.

"But the household revolved around him. We had to play quietly when he was home. We were encouraged to speak only when we had something intelligent or clever to say. But never to argue. So, in a way, his leaving lightened my life. A lot of the strictness from my childhood was relaxed. On the other hand, as I grew older, I would see parents and children—in a park, for instance—the father playing and delighting in his child, and I would mourn.

"One summer, when I was fourteen, I saw a lot of him. He had a boat and he was readying it for a cruise and he took me with him to work on the boat on weekends. I longed to go on the cruise with him. He expressed a desire to take me, but cited my mother's refusal to permit such a thing. Then, one day, after a lot of pleading on my part, my mother gave her permission. My father was stunned. He denied ever having expressed a wish that I go with him. Of course, he said, it was an impossibility, and he accused me of lying to my mother in reporting his desire for my companionship.

"Well, call it divine revelation, or having one's eyes opened, or what you will. But I saw in that moment that my father didn't love me, had no use for me, and that I could never trust him for anything. Ever since that summer, I have seen him only rarely. Once I was married, I felt that I no longer needed him.

"When he first left, I used to tell myself that if he had stayed a little longer, I would have been able to make him love me. If I had only been this or done that he would have changed his lifelong attitude of indifference toward me. I kept asking myself where I had failed him. Even after the initial excitement of my marriage, when I had convinced myself I didn't need my father, I found myself longing for him and wishing that he would have a sudden change of heart. I kept hoping that he would call me, express a desire to see me, be with me, want to know me. He never did. And now, finally, I hope he never will.

"When my marriage ended, I went through it all over again with my husband. I longed for him to want me back. I waited three years before starting divorce proceedings. But now, thanks in part to therapy, and in part to my own good sense, I don't mind so much.

"I'm very involved with my work, and I'm feeling a good deal happier now—except when I see a father love his child."

Valerie, who was forty when she filled out the questionnaire, said that she was thirty-nine and a half when she first fell in love . . . with the "wrong person." She declined to answer most of our questions about relationships, noting that she doesn't have any. For the decade preceding her recent brief encounter with the "wrong man," she was celibate. Before that, she had been married, "but I call myself 'single.' I have never dated very much in my life, don't like it, feel uncomfortable with it."

Her father left for overseas duty in World War II two months before Valerie was born. He returned three years later, lived with the family for six months, and then left for good.

"I don't remember his leaving, but I am told that I had a severe depression. My mother was not one for emotionalism, so I probably did a good job of burying my feelings. During my teenage years, I had anorexia nervosa, which wrecked my health and body. I still haven't totally recovered from the damage I did to myself.

"When I was twenty-two, I had my first sexual relationship, and a lot of my repressed feelings began to surface. The prospect of being rejected was overwhelming, and if a man left me I was filled with grief, depression, and suicidal feelings. I went into therapy, but it was a waste of time. I've only made it this far because I've done my own shrinking—without any outside help." (She heavily underlines these last two words.)

Valerie shuns the very notion of outside help. She is afraid of it, distrustful of it, ultimately unfamiliar with it. Her infrequent relationships are selected from among the "unsettled," "unavailable," "indifferent" men that she meets, because that is what she is used to. She feels that she gets emotional support from neither men nor women, and at least for now, the part-time clerical worker can live with this accustomed isolation.

"My mother rejected me at birth, and my father was never around. I had biological parents only: no mothering from any woman, no fathering from any man. I have never basked in the glow of the love a man and woman have for each other or for me, their creation. Of course, I would like myself more if my father had stayed. I certainly wouldn't be in so much pain."

Pain, an inevitable result of father loss, cannot be moderated if unacknowledged. The girl who never knew her father is usually assumed oblivious to her loss and, in trying to please, she goes along with the deception. In ensuing years, she will almost certainly allow the pain to surface, but her ability to integrate it will depend to an enormous extent on what she has been told about the man that got away. The void created by an ever absent father must be carefully and sensitively filled if daughter is to step over and beyond it.

The tendency of mother to idealize her dead husband may lead daughter to believe herself unworthy of all men. Like Faye and Betty, she will set impossible standards for men, so that she may be protected from her suspected shortcomings as a woman.

The tendency of mother to denigrate her abandoning husband reaps similar results: the sting of father's indifference is magnified by mother's acknowledgment of it. Feeling rejected herself, she may find it impossible to offer comfort to her daughter, the product and reminder of her failed relationship.

Amy, Evelyn, and Valerie, abandoned by living fathers, received little reassurance from the female parent. Deprived of affection during childhood, they are ill at ease with giving or receiving love as adults.

The importance of the mother's attitude cannot be over-stated. In her hands rests the difference between openness and alienation, confidence and self-doubt, adjustment and serious psychological damage.

Carol was four when her parents divorced. Within six months, her mother met and married another man. "She told me to pretend that my natural father never existed. I was so eager for a father that I went along with it. I even remember, on her first date with my future stepfather, I ran to him saying, 'Daddy, Daddy.' I was very happy when they got married, but I was always afraid that he would leave. I worshiped him.

"To keep up the pretense about my father, I was encouraged to lie to my younger sister about his true identity. When she was nine, she found out that we had been lying to her, and the effect was shattering."

Despite the presence of her stepfather, Carol felt responsible for keeping the family together. "My mother is an alcoholic and a drug addict who appears to function adequately on a superficial level. As far back as I can remember, she has felt more like my child than my mother, and since I was so afraid of abandonment, I did whatever she wanted. Even my stepfather, to whom my mother is still married, used me as a companion, always complaining to me about her. When I was nineteen and left home, he cut me off, stopped relating to me altogether. It was like I was being punished for growing up.

"It wasn't until I was an adult and out of the house, that I began to have strong cravings to meet my father. I guess those feelings had always been there, but I repressed them for fear of losing Mother. Obviously there must have been a very powerful pull between them if she had to deny me any contact or even overt thoughts about him.

"At twenty-eight, I finally did contact him and, indeed, he was the charming, engaging man I had imagined, but also totally irresponsible and unresponsive to his family's needs.

"Two years later, I told my mother I had contacted him, and she drove fifteen hundred miles to sleep with him, this man she hadn't seen in twenty-one years. It became clear to me why she had denied me my thoughts and feelings about him: She was in love with him! And if she couldn't have him, neither could I."

Throughout her childhood, Carol was required to pretend that her father didn't exist. He was no good, selfish, and to even think about him would antagonize her mother to the point of possibly estranging *her* as well. Gradually, however, her mother's insistence on forgetting her father began to suggest *her mother's* continuing attachment to him. She was still in love with this "good-time Charlie," and Carol's amnesia was imposed to help *her mother* forget. With the dawning realization of her mother's needs, Carol allowed herself to acknowledge her own.

In fact, she longed for her father, fantasized that knowing him would help her to feel loved and adequate. When she worked up the courage to contact him, however, his "narcissism," and "immaturity" were inescapable, even over the phone. No, he wasn't any good; he didn't care about her; her mother was right. But her mother also drove fifteen hundred miles to see him. A lifetime of being denied overt feelings had communicated a covert lesson: men who are bad for you are irresistibly appealing.

At thirty-five, Carol finds herself consistently drawn to frustrating, destructive relationships. Like her mother, she is attracted to men who are no good for her, men whom she describes as "inadequate," "unavailable," "indifferent to me because of certain narcissistic defenses they have"—men, in short, who are like her father.

These relationships, moreover, perpetuate the self-doubt instigated by her mother's refusal to offer unconditional love. To maintain her mother's affection, Carol had to do no less than deny her father's existence. That she continues to deem herself unworthy of unconditional love is illustrated by each of her three "long-lasting relationships."

"My husband was good to me, but he turned out to be gay. After the divorce, I became involved with a seemingly strong person—he was macho, athletic, intelligent—but he could be extremely cruel emotionally. He's very narcissistic. The third relationship, of five years' duration, ended recently. I still see him occasionally. He is warm, supportive, and nurturing in some respects, but he is a drug addict, with all that that implies.

"I've been in therapy off and on for twelve years. It has helped me to stop hating my mother, to see her as a sad, hurt, angry, guilty woman with a terribly poor self-image, who feels deprived and victimized. Talk about poor self-image, I'm still working through my feelings that only inadequate men would want me. I guess inadequate men are the only ones I feel worthy of."

Becoming involved with men like her father, Carol is reinforcing self-doubt by repeating disappointment, and trying to win parental approval by simulating the dynamics of her parents' relationship. But beyond these impulses, which we have seen in varying degrees in women throughout this book, Carol's emotional adjustment is complicated by her struggle to settle one important and self-defeating score: "if she couldn't have him, neither could I."

Her hostility toward her mother, allegedly outgrown, continues to dictate her choices. Thirty-one years after being denied contact with and feelings for the man that her mother loved and lost, Carol exacts her revenge: Mother can't have him—the irresponsible, narcissistic man—but I can. See how many selfish, hurtful, unavailable partners I have attracted?

Carol is a nurse at a psychiatric hospital—which gives her further opportunity to interact with "inadequate" people. Like all the women on whom we have focused in this chapter, she is a productive, contributing member of society, neither nonfunctional nor manifestly alienated. Yet she, and the others herein described, suffer emotional wounds that continue to defy healing. Owing to overblown visions of father/men, and underground guilt and confusion—all nurtured by ill-advised mothers —the psychological damage inevitably sustained by fatherless daughters has in these women created not a scar, but an unrepaired fissure. It is a barrier that separates them from certain aspects of themselves and ensures separation from others. An untreated wound, it hurts to the touch.

As these women's backgrounds attest, socioeconomic advantages neither help nor hinder healing. Whether reared in shack or mansion, the fatherless daughter deprived of subsequent appropriate care may later reside as Anaïs Nin's "spy in the house of love." As long as her neediness is undetected, she feels safe. She may work and earn, participate to a point. But owing to circumstances surrounding the loss of her father, the effects of his absence have been more serious and more pervasive than those most of us have had to endure.

*

"At this stage of my life," one woman wrote on her questionnaire, "as I watch grandchildren born and grow up into interesting young people, I realize at times that the emotional retardation is incurable for me. Often I wish I could have the same emotional reactions that other people seem to have. But that is just the way it is, and it is alright."

A surprising number of elderly women participated in our study. Their voices, rich and expressive, reminded us that a woman in her seventies or eighties is still somebody's daughter, and that if she grew up fatherless, the loss and absence, the unknown quantity of father's love, remain a lifelong facet of her selfhood.

The quotation above may be seen as a general statement of our fate: we will love, care, interact and produce, yet always we will wonder what tenderness may have been cradled in father's lap; how would our emotional life have been enhanced had we been allowed to rest there?

Doubts about our emotional responses are common in fatherless women. All of us were, in a sense, rejected; the vast majority of us were taught to value repression; and the mothers of most of us, even as they tried to keep us close to home, depended on us to be mature from an early age. Yet it is when these conditions of rejection, repression, and pseudo-maturity are perceived as our only choices that "the way it is . . . is [not] alright." Quiet resignation turns to hapless protest, tentative attempts at closeness yield to an active avoidance of intimacy; and the far-reaching effects of father loss go from subtle breaches in confidence to serious psychic ruptures.

Who are the daughters most susceptible to a severe reaction to father loss? Those, as we have seen, who never knew their fathers, as well as those whose fathers were blatantly indifferent toward them before leaving. But age at time of loss and father's attitude prior to loss, while significant, are not the determining factors in daughter's adjustment. Rather, the nature and quality of the subsequent fatherless home, the availability of support from outside quarters, and most important, the coping mechanisms manifested by mother, inform the extent to which rejection, repression, and pseudo-maturity will overwhelm normal development.

Based on a study of thirteen adolescent fatherless girls undergoing psychiatric evaluation, two researchers concluded, "There would appear to be a positive correlation between the quality of mothering and the adaptive adjustment made by the daughter faced with paternal loss."

In relation to children, one often hears of their "insatiable urge to suck." Freud called it the oral phase, and indeed, parents try to gratify their young with a steady provision of nipples, milk, and various nontoxic suckables. Yet the infant's viability as a living creature depends on the gratification of less tangible needs as well, and again, in the areas of affection, reassurance, and love, it is the parents' responsibility to provide.

A girl growing up without a father is definitely growing up without. But this lack of male attention and its attendant ramifications, though detrimental, will become disastrous only if compounded by further rejection. Misfortune, unattended, becomes evidence to the child of her worthlessness. This conviction of lack of worth—nurtured by mothers whom we have already heard described as "distant," "rejecting,"—will exacerbate the usual toll exacted by father absence, rendering the woman incapable of accepting affection, love, intimacy.

In his discussion of parental neglect, Dr. W. Hugh Missildine asserts that "absence of attention [may become] your way of experiencing life . . . Thus, in adult life, the neglected 'child of the past' maintains the security of this familiar emptiness and prevents the formation of any deep, close relationship . . . Closeness threatens the security of neglect on which [her] 'child of the past' has been nourished."

Rejection, a sense of which is inevitable following father loss, becomes something the subsequently neglected daughter anticipates. Avoidance of relationships is the common defense. But another way of protecting against emotional involvement —and the presumed rejection that results from it—is to pursue numerous, meaningless relationships. This alternative is particularly useful for the woman intent on denying her fear of rejection and repressing the existence of pain.

There is little question that repression is one of the major components of father loss. Of the fatherless women in our study, only 18 percent were encouraged to express their feelings at the time of loss. And even now, as adults, 30 percent say that they have not as yet accepted it. As long as feelings are repressed, the woman maintains a fantasized attachment to her father that precludes attachment to others, for just as acknowledgment is a prerequisite to mourning, mourning is a prerequisite to separation.

The daughter of divorce may be furious at her father, but until she has vented her fury, either directly or indirectly, at its rightful source, a succession of disappointing men makes a useful substitute. They reinforce her low opinion of men and herself while simultaneously distracting her from the ultimate separation from father.

The woman who has yet to accept her father's death also ensures a destiny of disappointment. Until she acknowledges the negative feelings evoked by his death, her father remains a saint—a regenerated and sanctified presence—against whom a loving relationship with another would be a sacrilege. These women try to become involved with men, but alas, no one measures up.

Long-term repression may be understood as a defense against rejection. Instead of contending with the self-denigration that follows a recognition of rejection, repressed pain allows us to denigrate others. The woman pursuing shallow relationships may deny her fear of intimacy, and her doubts about herself, while at the same time avoiding the final separation from father. The men she chooses will invariably assist her by reconfirming her belief that all men are inferior ("Father's absence didn't bother me") or that all men are inferior to him. Thus, in the midst of all her human contact, the repressed/promiscuous woman is just as alienated as the rejected/isolated one. In fact, her insistent denial may be so draining of energy as to leave her severely depressed.

Of the women in our study, 82 percent were discouraged from expressing their feelings at the time of loss. Repression, we must conclude, is a major component of loss. Yet, beginning with adolescence, most of us became acquainted with our grief, and eventually exorcised enough of it to be free of its dictates. Who are the women for whom repression is the only choice?

It is fortunate that there are comparatively few, for the consequences of repression can be, literally, fatal. Joy, hope, laughter are blighted, along with anger and tears. Denial of the death—of father or of the relationship with him—may exact denial of life.

"I was the one who found him," one woman wrote. "He was blue. I told my mother and soon afterwards, I was told that he was dead. He had died suddenly, of a heart attack. My mother told me, 'Daddy went to heaven to help God.' I was only five years old and couldn't grasp the concept. I assumed if my father went to help God, he'd return when he was done.

"I come from a very religious family. A lot of relatives came over and I knew something very serious had happened. But whenever I cried, I was called a baby. From the ages of sixteen to twenty-two, I was a certified agorophobic, wouldn't leave the house. It's only thanks to many years of therapy that I am now only merely neurotic."

Children from austere religious backgrounds are frequently instructed against the indulgence of emotionalism. They must accept "God's way," honor his mysterious acts without question or, God forbid, complaint. In the case of the woman quoted above, father had gone to help God. It would be selfish and wrong of her to consider her own feelings.

The daughter whose mother has been hurt and mistreated by an abandoning husband is in a similar position. She dare not miss him, not even privately.

The edict against feeling is in direct proportion to the repression that it spawns. Manifest sorrow is generally discouraged in children; if it is forbidden, the child, desperate for her mother's approval, is bound to obey. Even after it outlasts its usefulness—

the dependent child has become an adult and is presumably living away from her mother—repression, like Missildine's "absence of attention," has become a way of life.

The daughter's rage at being abandoned by the first man she ever loved is profound. Having been forbidden to vent, it sparks and sizzles within her, forcing her to perceive all the world through a glare of hatred, not the least of which is directed at herself. Taken to its extreme, so much hostility may convince the woman that she, and all the evil contained within her, are responsible for her father's death or abandonment. We saw this in the daughters of suicide victims, and indeed to varying degrees in several other interview subjects. Protracted suspicion of her own guilt, of course, will stimulate further repression, which, if submerging her to the deepest abyss, may render life itself intolerable.

Childhood despair is often cloaked in pseudo-maturity. Unlike repression, this is a strategy that may admit of the existence of negative feelings, but aspires instead to a higher calling: helping mother. The cloak becomes tattered with prolonged wear, however, a useless vestige capable of offering only surface protection from the elements.

Human development may be seen as a constant modulation of our dependence on our parents. As infants, we need them wholly and without question; disruption of reliable care may threaten our very survival. Then, as we become aware of ourselves as individual people, we begin to experiment with autonomy in what may be seen as a ritualistic dance:

Now the toddler steps away from the parent, now she hurries back, ever delighting in her ability to be the master of that return. Dependence, independence, step-together-step. If mother is usually the object of the dance, father is the leader of the band. His presence sets the tempo and confirms the fact that there is a dance in the world away from mother.

Throughout our childhoods, and culminating in adolescence, we fine-tune our viability as independent beings, daring to step farther and farther away from our mothers, and for longer periods of time, until, as adults, we find ourselves in the key of true autonomy. We are separate, functioning individuals.

If our partner, mother, has not been there to catch us as we leap back toward her—a common consequence of father's absence—the gratification of periodic reunion with her, the part that recharges our courage to step away, has been eliminated. Yet the compelling music of the dance plays on. The human being, the little girl, becomes her own partner, denies her need for her mother's support, and turns inward for gratification. The precariousness of independence fails to wane, as it would with the help of mother's steady hand, but the fatherless girl presses on, for she has a singular reason to maintain her balance: stumbling might result in the physical as well as the emotional loss of her one remaining parent. This danger must be avoided at all costs.

The cost of pseudo-maturity varies in proportion to the obstinacy with which it is practiced. Again, mother's behavior is the determining factor. If she has given her daughter *some* opportunity to be helpless as a child, *some* permission to express fears and vulnerability, and has from time to time herself provided a persuasive attitude of strength, then the child has had at least some acquaintance with her own dependency. And, of course, this is usually the case.

It is when pseudo-maturity is granted no respite, when the normal fears and doubts and confusions of childhood have been denied all expression, that the cloak of pseudo-maturity shelters a profound vulnerability indeed. The cloak tends to suggest a surface competence and invincibility, but the shredded lining offers little protection to the terrified, and perpetual, child.

As I have tried to illustrate with the "dance" of development, it is the early assurance of dependency that makes a true sense of independence possible. "I" evolves out of trusting in "we." And later, "we" becomes possible only if there is an "I." The consequences of *moderated* pseudo-maturity have been repeatedly observed in the priority that fatherless daughters assign to self-control. They keep the guard on duty, to be sure, but they value interaction as well, and eventually most of them partake of gratifying relationships.

Pseudo-maturity unabated, however, and for all its show of self-reliance, inhibits the formation of a self. Deprived of the trust in another, the growing child is incapable of trusting in herself. Without attachment, there can be no separation.

Uncertainty about her viability as a separate person—about her identity—makes it impossible for the pseudo-mature woman to relate to others. Their dependency is as distasteful as her own. And secretly, she is terrified of revealing the extent of her vulnerability, the fact that she needs to be mothered very much as a child does.

Playing the grownup, she remains an isolated, frustrated individual, wrapped up in the fruitless task of taking care of her self —an entity of whose existence she cannot even be sure.

Pseudo-maturity acts as mother to rejection. Up to a point, it is a useful tool for the child trying to cope with the exquisite pain of parental loss. Indeed, a certain amount of repression may be necessary if the child is to withstand the dramatic disruption of attachment inherent in father loss.

Yet when pseudo-maturity replaces the girl's own mother, when rejection is multiplied and repression demanded, father loss becomes an insurmountable trauma, its influence inhibiting emotional honesty, impeding relationships with others, and blocking the development of an identity. "Self" becomes a pretense, a taunting presence to be quieted with alcohol or drugs, or silenced altogether.

*

Anita's father was given to habitual disappearances. They were preceded by his announcing that he was "goin' up the street," and usually lasted for several months. He finally left for good when the girl was twelve years old. Her mother worked before and after his official departure, able to provide only the bare necessities for herself and her four children, of whom Anita is the eldest.

"My mother is only eighteen years my senior, and the dependent sort," Anita writes. "If there was any burden placed on anyone after my father walked out, it was me. My brothers and sister are much younger than I am, so there I was with three kids in diapers. I raised them, cooked, cleaned, had a job and went to school. I think when I was fifteen, my mother actually decided to change roles with me. But even before that, I was always the responsible one.

"When I was eighteen, I moved away. My mother was living with the man she would soon marry, so I was glad the kids had a father. As for me, I had no desire to get married, and certainly no interest in having children. I had already reared three and considered myself dangerously capable of child abuse. I guess my only ambition was to be an eccentric, and I've learned that you don't even have to try!

"I've had *a lot* of terrific affairs, starting when I was thirteen. I've traveled and enjoyed myself. A lot of the men I've had are married, but they were also rich, influential and took good care of me. We sometimes drank one martini too many, but I'm a resilient soul and open to all kinds of exploration. My father's like that too."

An exploration of her psyche did not prove too inviting, however. The thirty-eight-year-old unemployed artist did "try" therapy once, when she was twenty, but decided after one session that the therapist didn't understand her "reality," and never pursued it further.

The persona is definitely all confidence. Describing herself as "successful," "aggressive," "dynamic," and "outspoken," Anita epitomizes the façade of pseudo-maturity. She sees herself as a free spirit, but in fact is a frequent user of alcohol. Her attitude —brash, assertive, boastful—requires the use of drink, a well-known purveyor of false confidence.

She never wants to be a mother, she says, but the man she finally did marry, when she was thirty-one, is five years her junior. Her only description of him is that he's a "great bacon bringer"; and although she anticipates a lasting marriage, she still dreams about the one "great love of my life," a man who was twenty-one years older than she and as unavailable to her as her father was.

With the help of the façade, and the free use of spirits, Anita protects and nourishes the little girl deprived of nurturing parents. She never got to be a child, but was forced instead to mother not only herself, but her mother and three infants. The voice of independence is insistent and forceful, interrupted only once with a reluctant confession of vulnerability.

"I was quite a distance from home when my stepfather died. As usual, my mother couldn't cope, so I returned home to handle all the arrangements, feed and house attending relatives, and keep her as together as possible.

"The last night of viewing his body, before the casket was closed and all but I had gone, I remember kneeling beside him, taking his hand in mind, and thanking him for taking care of my mother after I had *had* to get out. Maybe I felt close to him, or grateful, for he had helped me shield Mama from the cold, cruel world. I don't know what it was, but the tears were streaming down my cheeks."

Mona, an only child, was nine years old when her mother died. Her father, to whom she was devoted, was a successful businessman and provided his daughter with all the necessities . . . especially after he left.

"Four months after my mother's death, my father decided to move to Arizona and leave me behind in Chicago with my grandmother. I've blocked my memories of my mother, but somehow I seemed to grasp that there was nothing that could be done about her dying. But my father *could* have taken me with him. This action on his part made me feel betrayed, unloved, alienated and rejected.

"He was a gregarious man. He had the talent to make even the most mundane into an exciting occasion. Whenever he was around (which was *not* often), life was a fun-filled adventure.

"He chose not to live with me but he was certain I had not only the necessities of life, but also twenty-pound boxes of candy, dozens of cashmere sweaters, etc. He must have equated things with love. He'd send money and insist that my grandmother take me on thousand-dollar shopping sprees.

"When I would visit him, he'd take me to nightclubs, gambling casinos—places my grandmother disapproved of. I would long for him to hug me and say how happy he was to have me with him. Instead, he always said, 'What the hell has my mother got you dressed in now?' I *never* fulfilled his expectations.

"When I'd return to my grandmother, she would say, 'Oh my, what has he dressed you in now?' They had totally different values and I was caught in the middle.

"When I was fifteen, a colleague of his called to inform us that my father was seriously ill. He urged my grandmother to bring me to Arizona to see him. We traveled two and a half days, and finally arrived at his apartment.

"He was surprised and *furious* that we came, saying that I was old enough not to have made such a rash decision. That same day, he took us immediately to the train station and waited for the first train out of town to put us on it. He never wrote or telephoned me again, and that was the last time I saw him alive.

"About six months later, I was in my high school algebra class when I was paged to the principal's office over the loudspeaker. 'Your father is dead,' the principal told me. 'Go home to your grandmother.'

"I cannot forgive my father for not sharing all of his limited life with me. But I cannot feel anything but great good fortune to have had him as a father."

After reading her account of her father's repeated insensitivities, it is startling to come upon this last sentence. Yet, at forty-four, Mona remains convinced that she is the cause, as well as the victim, of her father's rejection. Within a span of four months, her mother died and then he abandoned her. To a nine-year-old girl, such flagrant withdrawal of love would readily translate to her own unworthiness. Mona became the villain of the piece, the one who didn't look right, the one who upset her father when he was ill; and he remains the hero. She says that she cannot forgive him, but really she cannot forgive herself.

As we have seen, women who have never mourned their fathers remain attached to a memory that prohibits fulfilling relationships. They may, like Anita, affect an indifference that is validated by promiscuity; more often, they steer away from relationships as a way of avoiding vulnerability. Both of these defense mechanisms were exacerbated by a mother who, in one way or another, was unavailable for appropriate guidance.

Mona's mother was unavailable, period. And the little girl became the victim not of neglect, but of flat-out rejection. She was such a burden, so unfit for love, that both parents absented themselves. As a result, she is unrelentingly convinced of the inhospitality of life, and of her own unworthiness to enjoy it. The world, to her, is a hostile place, containing neither comfort nor pleasure. She and it are guilty, and even a semblance of contentment is unimaginable, undeserved.

"I, like Hawthorne's 'Young Goodman Brown,' having seen the evil can no longer see the good in life," writes the free-lance literary editor. "I have been married for twenty years, but I would *never* be responsible for bringing a child into this world. My major hope is that I die before my husband does. In fact, I must admit that I would welcome an early death.

"I've tried therapy, but it was helpful in only a limited sense. At least the prescribed anti-depressant helped me to function. I've never had trouble finding a job, but I tend not to respect anyone who admires my work. I suffer from chronic headaches for which I am on daily medication, and I live with all those who need a 'Clean Well-Lighted Place,' because Hemingway was right: 'Our nada who are in nada, nada be thy name thy kingdom nada thy will be nada in nada as it is in nada.' "

Irene has survived several suicide attempts. "The first time, I was thirteen, and my mother came along at just the right moment. Sometimes, I think, the wrong moment." The child of a very wealthy doctor and his very neglected wife, she was "raised on maids" and taught to keep a low profile.

Seated in her spacious hillside home, we talk matter-of-factly of her desire for death: she, the stoical reporter of life's injustices; I, the objective journalist there to record, not object.

"I have to begin by telling you that when I was first born," says the pale-haired, pleasant-looking woman, "he hated me. He actively hated me. I was his first daughter after two boys and he blamed my mother for having a girl. I am told that when I started to talk, he did a complete turnaround and doted on me, but I have no recollection of that. I only remember being starved for affection as a child, and as a result, I have the ego strength of about a six-month-old. I mean, I just have zero.

"As well as being quite successful as an M.D., my father was a playboy and gambler. We moved from Virginia to the Southwest when I was four so that he could be closer to Vegas—and so that my mother could be closer to him when he was in Vegas. He was an alcoholic and heavy into drugs, which he habitually prescribed for himself. The fact is, he was very rarely around.

Most of my memories of him involve watching him from a distance.

"He was an excellent tennis player and spent a lot of time on the court above the swimming pool of our house. I used to love to swim and I just lived in that pool so I could watch him. Once or twice, I was allowed up on the court, but then I had to be absolutely quiet as a mouse, no fidgeting, no fussing, no 'Gee, Daddy, that was a great shot.'

"Overall, I was not a particularly happy child. I was basically bored and isolated most of the time. My brothers ignored me, and my mother was caught up in her own problems. I vividly remember that she read a lot. She'd always be sitting in a chair reading, and I would go stand in front of the chair and look up at her. Eventually, she'd look at me and that would be that. She was just terribly preoccupied with getting her life together.

"By the time I was six, my father had been admitted as an outpatient at a psychiatric hospital, and I only saw him a few times after that.

"One summer—I was six or seven—my mother and I went to visit with him. The three of us stayed in a small house in the country, and, in the middle of the night, my mother came running out of the bedroom screaming. I was sleeping in a small alcove off the living room.

"My father came running after her and just started to beat the shit out of her. I tried to hold him back, but he just pushed me away. My mother was crying and crying and shaking, and apparently bleeding. I don't know how long it went on, too long, but finally she ran out of the house.

"A lot of this is a blur to me, of course. But I do remember that before my father left, he took a hammer and smashed all of the jewelry that she had with her, and took as many clothes of hers as he could get his hands on and took them out in the yard and set fire to them, and then he was gone. Somehow or other, my mother and I packed up and got out of there.

"The next time I saw him was several years after this incident. There was a knock at the door and then there was this man standing there with a woman obviously quite a bit younger. I looked up at him and I said, 'Who are you?' I didn't know who he was and it could have been that it was awfully late, but I really didn't recognize him. Anyway, he came in and it was like a stranger, a very drunk stranger.

"Once I realized who it was, I was filled with ecstasy. I started showing him the pool out in the back, how it looked so pretty with the lights on. I remember this gleeful joy, saying, 'Come with me, Daddy, come and look at this.' A little bit later, I realized that he had lived here, of course he knew how the pool looked at night, and I felt kind of sheepish and embarrassed. But he did humor me and I appreciated it. Of course, there was an ugly scene soon afterwards between him and my mother, and about a year later they were divorced officially. He remarried and moved to the Midwest.

"He called occasionally, but never asked to talk to me or my brothers. Sometimes, I would pick up an extension and listen for a little while, hoping to hear something about myself. I don't think I ever did, because I have a vague feeling of humiliation and disappointment when I picture listening in on those calls.

"My mother, meanwhile, was totally devastated after he left. She still loved him. It was around that point—I must have been about eight—that the whole family went into individual therapy. And I've pretty much been in analysis ever since."

The tale is told in cool and balanced tones, from the distance of a darkened swimming pool looking onto the heated action courtside. Children should be seen, rarely, and never heard; the forty-year-old with the six-month-old's ego has learned her lesson well. To keep herself from sinking, she has mastered the dead man's float: arms silently outstretched, mobilized by the occasional quiet kick.

The suicide attempts failed, as did her father's until his last one. "My mother gathered us in the living room on that particular afternoon and she was crying. She loved him until the day he died. I don't know that there was an official autopsy, but I've always kind of known that he died of a combination of booze and drugs. Maybe it was accidentally on purpose, not as obvious as the time he jumped out of a third-story hotel window.

"I didn't feel anything. I know an analyst would say I didn't *allow* myself to feel anything. But the next day at school—I was in seventh grade—I remember letting it be known that my

father had died and that I said it for the shock value, for the
attention I'd get from my friends.

"I've always had a tendency to behave in ways that will cater
to other people. I figure out what would please them, or interest
them, or appeal to them, and play the part. I know that everybody plays slightly different roles in different situations, but I
have an almost uncanny ability to do that. I think I have a fair
sense of humor, and I always try to make people laugh, because
that to me is a neon sign that says approval.

"The times I've come close to killing myself—the first time
was just before my father died—what happens is that I wake up
in the middle of the night and I'm just terrified. Nothing in
particular precipitates it, but I wake up having no idea who I
am, no identity. It's like I'm in some kind of criminal state, and I
go into a panic.

"It's interesting, I guess, that my mother has come to my
rescue twice. The other times it was drunk driving and I was
just lucky . . . or unlucky."

Irene has used dramatic measures to get her mother to look
up from her reading. As the interview ends and I say good-bye
to the twice-divorced advertizing executive, I feel uneasy about
leaving her alone in the house, with all its spaces. She identifies
with her father, she has told me several times, and regrets the
failures of her admittedly halfhearted gestures toward ending
her life. Has our conversation stirred the quiet waters of the
pool? Will she wake up this night in a state of panic, a "criminal," and not be able to reach her mother by phone?

"Drive safely," she calls out, unwittingly mocking my concern. "Take care," I respond feebly, and she disappears behind
the well-manicured rise of lawn that hides her front door.

In melancholia . . . guilt and hostility are too much for the
sufferer. It is as though the melancholic believed that whatever was lost, by death or separation or rejection, had somehow been murdered by him. It therefore returns as an
internal persecutor, punishing, seeking revenge and expia-
tion . . . This is the vicious circle of melancholia, in which
a man may take his own life partly to atone for his
fantasized guilt for the death of someone he loves, and

partly because he feels the dead person lives on inside him, crying out, like Hamlet's father, for revenge.

Melancholia, considered by Freud to be the pathological counterpart of mourning (and described above by A. Alvarez), is the most severe consequence of the combined forces of rejection, repression, and pseudo-maturity. The woman who felt guilty about her wishes for a rejecting father who ultimately left her, and who was neglected by an unavailable mother; the woman who masked her confusion and vulnerability behind a guise of independence and who therefore never developed a viable sense of self, may incorporate *as* herself the blatantly punishing figure, the father, who verified beyond question the worthlessness of her being.

Madeleine, whom we met in an earlier chapter, has emulated her rejecting father's suicide by all manner of self-destructive behavior. Jayne also feels guilty, also identifies with her father, but has escaped serious psychological damage because of her memories of a loving father.

Mona and Irene still fantasize about an imminent death. Haunted by fathers who were singularly uncaring, they idealize these men, rather than admit their previous hostility, and most important, perceive themselves as being like their fathers. What more concrete testament to their loyalty, what better absolution of their responsibility for father's demise than to use his murdered and murdering spirit as a substitute for self?

Mona and Irene, suffering from melancholia, continue to do battle with father's ghost. One of the most famous suicide victims of our time succumbed.

Volumes have been written on the untimely death of Sylvia Plath. Her poetry and prose, the chronology of her aborted life, have been analyzed, romanticized, plumbed for meaning. Regard for her work is almost unanimous, yet even among admirers, there are those who suggest that her literary stature rose with the gaseous fumes that put an end to her work. The voice resounds as much for what it said as for the way in which it was silenced. We read and reread Plath not only because we appreciate her talent, but because we are seeking an explanation, a presage of her choice.

Sylvia was eight years old when her father died. "God knows what wound the death of her father had inflicted on her in her childhood," muses one author. "She was looking for a self from which to shape her poetry," critics observed.

Thanks to Plath's bounteous canon, and the remembrances of those who knew her, we can eliminate the Lord from our investigation, and link the "wound" with that self for which she was looking, that elusive self whose taunting voice beckoned toward death.

Her father's death—following a leg amputation necessitated by his diabetic condition—had a tremendous impact on the girl. Her feelings about him and her mother, her rage and denial and inability to integrate the rejection, are everywhere in her writing, just as her search for self was manifest in her reported shifts in mood, attitude, presence. "Sylvia Plath was a person of many masks," writes her former husband, Ted Hughes, in the Foreword to her published journals. "I never saw her show her real self to anybody—except, perhaps, in the last three months of her life." As described by her friend, literary critic A. Alvarez, she was now the self-effacing housewife, now the assertive career woman.

To read her is to be pierced by pointed rage shooting from the page, momentarily to be moved by tender/soft confessions. She loved men, hated men; wanted to shine, shunned attention. She was quite obviously shattered by her father's death, yet, at the age of seventeen, wrote, "No one I love has ever died."

The eloquent prose of Sylvia Plath's journals may be read as the gradual unfolding of a revelation, a reluctantly exposed anatomy of the most severe effects of father loss. Rejection, feelings of neglect, repression and pseudo-maturity, a gnawing suspicion of a terrible guilt, plague and motivate the writer, urging her ever more insistently toward the ultimate punishment of reunion.

From *The Journals of Sylvia Plath:*
Reflections During Adolescence

God, who am I?

There is your dead father who is somewhere in you . . .
You remember that you were his favorite when you were
little, and you used to make up dances to do for him as he
lay on the living room couch after supper. You wonder if
the absence of an older man in the house has anything to do
with your intense craving for male company . . .

I am afraid . . . I will not let myself get sick, go mad, or
retreat like a child into blubbering on someone else's shoul-
der. Masks are the order of the day . . .

Later Reflections
On Father:

I rail and rage against the taking of my father, whom I have
never known; even his mind, his heart, his face, as a boy of
17 I love terribly . . . I lust for the knowing of him; I
looked at Redpath at that wonderful coffee session at the
Anchor, and practically ripped him up to beg him to be my
father . . .
Me, I never knew the love of a father, the love of a steady
blood-related man after the age of eight . . . the only man
who'd love me steady through life; ([Mother] came in one
morning with tears . . . in her eyes and told me he was
gone for good. I hate her for that . . .)

On Mother:

She had to work. Work, and be a mother, too, a man and a
woman in one sweet ulcerous ball. She pinched. Scraped.
Wore the same old coat. But the children had new school
clothes and shoes that fit. Piano lessons, viola lessons,
French horn lessons . . . The little white house on the corner with a family full of women. So many women, the house
stank of them . . . I felt cheated: I wasn't loved, but all the
signs said I was loved: the world said I was loved: the pow-
ers-that-were said I was loved. My mother had sacrificed
her life for me. A sacrifice I didn't want. I made her sign a
promise she'd never marry . . . Too bad she didn't break
it.

On Men:

I hated men because they didn't stay around and love me like a father: . . . Men, nasty lousy men. They took all they could get and then had temper tantrums or died or went to Spain like Mrs. So-and-so's husband with his lusty lips.

I identify him [her husband] with my father at certain times, and these times take on great importance . . . Ted, insofar as he is a male presence, is a substitute for my father: but in no other way. Images of his faithlessness with women echo my fear of my father's relation with my mother and Lady Death.

All my life I have been "stood up" emotionally by the people I love most: Daddy dying and leaving me, Mother somehow not there. So I endow the smallest incidents of lateness, for example, in other people I love, with an emotional content of coldness, indication that I am not important to them . . .

On Increasing Melancholia:

Read Freud's *Mourning and Melancholia* this morning . . . An almost exact description of my feelings and reasons for suicide . . .

Went to my father's grave . . . I found the flat stone, "Otto E. Plath: 1885–1940," right beside the path, where it would be walked over. Felt cheated. My temptation to dig him up. To prove he existed and really was dead . . . It is good to have the place in mind.

What good does talking about my father do? It may be a minor catharsis that lasts a day or two, but I don't get insight talking to myself. What insight am I trying to get to free what? . . . If I really think I killed and castrated my father may all my dreams of deformed and tortured people be my guilty visions of him or fears of punishment for me? And how to lay them? To stop them operating through the rest of my life?

Plath did not succeed in allaying her guilty visions. Rather, the accusing voice grew steadily louder, amplified beyond escape when she and her husband separated, in the fall of 1962. Without his buffering presence, she was left alone and reminded: a man she loved was gone. Four months later, so was she.

Can we attribute Sylvia Plath's suicide to her father's death? Millions of us have lost our fathers and endured it. Endured the rejection, the subsequent neglect, the guilt and the denial of all of these. Yet, as we have seen, the circumstances surrounding the loss, playing on the daughter's own makeup, determine the extent of damage sustained.

Certainly Sylvia's mother was no ogre. She was a hardworking schoolteacher bent on providing her children with food, clothing, a fine education. And the home, before and after her father's death, was a highly disciplined one, with a firm emphasis on scholarship, industriousness, and accomplishment—values that Sylvia obviously aspired to and admirably attained. She was a model student, a prizewinning author before she was twenty, a highly regarded poet in her own brief lifetime.

But hers was a passionate nature: there was within her a rebellious, sensual, questioning spirit from whose disobedient forcefulness she derived an agonizing guilt. She placed much of the blame for her unhappiness on her mother's pressures, but the real, killing, deafening pressure that pounded in her poet's skull was, of course, her own—periodically appearing as the death mask of her father.

To a soul so torn—between discipline and passion—father's death/rejection was unendurable. Four months after the breakup of her marriage, which forced a renewed confrontation with abandonment and powerless rage, her divided self gave up the battle.

Can the ramifications of father loss be so severe as to lead a woman to take her life? Of her first suicide attempt, Sylvia Plath wrote:

> At twenty I tried to die
> And get back, back, back to you.
> I thought even the bones would do.

THIRTEEN

"I'M THE GREATEST STAR"

Women Who Have Excelled

"The safe and general antidote against sorrow is employment."

The nearly six hundred subjects whose participation in this study has illuminated the world of fatherless daughters would surely agree with Samuel Johnson's maxim. Beginning with the period immediately following their loss, and continuing into their adulthood, fatherless daughters have seen employment as an antidote to sorrow, and to fear as well. As children, we threw ourselves into the task of growing up—often to the detriment of true maturity—taking care of ourselves and, to varying degrees, our mothers, too; we adopted a stance of helpfulness, industriousness, and self-control that led to early entrance into the workplace and an acceptance of responsibility.

As adults, less frivolous than women who grew up with fathers, we approach life with an earnestness of purpose and a resistance to self-indulgence that is discernible in the following table:

HABITS	FATHER:		
	DECEASED	DIVORCED	AT HOME
Drink	59%	63%	82%
Use drugs	12%	16%	20%

Though financial hardship curtailed educational opportunities
for many of us—80 percent of the women from intact homes
completed college, as compared to 49 percent of the fatherless
women—we earn only slightly less than they do. And regarding
our chosen vocations, as reported in Chapter Three, we tend to
be attracted by the personal interaction of the so-called "helping professions." Teaching, secretarial, counseling, and non-
M.D. medical work are the most common careers among the
fatherless women in our study. Those subjects who grew up
with fathers, on the other hand, are most often involved in
creative pursuits and sales.

Fatherless women are a hardworking group, leaning toward
salaried, steady employment in jobs that involve interaction
with and assistance to others. Not for them the high-pressure,
high-profile world of the saleswoman or the entertainer; nor
does the unpredictable, rejection/acceptance cycle of the creative artist hold much appeal. Moreover, of those who are married, their mates' careers tend to reflect this preference for
reliable employment: business executives and teachers are the
first and second most common positions held by husbands of
fatherless women; the control group was far more likely than
the fatherless group to be married to artists, salesmen, doctors,
and attorneys—vocations whose security may fluctuate with the
volume of clientele.

Just as the fatherless daughter's penchant for employment
may have begun as an antidote for childhood sorrow, so too may
her preference for reliable employment be traced to her childhood loss. She is not as confident as other women, or as bold.
Security—personal and professional—is a highly prized com-
modity, and she is loath to jeopardize however much of it she
has attained. To be conspicuous or competitive in the workplace is to make herself vulnerable to rebuke, disappointment,
rejection—experiences of which she has had quite enough.

Deprived of the ongoing encouragement of father, she is also
characteristically anxious about her femininity. Ambition and
its cohort, aggressiveness, pose a threat to her already shaky
sense of appropriate female behavior. The idea of prominence
in a male world makes her uncomfortable. Indeed, the very
idea of success makes her uncomfortable.

I WOULD DESCRIBE MYSELF AS:	FATHERLESS	FATHER AT HOME
Aggressive	30%	41%
Ambitious	45%	69%
Successful	51%	80%

In a Los Angeles *Times* article about fathers' influence on successful daughters, reporter Kathy Mackay wrote, "Psychologists studying motivation have found that many successful women were very much encouraged and influenced by their fathers; their fathers nurtured their talent and made them feel attractive and loved at an early age . . . when a father validates both a daughter's femininity and her achievement, she becomes clearer about her goals."

Mackay went on to cite well-known sports figures, politicians, and other luminaries—daughters all of actively encouraging, and often successful, men; women who have beyond question benefited from fathers who appreciated their female charms while at the same time reinforcing the qualities of excellence, persistence, and achievement.

But a subsequent observation in this article about the influence of the father on the successful daughter brings us to the focus of this chapter: the influence of the absent father on the successful daughter. Many notable women pursued careers, Mackay found, not only to emulate their fathers, but to avoid the dependency they saw exemplified in their mothers. Though she was speaking of daughters from intact homes, the relevance to our investigation is clear: maternal dependency is a characteristic feature of the fatherless daughter's background, and for a small, exceptional minority of fatherless women, it was enough of an impetus to motivate a fierce determination to succeed.

Daughter's perception of mother, and the drive that may derive from that perception, are indirectly influenced by father's absence. But the absent father—particularly if he was revered—can also have a very direct influence on his daughter's motivation. For many prominent women who grew up without fathers, achievement seems to have been a way of compensating for loss. Through the approval of others, they sought to fill

the gaping absence of father's approval. And by becoming the
greatest star, dazzling the public, they sought to gain recognition on a large scale, the only thing that might come close to
that longed-for recognition they could never have. "In *Yentl,*"
Barbra Streisand said of the movie dedicated to her father, "I
got to hear my 'father' tell me that he was proud of me. I've
always wished I'd heard him say that."

For the astonishing number of prominent women who lost
their fathers at an early age, employment probably did begin as
Samuel Johnson's "antidote against sorrow." But, as the poet
and literary critic also noted, "The applause of a single human
being is of great consequence." Employment, begun as antidote, may have come to be perceived as panacea; and achievement, the surest path to the man that got away.

Yes, the overwhelming majority of fatherless women conform
to the unassuming profile we have been describing throughout.
But, at the same time, we are most impressively represented
among women who have gained worldwide recognition,
women in whom the elements of mother's dependency and/or
a beloved father's absence created an urgent need for compen-
sation, independence, and applause.

Millions of women in the United States and abroad look to
Helen Gurley Brown, editor in chief of *Cosmopolitan* magazine, as the guru of feminine appeal. After all we have said
about the fatherless daughter's lack of confidence in her femininity, this is no small irony. Yet the essence of Brown's philosophy is self-help. Reaching out to countless young women in the
throes of growing into their womanhood, she preaches the kind
of vigorous make-over that she herself enacted and continues to
subscribe to. You're not born a desirable woman, she might say;
you've got to make yourself desirable. It takes hard work and
dedication. And it's worth it.

Perhaps it was the very lack of a father's male appreciation
during her adolescence that produced Helen's need to know
how to calculate charm. The zeal, articulated in a voice that
communicates empathy, has made *Cosmopolitan* the magazine
of choice when it comes to learning how to get, keep, and
continuously entice a man.

For all her emphasis on femininity, however, Brown would be the last person to endorse the tradition of male-dependent females. Allure may, in certain situations, require a kind of cutesy-cuddly come-on, but you, reader, know exactly what you're doing. You may have to appear to conform to the traditional image of subservience, but that's just a strategy, our little secret, sshh. *"Cosmopolitan,"* writes Nora Ephron, "makes its men mindless creatures who can be toppled into matrimony by perfect soufflés, perfect martinis, and other sorts of perfectible manipulative techniques." Helen Gurley Brown has mastered the techniques, and she is oh so willing to share them with a readership whose insecurities and small-town limitations she herself fought hard to overcome.

The Gurleys moved from the Ozarks to Little Rock, Arkansas, when Helen, the second of two daughters, was three years old. It was 1925 and her father had been elected to the state legislature. Her parents' marriage was not entirely harmonious—due to Mr. Gurley's objections to his wife's desire to work—but "He was a terrific father. He spent time with my sister and me and he played with us a lot. He always took us to the state fair, which is a very big deal in a small midwestern city. It is just heady even to think about it."

Nearly as heady as the lilt and cadence of her voice. Throughout our conversation, I am struck by its rhythms and inflections, undeniably familiar to anyone who has ever read *Cosmopolitan,* and calling to mind the oft-heard observation that Helen Gurley Brown *is* the magazine.

"He bought me a sink for my dollhouse," she continues, enthused. "It was all very well to have bedroom furniture and living room furniture. But a sink! It was very special.

"I know that one tends to gloss over the bad things very often when a relationship ends prematurely. I believe he was quite macho in terms of not wanting his wife to work. They were poor and he didn't want her to work, and that was heinous, because she had a lovely brain. But all I remember are the wonderful things, and everybody, even my mother, says that he was a terrific father. The neighborhood kids adored him. They always came to our house.

"I am deeply sorry for the things that happened to my

mother only because of living with my father, the fact that he hit her career in the head. But remember, this was the 1920s; *all* men were hitting *all* wives' careers in the head. There was no such thing as a working wife, so it is hard to be angry at him these many years later on her behalf."

Despite her conflicted awareness of the limits her father imposed on her mother's ambitions, the consummate career woman chooses to maintain an idealized image of her male parent. "I had a super relationship with him. Maybe it's because I was ten years old and still at the idealistic stage when he died. Yes, there are people in life who may not be first-rate human beings, but when they are wonderful to you, and they are adorable and friendly and generous, it is very hard to be mad at them because of what they did to somebody else."

Circumstances prevented Helen from ever having to confront her father on her own behalf. If he had lived, she ventures, "He probably would have been in government in Arkansas. He was a great charmer and he was smart and he was honest. He probably would have got to be governor and I would have been a politician's kid. I probably would have stayed in Arkansas, gone to the University of Arkansas, and married and had children like everybody else. His death really catapulted me into another world. I don't know what strengths I developed in terms of being a good person, capital G.P., but I certainly got strong in terms of coping and surviving and using whatever wits and talent I had to become whoever it is I became."

On a summer afternoon in 1932, Ira Gurley's younger daughter looked across the street and noticed that her neighbor was at home. She vaguely wondered why he had left work in the middle of the day . . . It wasn't long before she understood: he had come home early because he had to inform the family that a freak elevator accident at the state capitol building had killed her father.

"There was such a tremendous hullabaloo that I'm not sure if it really hit me. Maybe I just couldn't absorb what the loss meant. It's hard to explain, because he really was a hero as far as I was concerned. *He* was Mr. Wonderful.

"It was not until I was in my mid-thirties and undergoing analysis that I wept for him. Every Thursday for about a year, I

screamed my head off and finally exorcised the death of my
father. I really didn't go through it when it happened."

When it happened, the drama of a young healthy man on the
rise meeting such an untimely death was the order of the day.
Flowers, visitors, front-page stories in the local newspaper, an
outpouring of sympathy for the widow and her poor, fatherless
children made a much stronger impression on the ten-year-old
girl than the loss that had provoked all the attention. "Everyone
was making such a tremendous fuss over us and I guess I just
lapped it all up."

Predictably, the fuss waned, and with it Helen's attempted
obliviousness to its cause. "Our household was never the same.
It had been fun when he was there, but there was never any fun
in my household ever again after that. I missed the people; we
never had people around after he left.

"My mother had no money, but she made a prodigious effort
to keep our lifestyle as it had been. She insisted that we have the
same pretty clothes, go to parties. Finally, four years later, she
up and moved us to Los Angeles and broke the news that we
were out of money and she wanted to be with some relatives
who could help us a little bit. Within a year after we moved, my
sister was struck with polio and has been paralyzed ever since,
requiring constant attention."

Understandably, Helen suffered from some degree of neglect
at this time. But in typical pseudo-mature fashion—while vehe-
mently denying the epithet—her sympathies were with her
mother. "She was such a sad little person most of her life. Really
quite melancholy. I could weep for her. She had such a rotten
time of it. She had a husband who did not understand her, never
mind that he was adorable with the children and had a great
many friends; she didn't get to do what she wanted to do in life.
Then her husband dies, her daughter gets polio, the money runs
out. She was so sad, so desperately sad that there was really a
pall around our house for years. The three of us sort of huddled
together, my mother, my sister, and me, and I just came to
realize that if I ever wanted to have the good things of life and
to break out, and to be free of this sadness, I would have to get
out and do it on my own . . . The minute I got out of high

school, I started working, and I'd have to say I've been somewhat driven as a career woman ever since."

Compassion for her mother and the determination never to
be that helpless endowed Helen Gurley with a singular dedication to work. But complementing her conscientious climb toward financial independence was an equally fervent dedication
to enhancing her feminine appeal. "She tried everything,"
Nora Ephron writes. "Vitamin therapy. Group therapy. Psychoanalysis. Hair therapy. Skin therapy. Her persistent self-im-
provement dazzled her friends . . . but to hear her tell it, her
job always came first."

Had her father lived, Helen speculates, she would have married and had children like everyone else. Her mother's "feminist influence" would have been overridden by her father's
charm, and financial inviability would not have been an issue.
As it is, however, the job comes first. At thirty-seven, after
reveling in the fun-filled life of a "single girl," which is re-
counted in her bestselling book *Sex and the Single Girl,* she
married a highly successful man with whom she continues to
share a deeply fulfilling relationship. A key to their compatibility is his wholehearted support of her career.

"I never wanted to have children. I don't know whether that
was my mother's feminist influence, because she did feel that
having had children pretty much blottoed her own other life.
She always hastened to add that she loved my sister and me
more than anybody could love children. But when you have
children, your life changes. So maybe it was her indoctrina-
tion." . . . Or the fact that she was so sad.

The sixty-year-old editor-in-chief doesn't have time for sadness. It's way past closing at the *Cosmo* offices, and she really
must be going, she tells me, she has a million things to do. But
". . . I almost forgot this! It's very important: people in business, my bosses, I look to them all as fathers, even those who are
younger than I. Those people in business have always been
surrogate fathers. From my first job to the present.

"To this moment, I have never failed to like rich, powerful,
successful men. They are who I want to be with. I never wanted
to marry somebody just because I loved him. The person had to
make up for what I didn't have in terms of a strong person. He

didn't have to be that much older than I, but he should indeed be strong. I think that was definitely due to my father leaving so soon and to our being poor.

"And sometimes now, I think to myself, 'My word, I am married to a strong powerful man and we are certainly comfortable. I have a terrific career. I make a lot of money. Why am I still only interested in talking to rich, powerful men? Why don't I concentrate on somebody just because he has a nice brain or he's attractive, or has a great backside, or he's sexy? Why is my criterion still so rigid?"

"Did you get a father figure in your husband?" I hazard a presumably rhetorical question.

"Not exactly. There was never any doubt that he'd continue to be very important—he was a movie mogul when I married him—but I did not get a father. He's my baby, sort of. I do all the cooking and the creature stuff. No, I didn't really get a father. He got a mother, strangely enough . . . My surrogate fathers are at work."

In these few extra minutes of overtime conversation, Helen Gurley Brown, in the casual style nurtured by a pragmatic mind, enriches our understanding of what motivates the career-driven fatherless daughter for whom the job always comes first. To be sure, the world of work offers financial security and escape from mother's helplessness. But, especially in the high-stakes marketplace, it also offers a world of men: rich, powerful, successful men; men in a position of authority; men who, if you do a good job, commend, appreciate, and applaud your efforts.

It is debatable whether her husband does not indeed correspond to this description. What is definite is that the tireless, dedicated, visible career woman spends a lot of time in the world of work, where she may daily interact with, and garner approval from, father types.

*

The career-oriented fatherless woman starts out with an advantage that is characteristic of all our experience: an orientation toward achievement that dates back to childhood. Whether to maintain mother's love or to supplant her example of weakness, she gave priority at an early age to competence, responsibility, and performance. Helen Gurley Brown, for instance, was highly motivated as a result of her perceptions of a thwarted female parent.

The significance of achievement among fatherless daughters was cogently illustrated in a 1977 study of five hundred junior and senior high school students. Analyzing the performance of these students, it was found that ". . . there is a dramatic tendency for father-absent girls to have higher grades."* Furthermore, and poignantly echoing the importance they place on responsible performance at home, these fatherless daughters' very *self-esteem relied on their higher grades*. When this factor was eliminated from the computations, self-esteem dramatically decreased. Doing well, at home and school, provides us with confidence.

Several theorists have suggested that father's absence "frees" the girl from the typical behavioral and academic restraints placed on females. This may be true up to a point. Yet, as reflected in the subsequent findings of the 1977 study, ". . . the extent . . . to which the achievement advantage of these girls registered in the context of school can be translated into the realization of personal success goals in adulthood is questionable. Indeed, their lower sense of personal destiny control . . . suggests their own lack of optimism regarding their futures, despite current performance levels."

The historical dichotomy between femininity and achievement is clearly indicated in the fatherless daughter's tendency toward industriousness. A conscientious approach is her defense against self-doubt and suspected deficiencies in the traditionally female realms of attractiveness, domesticity, the ability to hold onto a man. But self-doubt and suspected deficiencies are not obliterated by employment; they are merely tempered. Hence the generally low frequency with which achievement orientation extends to goal orientation. We think in terms of "work," not "careers." Fewer than half the fatherless women in our study grew up believing they would have a career, as compared to 61 percent of the women from intact homes. The early

---

* This finding applied specifically to white female students. The authors went on to report that father's absence had no impact on the school performance of black girls.

valuing of achievement is indeed shared by most of us; only for a select few has it served as the foundation on which to build a great career.

Bella Abzug, Marian Anderson, Helen Gurley Brown, Isak Dinesen, Isadora Duncan, Geraldine Ferraro, Edna St. Vincent Millay, Martina Navratilova, Anaïs Nin, Anna Pavlova, Gilda Radner, Eleanor Roosevelt, Carole Bayer Sager, George Sand, Carly Simon, Wallis Simpson, Susan Sontag, Gloria Steinem, Barbra Streisand, Cicely Tyson—each of these women lost her father before eighteen years of age, owing to death, divorce, or abandonment. Yet, if most fatherless daughters tend to shy away from competitive, conspicuous vocations, what are the factors that distinguished these highly accomplished, world-recognized personalities, an exceptional group by any criterion, who constitute such a compelling exception to the rule? The variables noted above, and upon which we will presently elaborate, suggest an explanation for the impressive number of fatherless women among the ranks of women who have excelled.

The career-oriented fatherless daughter is well served by the emphasis on performance that characterizes most of our backgrounds. But in addition to that characteristic industriousness, she is urged on by an image of father that compels her to compensate for his absence. The loss, for her, cannot be denied, so, rather than repress the pain, she uses it, very much as fuel, to propel her full-steam ahead. Indeed, many well-known women who grew up without fathers have claimed his loss as the impetus for their productivity.

Among the "high achievers" in our study—women who earn more than twenty-five thousand dollars a year and/or received advanced degrees and/or married very successful men—an exalted image of father was very much in evidence. These women held their absent father in the highest regard and described him and their relationship as "special." These distinctly positive memories reinforce the significant connection between the sense of loss and the sense of striving. The impulse fueling ambition would seem to originate in a desire for restitution with a father whose presence was, or is imagined to have been, a great source of validation.

Isak Dinesen, the Danish writer, farmer, adventurous free

spirit, twice nominated for a Nobel prize, was nine years old when her father killed himself. According to her biographer, his death was the "central drama" of her existence, and his image the core of her inspiration. Dinesen's ". . . fantasy of union with her father . . . [gave] her a powerful, if imaginary, ally against despair." "Indeed, where Isak Dinesen uses the word 'life' it is often synonymous with the word 'father.' " And Dinesen herself, in a letter to her mother during a crisis in her later years, wrote, "If I can . . . make something of myself again, and can look at life calmly and clearly one day—then it is Father who has done it for me . . . Often I get the feeling that he is beside me, helping me . . ."

In their investigation of the restitution theory, several analysts have maintained that by exhibiting qualities generally associated with men—persistence, for example—the ambitious woman is identifying with her absent father, and thereby delaying separation from him. A contradictory view holds that most of us eschew ambition because success implies separation from father. Our overall findings support the latter theory. The sense of profound loss that distinguishes high achievers illuminates the former.

The abundance of fatherless women in artistic fields further illustrates the need to restore, create, render fantasized images into reality. A profound sense of loss doesn't breed talent, of course, but, nurtured by an early seriousness of purpose, it does seem to feed it.

The artist, alone within four walls, confronts blank spaces with an eye toward filling them. Manipulating clay or colors, words or musical phrases, she is making something that was not there before. Regardless of the instrument, her resource is her mind. While I personally do not subscribe to the notion that suffering is a prerequisite to the development of creative instincts—such an idea romanticizes deprivation and serves to discourage the pursuit of happiness—in analyzing the lives and motivations of prominent fatherless women, I repeatedly discerned a reflection of father's absence in the empty canvas; and in the urgent need to fill it, the hope of somehow finding him.

"The first defeat, the first loss is the one which stamps itself upon the soul," Anaïs Nin wrote at the age of fifty-two. "I did try to transcend [the loss] by making efforts to *become* the women he admired . . . I wanted to charm my father. The diary was not originally a depository for secrets only. It was written at first for my father to read, to make him share our life, think of us, want to join us." Deserted by her father when she was twelve, Nin is perhaps one of the most dramatic examples of a female artist seeking to regain her father's love through her work. The diaries, spanning more than forty years and considered by many to be the most accomplished of her writings, were in fact inspired by her father's abandonment of her, and conceived very much as a love letter that would entice, and then win him back.

The accomplished father-bereft daughter may have succeeded at turning deprivation to advantage. But even if she is highly regarded by an admiring public, she is not necessarily a woman who thinks highly of herself. If she is among those using ambition as a vehicle for restitution, and persistence as a means by which to identify with father, the ultimate separation, and hence, psychological adjustment, may be delayed. Her pain is bearing fruit, but the seeds are not replenishing. If she is disinclined to investigate the disappointing results of her harvest, she is likely to get caught up in the self-defeating task of frenzied sowing.

Through single-minded dedication to a goal, the ambitious fatherless daughter may be trying to overwhelm powerlessness with action, insecurity with accomplishment; in her zeal, she strives to replace loss with laudable gain, and prove beyond the shadow of her doubt that she is lovable. As elaborated by Dr. Gregory Rochlin in the paragraph below, her strategy is not unlike a child's, for tenuous self-esteem originates in childhood, its abatement seriously curtailed by the loss of a loved parent.

. . . the child holds the belief that disappointment, frustration, and therefore the neglect it experiences as a result of the loss signify its own worthlessness. The Mosaic legend exemplifies how these old conflicts can be overcome. According to this belief, instead of being forsaken, one is chosen; instead of being abandoned among the bulrushes, the emphasis is upon being found. Restitution of the self is made by being given a noble station in place of ignominy . . . No child wants to believe it is not wanted, hence the prevalent childhood fantasy and wish of being chosen or favored. Most important is that the entire device operates to elevate an otherwise doubtful or precarious self-esteem.

Indeed, when considering the factors that motivate ambitious women, psychoanalytic research substantiates these observations. A broadened worldview would seem to emanate from a slim view of self: the connection between father absence, low self-esteem, and career orientation in women resounds throughout the literature. For example:

Based on a 1957 study, a seminal paper on the relationship between self-concept and vocational choices in women reported that "Girls with career motivation tended to be individuals who came from homes in which the male parent was deceased or in which there was less communication between the girl and her parents . . . The dissatisfaction with themselves that girls with career interests expressed may be indicative of the strivings which propelled them toward occupations that deviate from typically feminine patterns . . . girls with liberal attitudes concerning the roles of women were insecure individuals with low self-esteem."

In our quasi-liberated society, female ambition is slowly being extricated from its association with low self-esteem. This still evolving change in cultural attitudes could explain *our* findings (quite different from those of the 1957 study and many others), which indicate that women from intact homes are *more* ambitious, *more* career-oriented than those who grew up without fathers. Most of the prominent women in this chapter, however, were reared in prefeminist society, where femininity and career orientation were very much opposed and father's absence had the effect of directing them toward the latter.

Still, what distinguishes them from other fatherless women is not a particularly low self-esteem, but, rather, a particularly profound sense of loss. Like the "high achievers" in our study, the majority of fatherless women who have excelled hark back to a "special" relationship with their male parent. The ending of that relationship must certainly have called confidence into question, but the memory of its support called daughter into action.

*

". . . [W]ithout the impulse of his loss, I would never have made the efforts that I made."

Many women who have risen to prominence in their fields have been driven by a need to compensate for loss, but unlike the women in the previous chapter, they had enough ego strength—in many cases bequeathed by a loving father—to maintain their own identities. One oft-mentioned and, I believe, mistaken impression of father absence is that it has the "advantage" of freeing daughter from the sex typing generally ascribed to father. Her confidence in her femininity may be weakened, this theory asserts, but so too are the constraints traditionally imposed by that quality. The preponderance of encouraging fathers, present or absent, in the backgrounds of prominent women persuasively disputes this so-called "advantage"; yet there is some evidence that the subsequent absence of a loving father may encourage daughter to develop her "masculine" side.

There is perhaps no better example of the rejection of femininity's trappings than the nineteenth-century French author George Sand. She was in fact more famous for her masculine dress and lifestyle than for her voluminous body of work.

Born Aurore Dupin, she was the daughter of an intellectual aristocrat and his rather less privileged, less educated wife. When Aurore was four years old, her father died suddenly in a riding accident, leaving her the unfortunate go-between in a perennial feud waged by her mother and her paternal grandmother. The former eventually left Aurore's upbringing to her husband's bereaved mother, who doted on the girl and provided her with the kind of vigorous education usually reserved for boys. Aurore thrived in her tutelage, displaying an eagerness for learning and a marked aptitude for literature.

Despite the flamboyant lifestyle for which she was to become known, the author of over one hundred volumes amazed her friends not by her trousers—which she proclaimed more sensible than long skirts—but by her discipline. She was a tireless, dedicated, serious worker who, from the beginning of her career, at the age of twenty-eight, was praised and paid well for her efforts.

The pen name, like the pants, was adopted for practical reasons, Aurore having been told by a colleague that a woman writer was a contradiction in terms. "Do not make books, make children," he told her. (In fact, she was a devoted mother.) To gain the respect and remuneration to which she aspired, "George Sand" became her signature.

A celebrity in her own time, it is not surprising that this unconventional champion of women's rights has continued to fascinate biographers and students of personality. Unabashed by masculine name or notoriety, she was equally unapologetic about her numerous romances. And while regaled by women as a spokesperson for their cause, she was outspoken in her disdain for the female sex. A well of seeming contradictions, the intriguing woman inspired at least one analyst to attribute her passionate nature to the conflicts aroused by father loss.

According to Freudian psychoanalyst Helene Deutsch, Sand adopted "masculine" habits as a way of identifying with her father. She despised her ill-bred mother for abandoning her, and the grandmother whose priggishness had driven her away. "Thus she turned from all that was feminine."

Deutsch went on to explain Sand's copious love life as an eternal search for a ". . . strong, powerful, godlike father who could restore her femininity." Indeed, in one of her published letters, Sand reinforced this conclusion: ". . . I have always felt that my infidelities were caused by fate," she wrote, ". . . by a search for an ideal which impelled me to abandon the imperfect in favor of what appeared to be nearer perfection."

Similarly, as suggested by her indefatigable dedication to her work, her writing may very well have been the nearest approximation to a "perfect" love that George Sand ever found. Unlike the many people in her life who had abandoned or disappointed her, her imagination and her inkwell could be relied upon. "Writing is a violent passion," she proclaimed, "virtually indestructible. Once it has got hold of you it will never let go."

Just as George Sand's conspicuous mode would seem to fly in the face of our overall profile (though her masculine façade might just as well be perceived as the ultimate personification of our unsure femininity), the striking number of famous wives who grew up without fathers would seem to contradict the finding that we tend to marry reliable, rather than ambitious, men. Again we are reminded that although father absence rendered most of us determinedly unassuming, it was also an impetus for distinction in many women.

Wallis Warfield Simpson shocked no less than the Western world by provoking the abdication of the British throne. Already married to her second husband when she met the future king, she had been, since childhood, fiercely determined to rise above the middle-class circumstances in which she had been born.

Her father, a county auctioneer in Baltimore, died five months after her birth. Sickly and generally undistinguished, he was yet a member of a wealthy Baltimore family of whose advantages he, and then his widowed wife and daughter, were denied full benefit. Several biographers have in fact attributed Wallis's notorious status consciousness to her early privations and the frustrations bequeathed by her father's absence.

"If Wallis's ambition to improve her lot seems to have been stronger than most, there were special reasons behind her drive. Here she was, after all, a girl of good family, in a class-conscious city, who was deprived, by what seemed a trick of fate, of the money that was expected to go with a proud name. With her father dead and her mother forced to work . . . she must have felt particularly cheated . . . For Wallis, high society represented a birthright she had been cheated of all her life. She had been on the fringes of wealth and substance, but never part of them, convinced that she was born to be first rate but forced to accept the second rate. She felt she deserved to share what lay behind the pillared gates and rhododendron hedges of the rich."

As a girl, Wallis was as insecure about her plain looks as she was about her inferior circumstances. It is said that she needed desperately to be liked, noticed, approved, by the opposite sex, and that most of her energy was spent in that direction. We can only speculate on how an attentive father might have improved the self-image that so fiercely motivated her ambitions, but surely it was her lifetime battle with insecurity that created the determination that would alter history.

Further investigation into the biographies of wives of famous men reveals that nearly one third of the women who have been married to United States presidents, and five of the nine most recent "first ladies," lost their fathers early in life owing to either death or divorce.† Behind every great man, there is a woman, we are told. Behind many of these women, there is a man that got away.

Eleanor Roosevelt is probably the most celebrated of all the women who have occupied the White House. Her involvements took her beyond those hallowed walls onto avenues of independent accomplishment, so that she became famous not only by virtue of the man to whom she was married, but on her own account. "Of all American women up to her time, she played the greatest role in national and international affairs," one historian asserted.

For the homely daughter of one of New York society's most beautiful women, childhood was made bearable by an adoring father. Only he could enliven her solemn countenance, or make her feel that she was anything more than a disappointment. "He was the center of my world," Mrs. Roosevelt wrote in her autobiography, ". . . and I never doubted that I stood first in his heart."

Lengthy treatment in a sanitarium, necessitated by his serious drinking problem, denied the girl steady contact with the man that meant so much to her. Then, when she was eight years old, her mother died; yet maternal loss was overshadowed by the prospect of a visit from her father. Recalling her anticipation of his arrival for her mother's funeral, Roosevelt wrote, "Death meant nothing to me, and one fact wiped out everything else. My father was back and I would see him soon . . .

† Margaret Taylor, Abigail Fillmore, Jane Pierce, Lucy Hayes, Ellen Arthur, Frances Cleveland, Eleanor Roosevelt, Bess Truman, and Rosalynn Carter lost their fathers to death. Jacqueline Kennedy and Nancy Reagan lost their fathers to divorce.

He sat in a big chair. He was dressed all in black, looking very sad. He held out his arms and gathered me to him . . . There started that day a feeling which never left me, that he and I were very close and someday would have a life of our own together."

Less than two years later, just before her tenth birthday, word of her father's death arrived. Following a night of weeping, Eleanor awakened with a feeling of renewed closeness to him, a feeling that never quite left her. "He dominated my life as long as he lived, and was the love of my life for many years after he died."

Her distant cousin Franklin D. Roosevelt was, of course, to become the more immediate focus of her attention. Yet, throughout her writings, she credits her father as a major source not only of comfort to her shaky self-esteem, but of inspiration in her unshakable dedication to social reform. He had introduced her at an early age to the plight of the unfortunate, and encouraged the active pursuit of equality among people.

Eleanor Roosevelt had promised her father that she would grow up to be a woman of whom he could be proud. Through her tireless efforts as good will ambassador cum U.S. representative in the General Assembly of the United Nations cum "chairman" of the Human Rights Commission—efforts often ridiculed in a society unaccustomed to such tenacity in a female—she made good on that promise and was, by her own admission, more than a little motivated by it. By persisting in her zealous dedication to a cause espoused by her father, she was, like many achieving women, validating and extending his existence through her own.

When she was seventy-six, and still active in the pursuit of human rights, she wrote, "As long as he remains to me the vivid, living person that he is, he will . . . be alive and continue to exert his influence, which was always a gentle, kindly one."

Studying the lives of women whose voices have transformed our own, one comes time and again to the influence of an absent father and a nearly conscious search for his approval. From poetry to politics, and in the worlds of sports, song, and stage, fatherless daughters have risen from the ranks of the deprived to the renown of great accomplishment, their efforts playing a significant role in changing the way that women think about themselves. A broadened worldview need no longer imply a slim view of self. It is perhaps ironic that women motivated by loss should have made such an immeasurable contribution to this gain in the female outlook. Yet father loss has had an undeniable influence on the lives of many women who have excelled and on the world that their determination has helped to fashion.

As of this writing, five and a half million American girls under the age of eighteen are growing up without fathers. Along with the countless others who have preceded them, they constitute a vital part of our population, a distinctive force that both participates in and contributes to society.

Until recently, father absence in females has been discussed only perfunctorily in psychoanalytic journals, earning scant mention in more popular pages. Now, with the emergence of interest in both women and fathers, and the ever-increasing incidence of female-headed households, one can hope that this omission will be rectified. When considering the lives of women —great or merely good, troubled or serene—it behooves us to understand that a missed relationship with father is at least as affecting as one that is still going on; that in impact and influence, in fact and in essence, the imperceptible relationship with father never ceases to go on.

*

I stand before the mirror, a fifteen-year-old girl, and belt out a song. Alone in that adolescent haven, my bedroom, I shed the self-effacing posture that is my daily accessory, throw back my shoulders, toss back my hair, and sing my heart out. "I'm the greatest star, I am by far, but no one knows it."

Behind the singing teenager's reflection, there is a smiling audience of one, one who, unlike all others, appreciates my starlike qualities. Here, in the cherished privacy of my room, I entertain a fantasy, and acknowledge before the mirror my longing for his applause.

Sometimes, now that I am grown and speaking of such things, I still find myself wondering, at the end of a chapter, for instance, "Daddy, are you clapping?"

Ya tibya lyublyu.

SOURCES

Foreword Page xi
E. Mavis Hetherington, "Girls Without Fathers," *Psychology Today*, February 1973, p. 52.

PART ONE
Chapter Two
Page 15
Anthony Brandt, "Father Love," *Esquire*, November 1982. p. 89.
Page 18
Sigmund Freud quoted in E. Janeway, "Female Sexuality," in J. Strouse, ed., *Women and Analysis* (New York: Grossman, 1974), p. 66.
"A fundamental part of the girl's sex-role development . . .": Henry B. Biller and Stephan D. Weiss, "The Father-Daughter Relationship and the Personality Development of the Female," *The Journal of Genetic Psychology*, 116 (1970), p. 82.
"Heterosexual femininity . . ." Signe Hammer, *Passionate Attachments* (New York: Rawson Associates, 1982), *passim*.
Page 19
Marjorie Leonard, "Fathers and Daughters: The Significance of 'Fathering' in the Psychosexual Development of the Girl," *International Journal of Psychoanalysis*, 47 (1966), p. 326.
"Crucial to the girl's development . . .": ibid., p. 333.
Pages 19–20
David Finklehor, *Sexually Victimized Children* (New York: Macmillan, 1979), p. 88.
Page 20
Judith Herman and Lisa Hirschman, "Father-Daughter Incest," *Signs* (1977), Vol. 2, no. 4, p. 73.
Page 21
O. Spurgeon English, "The Psychological Role of the Father in the Family," *Social Casework*, no. 35 (1954), p. 325.

Pages 22–23

Michael E. Lamb, "Paternal Influences and the Father's Role," *American Psychologist* Vol. 34, no. 10 (1979), p. 941.

Page 23

Henry B. Biller and Stephan D. Weiss, op. cit. pp. 82–83.
Judith Arcana, *Our Mothers' Daughters* (Berkeley, Calif.: Shameless Hussy Press, 1979), p. 129.

Pages 23–24

Ibid., p. 123.

Page 24

Mary-Lou Weisman, "Hers," New York *Times,* November 17, 1983, p. C2.

PART TWO
Chapter Three
Page 28

Sigmund Freud, *A General Introduction to Psychoanalysis* (New York: Washington Square Press, 1967), p. 211.

Page 29

Joseph Palombo, "Parent Loss and Childhood Bereavement: Some Theoretical Considerations," *Clinical Social Work Journal* Vol. 9, no. 1 (Spring 1981), p. 23.

Page 32

C. Janet Newman and Jeffrey S. Schwam, "The Fatherless Child," in Joseph D. Noshpitz, ed., *Basic Handbook of Child Psychiatry* (New York: Basic Books, 1979), Vol. I, p. 368.

Page 34

W. Hugh Missildine, *Your Inner Child of the Past* (New York: Simon & Schuster, 1963), p. 13.
"From the moment life begins . . .": Lily Pincus, *Death and the Family: The Importance of Mourning* (New York: Pantheon Books, 1974), p. 127.

Page 35

Ibid., pp. 171–72.

Page 36

Lynn Caine, *Widow* (New York: William Morrow, 1974), p. 131.
"Children are so observant of . . .": Erna Furman; *A Child's Parent Dies: Studies in Childhood Bereavement.* (New Haven: Yale University Press, 1974), p. 18.

Page 38

Robert A. Furman, "The Child's Reaction to Death in the Family," in Bernard Schoenberg et al., eds., *Loss and Grief: Psychological Man-*

agement in Medical Practice, (New York: Columbia University Press, 1970), p. 76.

Pages 38–39

"The death of a father may have a delayed effect": Lynn Caine reporting on the findings of Dr. Gilbert Kliman in *Widow,* p. 203.

Page 40

C. Janet Newman and Jeffrey S. Schwam, op. cit., p. 364.

Page 41

Adele Aron Schwarz, an excerpt from "Once," first published in *Response,* Winter 1975.

Page 41 fn

The Duchess of Windsor quoted by John Richardson, "Ghost Story," *The New York Review of Books,* February 21, 1975, p. 25.

Page 42

Erna Furman, op. cit., p. 34.
"Only in childhood . . .": Erna Furman, op. cit., p. 12.
". . . normally developed children . . .": ibid., p. 50.

Page 42 fn

Joseph Palombo, op. cit., p. 28.

Page 43

Bruno Bettelheim, *The Uses of Enchantment: The Meaning and Importance of Fairy Tales* (New York: Knopf, 1976), p. 8.

Page 44

C. Janet Newman and Jeffrey S. Schwam, op. cit., pp. 363–64.
Erna Furman: quote from "Children's Reactions to the Death of a Parent," an address to the American Psychoanalytic Association's workshop on "Children's Reactions to Loss," San Francisco, April 26, 1980.

Chapter Four
Page 58

W. Hugh Missildine, *Your Inner Child of the Past* (New York: Simon & Schuster, 1963), p. 250.

Page 59

Ms. Streisand's observation was made during a conversation with the author.

Page 60

Vladimir Nabokov, *Lolita* (New York: Berkeley Publishing, 1977), p. 261.
"It had become gradually clear . . .": ibid., p. 262.

Page 62

Selma Fraiberg, *The Magic Years* (New York: Scribner, 1959), p. 89.

Page 63

Martha Wolfenstein reporting on panel discussion "Effects on Adults of Object Loss in the First Five Years," held at the Annual Meeting of the American Psychoanalytic Association, Los Angeles, May 1975. *Scientific Proceedings*, 1975, p. 660.

Page 64

Anna Freud and D. T. Burlingham, *Infants Without Families* (New York: International Universities Press, 1943), pp. 636–37.

]Page 65

Dr. Mahler's remarks are quoted by Ernest L. Abelin, "Triangulation, The Role of the Father and the Origins of Core Gender Identity During the Rapprochement Sub-Phase," in Ruth F. Lax et al., eds., *Rapprochement: The Critical Sub-Phase of Separation-Individuation* (New York: International Universities Press, 1980), p. 152.

The comparison of girls and boys is noted by Ernest L. Abelin in "The Role of the Father in the Separation-Individuation Process," in Ruth F. Lax et al., eds., *Separation-Individuation* (New York: International Universities Press, 1980), p. 242.

Chapter Five
Page 71

A. Alvarez, *The Savage God: A Study of Suicide* (New York: Random House, 1972), p. 94.

Page 72

Albert C. Cain and Irene Fast, "Children's Disturbed Reactions to Parent Suicide," in Albert C. Cain and Edwin S. Shneidman, eds., *Survivors of Suicide* (Springfield, Ill.: Charles C. Thomas, 1972), p. 94.

Page 79

Edwin S. Shneidman, "Introduction," in Cain and Shneidman, op. cit., p. x.

Page 81

Albert C. Cain and Irene Fast, op. cit., p. 99.

Page 82

Albert C. Cain, paraphrased by Lisa Bergson in "Suicide's Other Victims," New York *Times Magazine*, November 14, 1982, p. 104.

Page 92

William S. Appleton, *Fathers and Daughters* (Garden City, N.Y.: Doubleday, 1981), p. 52.

Chapter Six
Page 102

From an unpublished short story, "The Tennis Bag," by "Patty Stokes."

Page 107

Deidre S. Laiken, *Daughters of Divorce* (New York: William Morrow, 1981), p. 15.

Page 109

E. Mavis Hetherington, "Effects of Father Absence on Personality Development in Adolescent Daughters," *Developmental Psychology,* Vol. 7 (1972), pp. 313–26.

"Being one with Mother . . .": Deidre S. Laiken, op. cit., p. 109–10.

Page 111

Deidre S. Laiken, op. cit., p. 36.

PART THREE

Chapter Seven
Page 125

William Shakespeare, *King Richard III,* Act II, sc. 2, ll. 55–56.

Page 126

Elizabeth Gould Davis, *The First Sex* (Baltimore, Md.: Penguin Books, 1972), p. 86.

Page 126 fn

Ibid., p. 87.

Page 127

Ibid., p. 117.

". . . to join in the tender and loving relations . . .: Judith Arcana, *Our Mothers' Daughters* (Berkeley, Calif.: Shameless Hussy Press, 1979), p. 120.

Page 128

Sidney H. Grossberg and Louise Crandall, "Father Loss and Father Absence in Preschool Children," *Clinical Social Work Journal,* 6 (1978), p. 127.

William Ulick O'Connor Cuffe (Lord Desart), "Mock Sermon: Old Mother Hubbard." 1877, *Bartlett's Familiar Quotations* (Boston: Little, Brown, 1955), p. 731.

Page 129

Bernard Malamud, *Dubin's Lives* (New York: Avon Books, 1979), p. 93.

Page 130

Clarence J. Kestenbaum and Michael H. Stone, "The Effects of Fatherless Homes upon Daughters: Clinical Impressions Regarding Paternal Deprivation," *Journal of the American Academy of Psychoanalysis,* Vol. 4, no. 2 (April 1976), p. 182.

Lily Pincus, *Death and the Family: The Importance of Mourning* (New York: Pantheon Books, 1974), p. 210.

Page 131

Signe Hammer, *Passionate Attachments* (New York: Rawson Associates, 1982), p. 263.

Page 139

"One effect of [father loss] . . ." Lynn Caine, reporting on the findings of Gilbert Kliman in *Widow* (New York: William Morrow, 1974), p. 203.

Chapter Eight
Page 144

Lucile Duberman, "Step-kin Relationships," *Journal of Marriage and the Family*, Vol. 35, (May 1973), p. 283.

Page 145

Ibid., p. 290.

Pages 151–52

Ruth Roosevelt and Jeannette Lofas, *Living in Step* (New York: Stein & Day, 1976), p. 81.

Page 152

Ibid., p. 79.

Page 153

Ibid., p. 96.

Page 154

Comparative studies cited by Duberman, op. cit., p. 289.

Chapter Nine
Page 167

E. Mavis Hetherington, "Girls Without Fathers," *Psychology Today*, February 1973, pp. 47–52.

Page 168

Ibid., p. 52.

"We may see . . . Martha Wolfenstein reporting on panel discussion "Effects on Adults of Object Loss in the First Five Years," held at the Annual Meeting of the American Psychoanalytic Association, Los Angeles, May 1975. *Scientific Proceedings*, 1975, p. 666.

Page 170

M. Esther Harding, *The Way of All Women* (New York: Harper Colophon Books, 1975), p. 38.

Page 171

Ibid., p. 46.
Ibid., p. 39.
Ibid., pp. 46–47.

Page 172

Richard A. Kula and Helen Weingarten, "Long Term Effects of Parental Divorce in Childhood on Adult Development," *Journal of Social Issues*, Vol. 35, no. 4 (1979), p. 59.

PART FOUR
Chapter Ten
Page 197

Henry B. Biller and Stephan D. Weiss, "The Father-Daughter Relationship and Personality Development of the Female," *The Journal of Genetic Psychology,* 116 (1970). p. 85.

Page 199

Marilynne Robinson, *Housekeeping* (New York: Bantam Books, 1982), p. 77.

Page 202

Martha Wolfenstein reporting on panel discussion "Effects on Adults of Object Loss in the First Five Years," held at the annual meeting of the American Psychoanalytic Association, Los Angeles, May 1975. *Scientific Proceedings,* 1975, p. 667.

Chapter Eleven
Page 207

Irene Mayer Selznick, *A Private View* (New York: Knopf, 1983), p. 133.

Pages 210–11

W. Hugh Missildine, *Your Inner Child of the Past* (New York: Simon & Schuster, 1963), pp. 56–57.

Page 212

E. Mavis Hetherington and Ross D. Parke, *Child Psychology: A Contemporary Viewpoint* (New York: McGraw-Hill, 1979), pp. 589–90.

Pages 213–14

Jill Johnston, *Mother Bound: Autobiography in Search of a Father* (New York: Knopf, 1983), pp. 96, 105.

Page 214

Gary Jacobson and Robert G. Ryder, "Parental Loss and Some Characteristics of the Early Marriage Relationship," *American Journal of Orthopsychiatry,* 39, no. 5 (October 1969), p. 782.

Pages 215–16

Saul L. Brown, "Reaction of Children to Deaths: Disruptions of Attachment and their Consequences" (unpublished paper delivered at Joint Conference of Loyola Marymount University and Southern California Psychoanalytic Society, LMU, July 16, 1982).

Chapter Twelve
Page 235

Clarence J. Kestenbaum and Michael H. Stone, "The Effects of Fatherless Homes upon Daughters: Clinical Impressions Regarding Paternal

Deprivation," *Journal of the American Academy of Psychoanalysis* Vol. 4, no. 2 (April 1976), p. 185.

W. Hugh Missildine, *Your Inner Child of the Past* (New York: Simon & Schuster, 1963), pp. 236–40.

Pages 247–48

A. Alvarez, *The Savage God: A Study of Suicide* (New York: Random House, 1972), pp. 105–6.

Page 249

Ibid., p. 19.

Ted Hughes, "Foreword," in Frances McCullough and Ted Hughes, eds., *The Journals of Sylvia Plath* (New York: The Dial Press, 1982), p. xii.

"No one I love . . .": Sylvia Plath, in *The Journals of Sylvia Plath,* p. 19.

Chapter Thirteen
Page 255

Kathy Mackay: "How Fathers Influence Daughters," Los Angeles *Times,* April 6, 1983, Section V, p. 1.

Page 257

Nora Ephron, "If You're a Little Mouseburger, Come with Me. I was a Mouseburger and I Will Help You," in *Wallflower at the Orgy* (New York: Bantam Books, 1980), p. 24.

Page 260

Ibid., p. 28.

Page 262

Janet G. Hunt and Larry L. Hunt, "Race, Daughters, and Father-Loss: Does Absence Make the Girl Grow Stronger?" *Social Problems,* Vol. 25, no. 1 (October 1977), p. 97.

Ibid., p. 100.

Page 264

Judith Thurman, *Isak Dinesen: The Life of A Storyteller* (New York: St. Martin's Press, 1982), p. 53.

"Indeed, where Isak Dinesen . . .": ibid., p. 7. "If I can . . . make something of myself again . . .": ibid., pp. 53–54.

Pages 264–65

Anaïs Nin, *The Diary of Anaïs Nin: Volume Six, 1955–1966* (New York: Harcourt, 1966), pp. 99–100.

Pages 265–66

Gregory Rochlin, "The Dread of Abandonment: A Contribution to the Etiology of the Loss Complex and to Depression," *The Psychoanalytic Study of the Child,* Vol. 16, pp. 454–55.

Page 266

Becky J. White, "The Relationship of Self-Concept and Parental Identification to Women's Vocational Interests," *Journal of Counseling Psychology,* Vol. 6, no. 3 (1959), p. 205.

Page 267

Margaret Drabble, *The Waterfall* (New York: Popular Library, 1977, p. 167.

Page 268

Quotes of George Sand cited by Ruth Jordan, *George Sand* (London: Constable, 1976), p. 56.

Helene Deutsch's analysis of George Sand paraphrased by Juanita H. Williams, *Psychology of Women: Behavior in a Biosocial Context* (New York: Norton, 1977), p. 45.

Page 269

Stephen Birmingham, *Duchess: The Story of Wallis Warfield Windsor* (Boston: Little, Brown, 1981), p. 12. "For Wallis, high society . . .": ibid., p. 32.

Page 270

Hope Stoddard, *Famous American Women* (New York: Crowell, 1970), p. 347.

Eleanor Roosevelt, *The Autobiography of Eleanor Roosevelt* (New York: Harper & Row, 1960), p. 5.

Pages 270–71

pp. 9–10.

Page 271

Ibid., p. 5. "As long as he remains . . .": ibid., p. xvii.

INDEX

Abandonment
  and divorce. *See* Divorce and
    abandonment, daughters of
  fear of, 198–99, 204, 227
Abzug, Bella, 263
Acceptance of loss
  with age, 204
  denial of, 199, 204
  and mourning, 43, 196
Achievement orientation, 131
  of junior and senior high school
    students, 262
  of successful women, 261, 262–63
Adjustment to loss
  and age, 235
  mother's role in child's, 44, 55,
    235
Adler, Alfred, 131
Adolescence, 7
  achievement orientation in, 262
  anxiety in, 172
  awkwardness of girls in, 167–68
  characteristics in men desired by
    women losing father in, 176
  for daughters of deceased fathers,
    168–69, 170
  for daughters of divorce, 168–70
  delinquent behavior in, 64–65,
    172
  and early object loss, 63
  examples of death of father in,
    165–67, 173–79
  father's role in developing
    sexuality in, 22
  independence conflict in, 172, 179
  self-esteem in, from achievement
    at school and at home, 262
  separation-individuation phase in,
    172, 173
  stress in, 172–73
Age
  acceptance of loss with, 204
  and adjustment to loss, 235

and social life of daughters with
    stepfathers, biological fathers,
    and none at all, 164–65
Alienation, and relationships, 225
Alvarez, A., 71, 248, 249
"Amnesia of childhood," 57–58
Anderson, Marian, 263
Anger
  death and, 48
  toward mother, 67–69, 130
Anxiety, in adolescence, 172
Apathy, 38
Arcana, Judith, 23–24
Arthur, Ellen, 270
Autonomy, father's encouragement
    of daughter's, 21–22

Barrett, Dr. Holly, xi–xiv, 20
Bettelheim, Bruno, *The Uses of
    Enchantment*, 43
Biller, Henry B., 197
Black women, 185–90
  attitudes toward men, 197
  examples of, 186–93
  statistics on, 185
Body image, self-description of, 184
Boy's loss, father's death as, 37
Brontë, Charlotte, 195
Brown, Helen Gurley, 256–61, 262,
    263
  childhood, 257–59
  drive to succeed, 260–61, 262
  recollections of father, 257–58
  Sex and the Single Girl, 260
Brown, Dr. Saul L., 215
Budhias, Bobby, 163–64

Cain, Dr. Albert C., 81
Caine, Lynn, *Widow*, 36
Careers, 254
  counseling 31–32, 254
Carter, Rosalynn, 270
"Cathect," 40

importance of money to, 111, 112

perceptions of father, compared with daughters of diseased and at-home fathers, 170

reconciliation wish, 95, 97, 108–9, 114

relationship with mother, 109–10, 114

repression of feelings about, 236

security through religion, 112, 113

self-esteem of, compared with daughters from intact or widowed families, 109

vs. daughters of deceased fathers, 102, 108, 109

Drinking habits 253

Drug use, 253

Duncan, Isadora, 263

Dupin, Aurore, 267–69

Education levels, 206, 254

Elderly women, 234

Emotionally deprived children, and avoidance of mourning, 35

Employment

as antidote to sorrow, 253, 254, 256

and career choices, 31–32, 254

English, Dr. O. Spurgeon, 21

Ephron, Nora, 257, 260

Esquire, 15

"Family myth, the," 79

Fantasy

in children, 38, 44

of idealized parent, 58

Fast, Dr. Irene, 81

Father, as head of household, 126, 127

Father as rescuer, 22, 23, 65

Father-daughter love, 15

"Father hunger," 57

Fatherless households, 125–26, 127

Fathers at home, daughters of

characteristics in men attracted to, 213

description of father, 170

description of self, 198

drinking habits, 253

drug use, 253

education levels of, 206

perceptions of father, 170

Fear(s)

of abandonment, 198–99, 204, 227

of commitment, 39

of death of spouse, 204

of intimacy, 226, 227

of love, 140

Feminine identity, in women never knowing fathers, 68

Femininity

anxieties about, in successful women, 254

confidence in, and father's approval, 60

doubts about, 216

father's role in encouraging, 18–19, 22

Freud on, 17–18

and independence, 22–23

Feminists, 23

Ferraro, Geraldine, 263

Fillmore, Abigail, 270

Financial insecurity, 53

Financial security, as driving force, 111, 112

Finklehor, David, 19

Fraiberg, Susan, 62

Freud, Anna

on children and mourning, 40

on effects of absence of father, 63–64, 172

Freud, Sigmund

on "amnesia of childhood," 28, 57–58

on death of a father, 40

on femininity, 17–18

on girls' relationship with men, 212

on incest taboo, 19

on infantile memories, 57–58

Interpretation of Dreams, 40

on "latency" phase, 37

on mourning, successful completion of, 82

Mourning and Melancholia, 40, 248, 251

on mourning in children, 40

and Oedipus complex, 16, 62, 66–67

and oral phase, 235

on sexual development in boys and in girls, 16–17